THE ABUSING OF AMERICA

Steven Diamond

Bloomington, IN

© 2003 by Steven Diamond. All rights reserved.

No part of this book may be reproduced, stored in a retrieval system, or transmitted by any means, electronic, mechanical, photocopying, recording, or otherwise, without written permission from the author.

ISBN: 1-4107-3011-5 (e-book)
ISBN: 1-4107-3010-7 (Paperback)

Library of Congress Control Number: 2003092194

This book is printed on acid free paper.

Printed in the United States of America
Bloomington, IN

Published by 1st Books Library –Bloomington, IN

For general (non-ordering) correspondence or to contact the author write to :
P.O.Box 42367
Cincinnati,OH 45242

1stBooks – rev. 09/11/03

CONTENTS

INTRODUCTION 1

Chapter 1   **GOVERNMENT** 6

    Debacles of Economic Lawlessness 7
    Accumulating Debt 12
    Out-of-Control Mismanagement 16
    Social Services 19
    Burning the Candle At Both Ends 20
    The Homeless 24
    The Two-Party System 26

Chapter 2   **INDUSTRY** 31

    Government and Big Business Are Synonymous 31
    Shifting Facades of Corporations 33
    Cost/Benefit Psychology 35
    Molding the Employee and Consumer 37
    Consumer Advertising 41
    Crunching the Workforce 45
    Re-engineering 49

Chapter 3   **EGO, GREED & SOCIETY** 54

    Wealth As A Measuring Stick 56
    The Inner Emptiness of Self 60
    Advertising and Society 64
    Two Sides to Success 68
    The Individual In the Information Age 69

Chapter 4   **INDIVIDUAL ABUSES** 76

    Reasons Why We Abuse 76
    Alcohol Abuse 88
    Animal Abuse 91
    Child Abuse 95
    Communication Abuse 101
    Drug Abuse 106

    Elder Abuse 109
    Relationship Abuse 111
    Spousal/Sexual Abuse 115
    Suicide 118
    Work Abuse 120

Chapter 5   HEALTH CARE 123

    Managed Care 125
    Physicians 130
    Hospitals 132
    Mental Health 134
    Drug Companies 137
    The Future of Health Care 141
    Realizations and Suggestions 149

Chapter 6   GUNS AND CRIME 153

    The Effect of Gun Controls 153
    The Second Amendment 156
    Crime and Dysfunctional Families 157
    Violence and Television 160
    Children and Guns 164
    Societal Costs of Guns and Crime 165
    What Can Be Done To Lessen The Danger? 169

Chapter 7   NATURE AND THE ENVIRONMENT 172

    Scientific "Progress" vs. the Laws of Nature 173
    The Relevance of the Geochemical Cycles of Life 175
    Examples of Man's Abuse of Nature 178
    Consequences of Adverse Environmental Change 181
    Playing Environmental Politics 187

Chapter 8   THE OVERPOPULATION EFFECT 192

    Increasing Populations vs. Limited Resources 192
    Proliferation of Old and New Diseases 198
    The Biggest Paradox of All 200
    Is Imitation the Sincerest Form of Flattery? 206
    Our Lost Sense of Who We Are 209

Choices And Priorities Determine Our Destiny...................... 212
APPENDIX... 227
NOTATIONS 229
BIBLIOGRAPHY 237
INDEX 247

INTRODUCTION

After World War II, in our haste to move ahead and prosper, all of our logical thinking and sensibilities were left at the starting gate. In the almost 60 years since then, nobody has ever taken the time to go back and retrieve them. With the end of the War, everybody and everything sped up in order to make up for lost time. This speed was exhibited in: pent-up emotions and expectations; physical demands; rebuilding and unprecedented economic growth; material wants; and the unending advancement in science and technology. In short, propagate and prosper was the order of the day.

But, in retrospect, we overreacted by "fast-tracking" in so many ways and at so many levels of society. Parents who had known the hardships and deprivations of the Depression and then the War, were not going to let their children want of anything. The rationalization was that if you could especially provide and meet people's material needs and wants, the future generations would never have to feel the pain of any such deprivations, and could live with relative contentment. This notion was understandably expected and even necessary for a period of time. But, one must question whether we have "overshot our mark" by extending this trend so many years into our present, and whether it has severely compromised our own personal development and humanity towards others. With the advent of the Industrial Age followed by our current Information Age, we have gauged progress only on a technological level—at the expense of overlooking how they affect the human factors within all of us.

I set out to write this book, because even though we see our country as the most successful on Earth, I cannot help but think that somehow (and in some way) we have lost our way, individually and collectively. Why do I feel this way? Because, although we all might not fully be consciously aware of it, abuse in this country has festered over the years to become endemic and systemic at all levels and areas of society. That is, we have taken what was originally a "good thing" (i.e., meeting our needs), and have taken it so far to the point that "diminishing returns" have resulted. Development, productivity and prosperity would have all been healthy things in moderation, but instead they have gone amok in our obsessive, unidimensional path that we have followed.

The word, abuse, will be used in different contexts to describe the many areas of society in which it is found. By definition, it means "to treat or misuse a person or thing wrongfully, improperly or harmfully." Abuse is often carried out by: deception, corruption, maltreatment, misleading, or simply neglecting conditions or facts. We are going to determine the real *causes* of abuse and distinguish them from the *symptoms*. In the discussion, twenty paradoxes will be brought to light of how obstacles (many of them self-imposed) hinder our ability to deal constructively with lessening (if not eradicating) abuses.

We will discover how abuses become more acute through wrong choices and misguided priorities that detrimentally lead to: waste, mismanagement, greed, and significant amounts of heartache and grief in many people's lives. In addition, instead of taking preventive measures in order to avoid the problems altogether, we often end up having to "burn the candle" at both ends in our attempts at resolution. It then becomes incumbent upon us to have to straighten out wrecked, personal lives that have been destroyed after the fact.

For all of these reasons, a tidal wave of untreated abuses are continually flooded down upon all of us by: institutions, industries, other people in society, as well as by ourselves. It is incredible the number of vices that are promoted, whereby one's gain (or fortune) can only come about as the results of taking advantage of another person's loss (or misfortune), indiscretion or acquiring of an addiction. Some examples that come to mind are the respective manufacturers who proliferate the sale of: handguns, cigarettes, prescription drugs and alcoholic spirits, as well as state-sponsored lottery-game fever. Since such interests are generally deep-rooted (by all involved), the resultant perpetuation of such abuses becomes that much harder to eradicate. Consequently, we live within a society that is often out-of-balance and tragically skewed.

Abuses also amass from the fact that we have become a society that has chosen to overemphasize "competition rather than cooperation, development rather than stability...profit rather than compassion, and [unrestrained] individualism rather than group identity."[1] We have completely bought into the notion that our concentration should be in attaining the "fluff" of life, and only a rather paltry amount in furthering our natural and humanistic qualities of life. Our cost-benefit analyses and unrelenting "playing to win" attitudes lack any specific commitment to human factors or overall values.

Greed, materialism, and overcompetition have contributed greatly to rotting our brains from the inside out and have severely compromised our humanity for each other. Accumulating wealth and material goods have become the very purpose for our being. Consequently, each of us has confused the conceptual difference between our "needs and wants." With our longing to impress others with our material "extras", we have compromised to a great extent our inner sense of meaning, purpose and values. But, with our portrayed images overshadowing our ideals, we have paid a high price with a dismal dirge of inner emptiness and unsatisfied selves.

Not only that, but the overcompetitiveness of our society (and the acquiring of the Almighty Dollar *at any cost*) has made us an abusive society—institutionally and individually. In the process, such a reality has allowed us to excuse a whole range of our indiscretions and indulgences, while at the same time has seriously compromised our values. Accordingly, there has increasingly become a general starving of our "social infrastructure."[2] While each one is doing what's best for one's own individual self-interests, there has become a widening disrespect for what is best for the greater "whole" .

In short, consumerism is replacing humanism. In order to keep the economy growing (which has become our single most important goal—societally and individually), we all must continue to always push for more and more consumption. We have created a society where our expanding and never-ending expectations and avarice "wants", by any and all means, must be satisfied. Furthermore, we ourselves are becoming commodities (more and more) that can be bought or sold—in the workplace, the marketplace (through advertising), in our individual relationships, and through our overabundance of compensatory lawsuits against each other.

Our very ability to act with any reason is increasingly becoming limited and compromised. In our impatience for attaining our "commodity lives", we have lost sight of the "natural ways of life". We have intrinsically linked personal happiness with material goods so strongly, that we have refused to acknowledge the restrictive limitations of equating inanimate objects with inner happiness.

In addition, the accelerating urgency in the expectations and pace of our lives has created a climate ripe for frustrations and anger, which can (in turn) manifest themselves into abuses. Moreover, the stimuli overload and the impersonality of the Information Age has further decreased our sense of human identity and purpose, so that we are losing touch of who we are. We are slowly becoming empirical robotons in this high-tech age. One could go as far as to say that we no longer are a society made up of unique (yet cooperating) individuals, but rather merely one-dimensional economic entities pitted against each other.

The lifestyles that we have chosen today have fragmented our lives to such an extent that our dependence and trust of others (even "significant" others) have been compromised. Consequently, we end up having to use much of our energies to "look out for #1" (ourself). This fact takes its toll on each of us through stress, individual abuses, and an overall lack of cohesiveness with others.

Meanwhile, our government and industries keep pushing the mantra that we as a country must stay #1 in everything. But, their prophetic vision has a price, because we are #1 (or near it) on all of the following as well: murders, teen suicides, gun possession, violent crime, domestic violence, drinking-while-driving accidents, smoking-related illnesses, drug-related deaths, unwanted pregnancies, child abuse and, of course, excessive consumption of just about anything that you can think of (as evident by our excessively large, foreign trade deficit).

And, we can't expect to look for answers from the Nation's Capital either, because the two-party system has become stale and stalemated. The government is only adept at using hindsight, not foresight. Instead of taking steps to *initiate* bold, new ideas (so as to keep one step ahead), it always *reacts* to circumstances, when it is either getting too late or is already too late (e.g., the savings and loan debacle, social security, health care including catastrophic health care). If we wanted a representative (who would not be free thinking) to go to Washington to simply tow the respective party line on issues—we could have sent the family pet.

Special interest groups have such a hold on our representatives, that any consideration of how the whole public-at-large is affected by our representatives' decisions is rarely (if ever) taken into account. In turn, the nation's higher priorities aren't addressed because of the influence of Washington's power brokers. Accordingly, we don't move forward, and we don't move backward. We become locked into a "time warp", where time stands still and we resultingly end up doing the same thing over and over again.

On a different front, we humans are trying to become greater than Nature itself. We downplay the potentially harsh consequences and unpredictable outcomes of altering Nature. We refuse to accept that although Man's science is powerful, it is no match for Nature. Sudden and severe climate changes are certainly indicative of this fact.

But, such an oversight could very well test our very own survivability by the middle of the 21st century. That is so, because the world's irreverence and desecration of Nature will only get worse, as developing countries that had exploding populations in the 20th century (e.g., China and India) now seek to obtain unrestricted economic growth for their respective people. We all must wake-up to the reality that this most lethal of combinations (the ravaging of a once most habitable planet, along with unrelenting population growth) must be averted. We must set our priorities (individual, societal and global) straight before it becomes too late for all of us.

Chapter 1

GOVERNMENT

Although it would be fair to say that we still live in a democracy, it cannot be denied that our governmental decisions are increasingly being detrimentally altered by a plutocracy, a consortium of people that don't have the best interest of America as a whole at heart. The definition of plutocracy is government by the wealthy—a group of wealthy people who exert control or influence over a government to an excessive (even at times unrestrained) degree relative to their few numbers. Needless to say, with this ever-increasing type of negative influence, the priorities and concerns of our government have changed dramatically over the years.

The clout of such a group has often swayed our governmental representatives to use imprudent judgment and implement unsound choices in their decisionmaking. Furthermore, the government has had to resort to daunting cover-ups in order to perpetuate this "false sense of normalcy" to the American people. More concisely, the Congresses of the past, present (and most likely the future) have not had the wisdom nor willingness to vote their best conscience for what is "good for America as a whole." Part of the reason may well be because almost 50% of the Senate consists of millionaires, and, therefore, are members of this existing plutocratic group. Government has often not been accountable to the general public for its decisions or actions—and without accountability, a true democracy is on shaky grounds.

Congress has become an institution adept at delaying in dealing with potential crises until they inevitably actually occur, and often with an even higher price tag. It uses a "hindsight approach" to solve problems (maybe because Congresspeople are so adept at covering their backsides for re-election or higher office)—rather than using foresight to avoid problems before they happen or while they are "in the making." This "dragging of the feet" has left open a large "window of opportunity" for corruption by insiders and outsiders all along the way. The following illustrations spotlight the dilemma.

Debacles of Economic Lawlessness

One of the worst examples of government's complacent character was the debacle of the collapse of so many savings and loans in 1989. Its laissez-faire behavior made it advantageous for the officers and decisionmakers in any S & L to make a mockery of the national financial system by whimsically using the "federally guaranteed" cash in their coffers.

The savings and loan scandal was a classic case of the government trying to arrive at justifiable "ends" via corruptible "means". In order to compete for clients in the marketplace with other institutions' higher yield financial options, deregulation helped lift the ceiling on thrifts' interest yields and allowed them to make business, consumer and real estate loans. Moreover, it thoughtlessly (and rather hastily) increased the federal protection insurance from a maximum of $40,000 to $100,000 per deposit.[1]

In essence, deregulation "dramatically expanded the investment powers of savings and loans, moving them farther away from their traditional role as providers of home mortgages...[and] allowed thrifts to provide 100 percent financing, requiring no down-payment from the borrower, in an apparent effort to attract new business to the desperate industry...it was a false solution that made the problem worse".[2] This situation was even further aggravated by permitting a single entrepreneur (without any stockholders) to own and operate a federally-insured savings and loan. Having set the mold in place, the door was left wide open for any unsavory characters to come right through it.

So succinctly, this deregulation that was pushed during the Reagan years bred two forms of leeches. One group was a truly criminal element that took over thrifts for the mere fraudulent purpose of embezzling millions of dollars for personal gain. This systematic fraud occurred in 60 percent of the cases. The other group were "high roller" entrepreneurs that remained within the "defined" law (but not within the "moral" code of conduct), and who invested in risky junk bonds, loans and real estate with the explicit goal of making windfall profits. The ultimate cost to the American people for such openly blatant abuse was to be $500 billion (after including "the interest payments on government bonds sold to finance the industry's bailout.")[3]

The shameful part of this whole situation was that it did not go unnoticed before the actual catastrophe happened, it simply went unchallenged. The Reagan Administration was dead set on pushing for a policy of deregulation in order to get the government off the back of the American financial institutions. So, when it was noticed that executives at savings and loans, suddenly were driving Rolls-Royces, buying high-priced mansions and wearing expensive jewelry—the "Reaganites" portrayal was that these luxuries demonstrated that their plan was working. These rewards were proof positive that successful entrepreneurism was well in America.

In reality though, it was a manipulative cover-up of how insolvent the thrifts had become after the "looting" by their own executives. Of course, this extremely superfluous and myopic viewpoint was held for such a long time that it ended up costing the American public "big-time"! In retrospect, deregulation: (1) not only permitted the legitimizing of exorbitantly speculative investments and loans but (2) obligingly created an atmosphere of hiring fewer examiners—people who could have actually solved the problem before it ever happened.

Moreover, we did not learn our lesson from the Savings and Loan Crisis. Lo and behold, about a decade later in 1998, the government had to financially bail out the banks and brokerages, that had loaned huge amounts of money to a relatively small number of sophisticated investors, who then turned around and invested those very loans into hedge funds. These are basically highly-risky (yet lightly regulated), computer-formulated speculations of projected yields on foreign countries' bonds in global financial markets.

In other words, the computers (and investors) would look for discrepancies in countries' historical bond yield relationships in comparison to their present yields. When any discrepancies were found, they would invest accordingly—betting that present low yields would return to their higher historical norms. But, all of these computer-derived formulas were worthless, since they could not forecast the global financial crunch (that happened to unfold at that time), and which spread from Asia, then to Russia and Latin America. This occurrence spelled disaster for these hedge funds.

In addition, these investors had highly-margined accounts, whereby the hedge funds had highly-leveraged debt loads in comparison to their net assets (or ownership capital)…in some cases, a debt/asset ratio of 100 to 1. So basically, the foundation for many of these hedge funds was a "house of cards." Nonetheless, the U.S. government had to put out huge, financial outlays in order to cover for all of the hijinks of this relatively small group of high-stakes investors. Why? Because there were so many billions of dollars involved, the losses could have had repercussions throughout the already shaky financial markets. With this necessitated government bailout, this whole charade was the equivalent of these investors going to Las Vegas, and being completely assured (and federally insured) ahead of time that any amounts (even billions of dollars) that they lost—was not going to be their money. Yet, it is ironic to note, that when all of this was occurring, the Senate was passing a bill that, on the other hand, would make it more difficult for the average citizen (who had to declare bankruptcy) to receive protection from banks and other creditors. If this is not the epitome of a double standard, then I do not know what is.

Even after the savings & loan and hedge fund debacles, the bloodletting from a lack of governmental regulation still continued. In fact, scandals have taken place with such rapidity and to such extreme degrees, that one must question whether there is any authentic credibility and accountability within the very core structure of our modern business culture.

There was no clearer example of this denunciation of responsibility than in the Enron Corporation meltdown, after it began running a basically unregulated energy-derivatives trading business. Even though overall governmental regulation was lax, this meltdown still would probably not have occurred, if the accounting auditors from Arthur Andersen had been unbiased in reviewing Enron's financial books. But, with the advent of the Information Age, accounting firms have branched into consulting, in order to supplement the auditing portion of their businesses. Thus, in the

1990s, with this added business option, consulting by the big, national accounting firms resulted in the acquisition of three times as much revenue as the auditing segment of their businesses was bringing them.

Needless to say, in light of this fact, auditors in these firms started feeling the pressure to attract non-audit business. In fact, auditors' compensation started to depend upon their own ability to sell such services to their client companies, who they were actually supposed to be independently auditing. Of course, this dual function was bound to cause a major conflict of interest. In essence, the supposedly independent accounting firm became an inside business partner of its own client. Andersen's duty was to make it appear that its client's profits were greater than they really were (i.e., through overestimates of the company's earnings and financial statements). In return, the accounting firm would collect large, additional fees from future services and projects, that it would be destined to receive from its "partner." In short, the "greed-is-good" mentality was alive and well.

The other key element in Enron's downfall was its off-the-books' partnerships that a few key Enron executives and outsiders (unrelated to the company) had with each other. When Enron's stock was still high, this handful of Enron executives, not only cashed in on their stock options, but independently devised a scheme (obviously without stockholders' consent) to use Enron's stock as collateral in order to borrow billions of dollars from institutions. These loans were to be used by themselves along with their outside partners to rake in millions of dollars in off-balance-sheet deals—borrowed money that would never be used in any way to benefit Enron or its unwitting stockholders.

But, when the stock unexpectedly started to precipitously drop (because of negative public rumors about the company's finances), the chagrined, deal-partnering executives realized that the repayment of their loans could not possibly be met—either through cash payments or the issuance of new stock. Moreover, in early Fall, 2001, Arthur Andersen (because of the out-of-control degree in which the whole situation had become) was necessarily compelled to reveal that it had knowingly certified Enron's financial statements over the last three years. Even more embarrassingly, it had to disclose that it didn't just falsely inflate the company's net income by just a small amount, but rather by nearly $600 million. They also admitted to brazenly destroying incriminating Enron documents. With all of these combined shocking revelations, Enron filed for bankruptcy; its stock accordingly plummeted; and investors ended up losing an estimated $93 billion. To add insult to injury, the assets from the 401(K)s of Enron's 20,000 employees—which were mostly tied up in company stock—literally evaporated from all the bad news that had come out about the company.

Hence, the combination of Enron's profits being greatly overstated (through the help of Andersen's accountants), while simultaneously having its debts being grossly understated (from the off-balance-sheet partnerships), added up to complete doom for the company...Whoa, what a scheme! One could easily argue that these scandalous executives at Enron (as well as Andersen) were the lowest of the low, a true scourge on our society. These people sank so low, that they would have had to stand on tiptoes in order to reach bottom!

In retrospect, the real question is where were the politicians when this whole blasphemous mess was occurring? At least part of the answer was that in the year, 2000 (alone), the accounting industry contributed over $10 million to political campaigns and over another $12 million on Congressional lobbying. Why? Because that happened to be the year that the Securities and Exchange Commission announced that it was going to propose drafting new rules that would greatly restrict accounting firms' ability to do both consulting and auditing for the same company. Thus, the fight for the private interest versus the public interest had commenced. After the accounting lobby was able to gather the necessary votes in Congress to overrule this proposed legislation, the accounting industry was able to maintain their right to continue consulting for the same companies that they audited. Ironically, if this political power play had not been successful at this critical point in time, it is very likely that this whole Enron debacle would not have been able to occur, in the first place.

There is a common lesson to be learned in all three of these scandals that have been addressed here. That is, unless government regulators have the ability to do their job, investor confidence and participation — a crucial element in our economic system — will become non-existent due to the apparent lack of fair and honest practices and corporate openness.

Accumulating Debt

Over the years, Congress has rather lackadaisically tried to balance the federal budget. Finally in 1998, the economic conditions of the nation allowed Congress to proudly make much ado that the yearly federal budget was going to be able to be balanced for the first time in a long time. Even a small surplus was expected. But in comparison, the balancing of a federal budget for one year to the balancing of the total accumulated national debt is like comparing apples and oranges. The fact that we were fortunate enough to have the best economic conditions (that this country had seen in 30 years) is little consolation, because to use such an extraordinary year as the standard norm for future years is sheer, unrealistic hopefulness. Chances are that most likely 1998 was the year that the economy was nearing the very apex of the economic productivity curve, and that it would gradually go down from there in the early 2000s.

In fact, the general framework that portends yearly deficit spending is starting to form once again. Recent economic scandals, political decisions and new governmental outlays, will all force the nation to revert back into deficit spending—making it virtually impossible to visualize any return to surpluses in the foreseeable future. Furthermore, because of the public's lost confidence in the whole investment industry and the current lack of corporate capital spending, overall tax revenues from capital gains will likely remain in the doldrums. President Bush's excessive tax refund program for this decade will give us absolutely no "wiggle" room for surplus revenue, that could help meet new national needs that always come to the fore yearly. Pressures to increase hospital and doctor reimbursements for Medicare; a seniors' drug benefit package; and general inflation of the entire health care system—will all put pressure on the system to increase spending outlays by hundreds of billions of dollars. Billions more will be needed to fight the war on terrorism; increase homeland security; improve as well as ramp up the military; and pay for the Iraqi War and our subsequent rebuilding of that country. A new farm subsidy bill will cost us an additional $73 billion over the next decade, and the costs to cover the depreciation of national infrastructure (e.g., highways) always increases annually.

Nonetheless, the overall point to be made here is that the total accumulated debt of the federal government through 2002 was approximately $6.3 trillion dollars. More unbelievably, $5.6 trillion of that has been amassed in just the last 25 years. Conversely, it took us over 200 years (since the inception of the country) to charge up the remaining "paltry" $0.7 trillion—and this was a period that included the costs of the Civil War, two World Wars, the Great Depression and the Korean and Vietnam Wars. So in actuality, an astounding 88.8% of the total debt (since we became a nation in 1776) has been accumulated in the last 25 years. See the chart in the Appendix that shows the incremental increase in the federal debt by year starting in the year before the Civil War.[4]

If you want to talk about something being "out of whack," simply take a minute to think about the comparison of these statistics. In essence, it should have taken the government 1600 years to accumulate the amount of debt that it has added in only the last 25 years—if you use what it accrued over the first 200 years as a "measuring stick." Furthermore, one cannot blame it on any "runaway inflation" that has occurred in the last 25 years.[5]

One of the main reasons that this is so, is because of the large percentage of the yearly total expenditures that must go to pay just the *interest* on the debt. Of course, it is a compounding interest charge year after year, and, therefore, the increases are more exponential (rather than arithmetical) in nature.

Yet, the government tells the public that it is not concerned about the total federal debt increase—that it is a common practice for governments to let debts balloon. Then, why if it could pay the debt off, would it allow the *yearly interest expense* that is paid on the debt to climb to over $332 billion [6] (as of 2002)? If one were to accept this logic, one could only assume that it is a "good thing" to throw away one-third of a trillion dollars per year. If the American people were to demand a response to this inference, what would the government's answer be?

In actuality, our wealth is built on the quicksands of credit, debt and overconsumption (as evident in our bloated foreign trade deficit). This condition is aggravated more by the fact that families are going into even more debt just to maintain their standard of living—in essence, "borrowing" from their children and grandchildren because of their inability to save. Increasing credit card debt in just this past decade is indicative of this fact.

Total Credit Card Debt (in billions of dollars)
1990..........................236.4
1996..........................510.0
2002..........................729.0
Source: U.S. Department of Commerce

Notice how we more than tripled our overall credit card indebtedness in a mere twelve years time. Because of this "sea of accumulated debt," if economic conditions were to take even a slight downturn, the demand for individuals to pay back borrowed money could necessitate a significant increase in foreclosures, defaults and liquidation of assets.

It is also significant to note that corporate debt is at an all-time high. This fact puts a real restraint on companies from hiring additional employees, because revenue must be used to repay corporate loans. In addition, excessive product inventories will keep companies from investing in any substantial new capital in order to increase production. On top of all of this restraint, banks are very reluctant to lend money for new venture capital for start-up companies, because they took a real hit in the late 1990s, when the tech bubble burst on the huge numbers of fledgling Internet companies.

But, it is still the consumers' overwhelming debt load that is the key element here, because they fuel two-thirds of GNP through their purchase spending. There are at least a few factors contributing to this reality. First, unlike the past, Americans are nonchalant about going into debt today, because it has been made so easy for them to borrow money. It is now possible to receive a low-interest mortgage with literally "no money down." The catch phrase of many loan companies and car dealerships is, "If you have a job, we'll give you credit in a minute."

Second, credit card issuers are aggressively marketing their cards through solicitations, in order to garner a greater share of the extended credit. New credit cards arrive in the mail daily often pre-approving you for a line of credit in the thousands of dollars. Furthermore, card issuers readily offer you the opportunity to use their credit cards at "teaser percentage" interest rates to pay off the debt from other competitors' cards, which you have accumulated. The net effect: More people end up carrying multiple cards with multiple debt balances.

Third, there is a social-psychological element at work here. We, as individuals, overspend in order to meet our instant-gratification needs and wants. The larger the amount of money that we can spend, supposedly conveys a sense of how "special" we are in relationship to others. This motivation of our behavior is exploited in credit card commercials, where come-ons relate to images of a materialistically better life..."Visa, it's everywhere you want to be"..."There's always something more to discover with your Discover Card"...or the American Express' credo, "Membership has its privileges."

In 2000, for the first time ever, total household debt (which include credit cards, car loans, mortgages etc.) surpassed 100 percent of disposable annual income. Conversely, personal savings has fallen to the lowest level in history—virtually a monthly level of zero. And wouldn't you know it, all of these happenings are occurring as Congress is getting ready to pass a reform of the personal bankruptcy laws, which would make it harder for an individual to get out of debt by declaring bankruptcy. In addition, many of us cannot rely on the safety nets that we have historically used in the past. With the tumble on all stock market indexes, individual portfolios currently can hardly even be counted as a real equity for debt repayment. Likewise, in the last decade, we have used home equity loans in order to pay off individual credit card debts. Many individuals have even extended their credit card debt, since they feel that they can use the equity in their home as a safety net. This could be a false assumption given the fact, that real estate markets have the potential to fluctuate just like any other market investment. In fact, home equity experts feel that we are setting ourselves up for a foreclosure crunch, if the current high prices of houses begin to fall even moderately.

Moreover, costs continue to climb (beyond the average inflationary rate) for such critical, individual necessities as: child care, education, transportation, suitable housing, and health care premiums/out-of-pocket costs. Furthermore, in order to cut costs, companies will continue to merge, thereby eliminating even more of the higher paying jobs. Meanwhile, the rest of the workforce's wages look to remain stagnant in the foreseeable future. It has also been estimated that Americans (on the whole) are saving only about 40-50% of what they will need for their retirement years. Needless to say, all of these factors will not only continue to place a real financial squeeze on many American families, but could be the initial, ominous signs of a cataclysmic, financial crisis sometime in our future.

All of the factors that have been discussed here should be a "wake-up call" to us all. It has been shown that our government, characteristically, does not seem to acknowledge financial crises and scandals, until it is too late. Even when it finally recognizes a crisis, the public is led to believe that the problem is controlled, when it really is not. Likewise, can we all (government, corporation, and individual) collectively learn something about overextension of our debt load, or are we all destined to continue to go down this predisposed, destructive path? Can we fully realize that even if one of this group of three was to have problems making timely payments on its respective debt, the corresponding effect would automatically have negative consequences on the other two?

Out-of-Control Mismanagement

Government mismanagement occurs even though it is commonly agreed upon that the governmental monitoring agency, The General Accounting Office, does a fairly respectable job at identifying waste and fraud. In the past, the GAO has written notable incriminating reports on agencies including: unneeded military surplus and excessive overpricing of contracts in the Defense Department; waste and fraud in Housing Urban Development; and the warning that the savings and loan solvency fund had significant problems four years before it collapsed.

But, generally the thousands of recommendations that it has made over the years for cutting such waste and fraud have (for the most part) been ignored by Congress and, in turn, by the very agencies that they review. So, in effect, you have a "designated watchdog" who is watching—but reporting back to a family of purposely-blind German Shepherds. Why? Because, those in charge of expenditures (the politicians) are rewarded for their "pork" spending with loyalty and financial support from industries, influential lobbyists, and key constituents. This occurrence (of purposely ignoring uncovered waste and fraud, which I'll call *Paradox #1*) is just the first example of many paradoxical behavior patterns which will be enumerated throughout this book.

Donald Wood alludes to an additional reason in his book, *Post Intellectualism and the Decline of Democracy*: "A characteristic of bureaucracies is Institutional Momentum (IM)—the inertia that keeps institutions and bureaucracies…doing what [they] have always done. Whether or not it makes any sense…Legislatures keep passing laws (whether or not they are needed);…banks keep making loans (even when they are on the verge of bankruptcy); and judges keep on sentencing criminals to jail terms (even if the prisons are overflowing and criminals are immediately released to the streets)."[7] One could also add the inertia that keeps the Defense Department continuing to buy more weaponry, warships and jet fighters (even though we already have enough of these to repeatedly blow up the world umpteen times over).

Our continual emphasis on IM in solving our problems, counteracts (or diffuses) all suggestive hints (when made), that change away from the status quo just may be more beneficial in the long-run. IM allows the proliferation and continuance of overbearing power by special interest groups, and it gives security to bureaucrats that their jobs will remain in place. These two groups have a vested interest in convincing us that the notion of change is too scary and, correspondingly, not a viable option. Subsequently, the pressure of IM doesn't allow us any change in focus and priorities—that very well might make our society a more accountable and better one.

Let's take a look at a few illustrations of governmental waste over the crucial period (from the mid-70s to the mid-90s), when the national debt skyrocketed, in order to demonstrate how our lack of "sensible" spending had become totally out-of-control, and how it still affects us to this current day, because of our inability to meaningfully pay down the national debt:[8]

* The Pentagon was billed $7417 for a 3-inch length of wire that an electric supply store would probably have given away.

* The Air Force paid $7600 for a coffee maker similar to one purchased for about $200 by commercial airlines.

* During the 1980s, the Reagan Administration spent over $1 trillion on armaments [alone]; [Note: He must had been under the illusion that we were preparing for an intergalactic war]; investigations [had] revealed thousands of fraudulent overcharges, billings for non-existent work, double sets of books, kickbacks, illegal gifts to government personnel, and the widespread misuse of funds, including support of the flamboyant lifestyles of defense industry executives.

Meanwhile, John Kohut cites other examples in his book:[9]

* Whistleblowers in the U.S. Navy said that the service was charged $544.09 for a spark plug connector that was available at local hardware stores for $10.77.

* The Senate Budget Committee determined that during the 1980's Defense Department efficiency experts saved between $27-136 million each year. The "catch" was that the actual work of these experts themselves had cost between $150-300 million each year.

* In 1993, it was revealed that the Resolution Trust Corporation had paid 1300 workers an average salary of $35 an hour in order to photocopy files of loans at a failed California savings and loan association. Consequently, the labor costs to photocopy millions of pages averaged 67 cents per page.

Finally, two examples (not about waste) but rather about bureaucratic rules governing postal employees. Maybe these will shed some insight into why some postal employees are susceptible to "cracking up."

* A postal employee in Seattle won the right to sort mail with his left hand. The postal regulations manual specifically said that mail had to be sorted with the right hand. After the employee won, the manual was amended.

* In the 1980's, a Des Moines postal clerk was suspended for one week and docked $400 in wages for not cooperating at a training session for 800 postal clerks. He was being taught to hold letters at a 45° angle, and he claimed that he could sort mail as quickly at a 90° angle.

Social Services

In this age when the government is trying to cut welfare services because of the increased costs for such programs, the question must be asked, "What is to become of the programs for the people that *truly* need them?" The elimination of the "waste" is still going to leave a large financial gap for fully funding the expanded responsibilities that have been thrust on welfare departments. These are services that so many people still direly need as "safety nets". In our haste to cut spending, this country must, be sure to do a careful "balancing act," and not actually "defund" the crucial social programs for those people who truly need them the most. Each American must reconcile his or her individual heart with the individual mind, in order to determine the final resting point between the dually-committed priorities of society versus self-interest.

This dilemma is aggravated further by the different misconceived notions of our two major political parties. On the one hand, Republicans' legislation is based on the invalid premise that every American has a couple million dollars in his or her bank account for any (and all) personal hardships and contingencies (that one might encounter). And if not, charities are the panacea (even though they are not) that can help every person with any problem. Meanwhile, the Democrats base their legislation on the illogical rationale that if you continue to throw money at a problem, it will eventually be solved. Yet, we have decades of evidence that the way such programs are designed, the monies go more for the bureaucratic administrators and to the implementation of the programs themselves—rather than the people for whom the programs were set aside for in the first place.

Meanwhile, here is a list of the overwhelming number of services that fall under the jurisdiction of the Health & Human Services Department: (1) aid to families with dependent children (2) food stamps (3) protection of child and spouse-abused victims (4) alimony and child support collection (5) housing of the homeless (6) providing shelters for the more than one million children and adolescents who run away from home each year (7) facilities for the mentally and physically disabled (8) juvenile delinquents (9) services and care for bedridden seniors (10) maintenance of AIDS patients (11) rehabilitation of drug addicts.

Keep in mind, that all of these functions must be done "professionally" with ever-decreasing staffs. I emphasize this word, professionally, because with smaller and smaller staffs, there is a real susceptibility to scrimp on the type of care that is actually needed to resolve a person's problems (rather than to "temporarily mend" problems for the sake of expediency and convenience). After all, the resolution of social problems is only successful when given time and understanding. The value of this point can be overlooked in this fast-paced age "where time that is 'lost' is considered money that is wasted". By overextending awesome responsibilities to one centralized department while at the same time cutting waste (if not done responsibly) is a formula for disaster.

Burning the Candle At Both Ends

Government has never taken a "holistic approach" to solving problems of the populace. It has always taken a "patchwork approach" in dealing with symptoms and de facto consequences rather than addressing the root causes of problems. This behavior forces it to continually try to "fix" two major problems instead of one. On the one hand, government must try to help the current generation with its problems (after the fact). At the same time, it must discourage and prevent "socially unacceptable" and abusive behavior patterns from ever coming to the fore among the upcoming generation (before the fact). In turn, a tremendous amount of strain is placed on its already limited financial and helping-professional resources. Inevitably, we end up having to burn our valuable energies at both ends of the spectrum. So, is it not incumbent upon all of us to encourage a much more open accessibility to the appropriate helping agents and stepping-stone programs before "the roots have a chance to take hold?"

It is obvious that something has to be very wrong in how we are approaching the problem—if many of our children are emerging "on the other end" of their childhood years, so unable to deal with everyday life without submitting to some type of personal abuse. We must convey to every child, adult and/or family (in every socioeconomic class) the feeling that, whatever their problem—no matter how deep and desperate—that we as a people do care about their plight, and that we are willing to help them to redirect their energies with empathy and without judgment. Because when you get down to the bottom line, that's only what all of us really seek—someone who cares about us (and vice-versa). Unfortunately, the actualization of such a simple element is missing in so many young people (and even adults) today; both urban and suburban, rich and poor.

An alternative to meet these purposes—"holistic helping centers"—not on the national, state or even local levels, but rather on a suburban, township or borough level. Why on this level? Because, when it is placed virtually on a neighborhood level, there is a real atmosphere that the community at-large does truly care, as long as the ones that are seeking help are motivated enough to work at solving their problems. And, where there is genuine care, there is almost always incentive to work at changing that which is hurtful or wrong.

These "helping centers" would specialize in dealing with a client's complete mental and emotional natures including:

(1) stress management
(2) child and family therapy
(3) peer group counseling
(4) drug awareness groups
(5) self-esteem and positive reinforcement workshops
(6) hobby formation alternatives and involvement

(7) job skill workshops and bona fide job searches linked especially with socially progressive and/or socially responsive companies
(8) financial counseling and easing of credit limitations based on individual cases
(9) teaching the consequences of "socially unacceptable" behavior (e.g., role-playing where they could see how it feels to be a victim in such situations; teaching the personal wastefulness of prison life)
(10) emphasizing the need to make sound choices in life (This area would especially apply to enumerating the enormous responsibilities and consequences that are intrinsic with bringing a newborn baby into the world. Additionally, in order to accentuate this point, public and private schools could also start drilling this fact into their heads as early as fifth-grade. Even if students still could not locate the U.S. on a world map, they certainly would be taught to have a full understanding of the important reality of giving birth).

Furthermore, these establishments would be well-staffed with competitively-paid, caring professional people. These "helping centers" would eventually replace the mental health clinics of today, clinics that are: (a) understaffed and have six month waiting lists to deal with problems that are immediate and dire (b) glutted with "novice students-in-training" who have enormous caseloads with limited time and resources.

Since most of these people would not be able to afford such "holistic" care, the next question (which is customary without fail) is how to pay for such a program. Well, let me ask you a question. What do we, the American public, receive for the $332 billion which the government is compelled each year to pay just on the interest expense of the total accumulated federal debt? Absolutely nothing! You might as well have money coming right off the Treasury printing press and being dropped directly into a pipe that is connected to the Washington, D.C. sewer system. There is only one logical message that we can infer from this fact. That is, our government is more concerned about strengthening the position (through these "bank welfare benefits") of the already "fat-asseted" banks in this country and throughout the world—rather than concerning itself with the welfare of its own people.

So, just maybe that wasted $332 billion dollars might be a good starting point for us to get something for our money. It is sometimes hard to envision how much one-third of a trillion dollars really is. This amount is so enormous that every man, woman and child in America could be sent a check every year for about $1200—or for a family of four, almost $5000. Moreover, it would be tax-free because that is already collected-tax money that has been actually delegated to be spent by the government for interest on the debt.

An independent audit by, for example, each respective local community board could prevent, any additional money from being wasted for the helping centers (once the money was actually allocated to the community). There is much more incentive to control waste and fraud when it affects the very community in which you and your neighbors live. There would be virtually total accountability for all monies that were expended. Furthermore, money could be directed to specific services that each community deemed most necessary for its particular situation. After all, if you had a patch of weeds in your backyard, it would be totally wasteful to spray the whole country in order to correct your one locale.

Hence, you would not have people being paid simply for being in some unneeded bureaucratic job category, that some far-away federal government agency blindly authorized based on some overgeneralized Congressional legislation. So, by propelling federal money directly to the townships and boroughs, much waste could be avoided—because there seemingly has always been a relationship between "lost money" and the number of governmental levels that have access to it along the way. The only thing that the federal government would have to watch out for would be that the money was honestly and fairly apportioned without fraud at the starting point.

But, the government here is in yet another paradox. *Paradox #2*: If the government cuts or eliminates federal agencies or departments to save bureaucratic waste, it will be seen as insensitive to federal workers and their jobs. So, each Administration ends up "talking big, but carrying a very small stick." What is good for the public at-large is once again compromised.

The Homeless

It is beyond comprehension why the richest country in the world has so many homeless people. It would seem that every American citizen should at the minimum be ensured health care, food and shelter. Yet, one of the major reasons that we have homeless people is because of the lack of available and affordable low-cost housing. While the supply of such housing has gone down, the demand for it by the homeless has gone up. Meanwhile, the government has reduced many of the tax and investment incentives for the building of low-cost housing by real estate developers. Furthermore, competition in the rental market has driven up rents, thereby leaving the poor behind in the dust. There is becoming a widening gap between their ability to raise their incomes in comparison to the rest of the population.

City councils and managers, knowing full well which "side of their bread is buttered on" (and by whom), allow inner city parcels of land to be demolished and converted to "upwardly mobile" facades (with upscale shops and cafes). Thus, most of the city planning goes for the convenience and comfortability of the downtown weekday office workers, even though they don't live there, and who quickly retire to their suburbs after work. Thoughtfully-designing and constructing, livable, inner-city communities for the poorer people (who actually live there) is often way down on a city government's priority list.

The plight of the homeless extends to rural areas, too. Generally, little federal funding and resources end up reaching rural areas, and small towns cannot usually afford to pick up the slack in aid. So, oftentimes the homeless have to improvise and fend anyway that they can. They may stay in campgrounds or state parks (even in their cars), or if it is a homeless family, they may "double up" and live with relatives or friends. Such types of homelessness aren't generally counted into the homeless figures, and therefore the overall problem is downplayed even more.

A large part of the reason for rural homelessness is because the loss and/or changeover of rural economies. Family-owned farms have been declining for quite awhile; migrant or seasonal workers are generally only temporarily employed and housed; and mass discount merchandisers have invaded small-town America with the clout to significantly underprice "Main Street Mom & Pop" shops.

The continuum of overall homelessness is also aggravated by the "failure of the needs-meeting structures of our society"[10] to function practically and efficiently in the organization and distribution of services. We could do better in addressing the different individual needs and situations of the homeless. Each person is affected by different types of vulnerabilities from the past and present. One could be homeless for any variety of reasons: economic difficulties; mental/physical disabilities and illnesses (e.g., there was a period of time when there was an emptying out of mental institutions without adequate support systems in place to ease the transitional difference); disruptive childhood and developmental histories; lack of access to family, friends and employers who could make a difference; inability to overcome tragedies; and personality characteristics (e.g., lack of self-esteem).

Although our country's leaders zealously "trumpet the horns" when we have economic growth, higher employment rates are not changing the trend that has been created, where new jobs (for the most part) are ones in the lower-paying service sector. Even though the country has more capital, and it may be in the hands of greater *numbers* of people than previously, overall it consists of smaller *percentages* of people. The structural economic transformation from manufacturing jobs to service/information jobs (that, our society has undergone) has increased the number of people trying to find affordable housing.

It should be especially noted that a significant segment of the homeless (who live in shelters) are actually hard-working poor who are stuck in low-paying, stagnant-waged jobs. Their employers believe that an honest day's pay for such employees should *not* be what it "takes for them to live on." Admittedly, many homeless are often less educated with less job skills, but (in this country) this should not be a good enough reason to pay someone an "unlivable" wage. Of course, such employers always use the excuse that, "If they were to pay them a living wage, they would go out of business." But, the other side of the coin, is that if they can't pay good employees a living wage, then they probably shouldn't even be in business. These type of employers are the same people who hypocritically rationalize that the reason (the homeless are in their situation) lays in the homeless themselves.

There is an ever-worsening dichotomy in our economic system, and it is even starting to affect the middle class. This problem will only grow worse as long as we distribute wealth in such *excessively* lopsided ways. The polarization of earnings as well as the increasing concentration of jobs at the extreme ends of the wage scale will produce an ever smaller middle class.

In summary, the homeless and the working poor are simply vulnerable groups that happen to stand out more, as the country's distribution of income becomes more glaringly disparate. The homeless problem has become "nothing but a form of withdrawal and avoidance: 'You've got your problems, I've got mine' "[11] Yet, a relatively key element that could change the plight of the homeless would be affordable low-cost housing (including single room occupancy units for the lone homeless). It could very well give them the needed stability in their lives to be able to better attempt to solve many of their own individual problems and to heal traumatic wounds that have been patched over. It is amazing how the psychological change from outcast to self-respected individual can move a person in a more positive direction.

The Two-Party System

The two major U.S. political parties have become so intertwined with government today that, they have convinced the public that they *are* actually government. Yet, the words, "political parties," are not mentioned anywhere in the Constitution. In Martin Gross' book, A *Call For Revolution*, he quotes John Taylor in a letter to John Adams in 1814 as summing it up best: "All parties degenerate into aristocracies of interest. He warned that the public remain watchful about where the party 'integrity ends and fraud begins.'"[12]

Democracy is compromised when each of two parties have such a strong hold on one's respective party members as well as the government. Strong party discipline can weaken the power of elected officials by forcing them to rescind the true wishes of the voters that they represent. Congresspeople cannot fully think or legislate "independently" because of possible repercussions by the respective party for not voting the "appropriate" way. In fact, today this lack of an independent mind has gotten so bad, it almost seems that before voting, each politician must feel compelled to first check with the Party's leadership for the politically-correct answer.

Furthermore, because there are so many different constituencies within the electorate, Congresspeople end up approving "watered-down" legislation, so as not to alienate any particular key constituency. The instinct for one's own self-preservation outweighs taking an articulate, heartfelt position on a specific piece of legislation. In turn, one must naturally wonder whether the normally low voter turnouts in elections are because so many independent voters (which are almost approaching a majority number of Americans) do not feel represented.

Therefore, it is understandable that if our country had a three or four party system, it would be easier for inter-party alliances to form based on the "rightness or wrongness" of an issue (of what is best for America as a whole), rather than because of party allegiance. An additional advantage of this expanded system is that it would create competition for any particular political group's control over legislation. Politicians could not so readily play "favorites" (whereby they are influenced by interests of some corporate lobbyists), who often can afford to "straddle the picket fence" and play one political side against the other. Under these circumstances, the lobbyists come out winning either way, generally at the expense of the American people. A perfect example of this concept is when so many "riders" are placed on a main piece of legislation by Congresspeople, that one has to read the fine print in order to locate the central issue, which the original piece of legislation was designed for.

This practice occurs so often today that, unfortunately, one could rightly argue that an ever-greater number of Congresspeople seem to view the concept of public service as the public serving Congresspeoples' own self-interests (and the partisan lobbyists) rather than vice-versa. In essence, the true meaning of the term, "public servant," has become lost. Sadly, the discontinuation of such practices will only be addressed when the effects of formulating national policy in this manner becomes so dysfunctional to the overall fabric of society, that they will have to be addressed.

A possible solution for giving the term, public servant, meaning again would be to limit Congresspeople to a single four (or conceivably five)-year term. This period should allow them enough time to do what they came there to do. Each American elected would do his/her public duty, and then move on, so that other Americans could be elected to do theirs. It would not only build confidence (that is presently lacking) in the public-at-large that the people they were electing were truly in Washington, D.C. to do their civic duty, but it would more than likely increase citizen participation. Just as importantly, it would be a way of assuring us that no elected representative would have the time or motivation to become entrenched with (and obliging to) special interest groups—but instead be there strictly for working on solving the issues and ills facing our country.

The increase in the number of issues in the electorate today is slowly leading to an erosion of consensus and, therefore, a lesser affiliation to any one party's ideology. Consequently, the result is "an agenda too diverse and too divisive for the parties to embrace."[13] These greater concerns among the electorate has caused it to at least consider a third party in the last three Presidential elections.

The intrinsic nature of the two parties (as well as the growing number of citizens who are affected by the irresponsibility of government) has forced many in the electorate to seek such alternative choices. This happenstance occurs because each party (in their pursuit for votes) must continually deal with two different, yet interrelated, sets of pressures—those arising internally; and others, emanating from the external environment. Each party is symbolized by a set of specific values and principles, and if they stray too much from them, each one risks disrupting the cohesion and loyalty of the Establishment within the respective party.

Resultingly, you have two parties that are each in a paranoiac quandary. ***Paradox #3***: On the one hand, in order to keep their "bases of support", they must, go away from the "center" on the political continuum toward the more liberal and conservative ends, respectively. Yet, on the other hand, a majority of the electorate is somewhere in the "center." Therefore, if the two parties' dogmas and/or platforms begin to wander toward the "center" they alienate their respective "bases of support" and, moreover, begin to resemble each other. Consequently, the electorate "shrugs its shoulders" and says, "We want a real choice," and accordingly seeks alternatives (e.g., third parties) to represent their public opinion when it comes to decisionmaking.

But, it is not that simple of a concept, because the formation of third parties is not without difficulties of its own. The very reason why third parties are generally begun in the first place is founded on a single-interest or topical cause rather than a wide, organized platform. Hence, the philosophical base is too restrictive in order to attract a wider electorate that could become competitive with the two major parties. In addition, the pushing of the one issue to the forefront becomes so all-encompassing that it subordinates many other meaningful issues that would allow a widening of the fledgling party's base.

This was the case with the third party that Ross Perot formed for his candidacy for President in 1992. This statement is said with reservations, because there is some uncertainty whether it was an actual party or an amorphous aggregation of voters that simply wanted a third choice for the Executive Office. Nonetheless, the point, is that this third party really only had a single issue & topical cause platform—the resolution of the national debt at all costs and to cease the trend of American jobs being lost to foreign countries. Although this issue/cause appealed to a wide range of people, it was not a real platform of many issues and principles—that voters (for the most part) need to see, if they are to end up casting their ballots for any particular candidate. Of course, the result was that Perot received a single-digit percentage of the vote overall in the election.

In short, the two major parties have a defined social base and, therefore, can prosper by adding these "floating voters"[14] to their firm cores. Conversely, third parties are vulnerable because they generally have no wide social base to begin with, and accordingly cannot compensate for the crucial loss (in their case) of "floating voters." The only way a third party could successfully compete would be to gather a strong, steady base of supporters over a period of years that would give it the necessary credibility in the eyes of the larger, general electorate. Inevitably, a majority of us Americans are susceptible to "political malaise" as we continue to get at best "lukewarm representation" and fundamentally irresponsible government as long as the "two-party beat" goes on.

Chapter 2

INDUSTRY

Nearly every decision and action undertaken by the corporate world today is motivated more than ever by the following criteria: (a) the "bottom line" profits obtained in any way possible (b) cost-benefit analysis irregardless of any human factors (c) "playing-to-win" attitude that lacks any specific commitment to overall values. Of course, the reason that industry implements these corporate operational factors is partially because they must function in a fiercely competitive global marketplace. But, a key question that must be asked is whether the corporate world has really pondered if they have chosen the correct "means" to arrive at the desired "ends"—and furthermore, whether a tremendous amount of abuse that has been thrust upon the victims of the fray could have been avoided through the utilization of more thoughtful and creative approaches. Such a path to success can often leave a lasting aura of fear, suspicion and hostility within the organization. It makes one wonder whether our overemphasis on corporate well-being and wealth leaves a deficiency and distortion of values and "true community among people."[1]

Government and Big Business Are Synonymous

In today's global economically-competitive world, our governmental and corporate concerns have become interconnected like never before. Understandably, one's own financial well-being is important to every individual. But because of this fact, the corporate world has seized this opportunity to take ever-increasing control over the political structure of this country for its own benefit. "The monetary connection between corporate interests and politicians grows ever tighter."[2] Even "our education system is judged by its success in making us economically competitive; students are viewed primarily as potential employees (not as potential citizens)."[3] The Gross National Product (GNP) is supposed to be a measuring indicator of our well-being. But, while it may be symbolic of our economic soundness, it is not a measure of our happiness, personal satisfaction or sense of individual freedom. Consequently, we must be vigilant not to lose sight of a human value system in a country patterned for the sake of economics and "money-making-as-the-highest-good."[4] We as citizens must make decisions responsibly and which takes into account the well-being of society as a whole that projects well into the future.

Meanwhile, corporate special interest groups continue to take advantage of the government's complexities (i.e., its widespread bureaucracies, expenditures of money in the many nooks and crevices within the budget and the implementation of special or emergency programs) for the betterment of their own clients' biased agendas. Well-placed lobbyists can influence the making of small adjustments to be made in regulations or laws, that will either allow their clients to reap large financial benefits or enable the passing along of costs to another participatory faction or group.

An example of this latter practice happened in Florida's sugar industry. Its special interest lobbyists were able to finagle last-minute changes in a legislative bill that, in turn, allowed sugar growers to pass on to the government much of the cost for the clean-up from their industry's crop-fertilizer runoff that flowed out into the Everglades. Since the Everglades was a National Park (and was on the government's agenda to be cleaned up anyway by using taxpayers' money), the sugar growers basically shifted responsibility of their clean-up costs to the government, by letting it pay the brunt of the overall costs. In essence, they "rode the back" of the government sector's public responsibilities in order to shirk any large payouts of their own.

Furthermore, many corporations and individual contributors are "hedging their bets" today by making large donations to both political parties, so that they can't lose either way. The rationale for this type of thinking is twofold. First, there is no partisan political permanency in Congress or the White House. Therefore, if you contribute to only one side, you can't get the access and influence for your interests when the other side comes to power. Second, "policy differences between the two parties have begun to decrease" [5]—possibly (at least in part) as a direct outgrowth of both having attracted such similar financial bases from the very same contributors.

It doesn't seem like such tactics (or any similar ones) are going to disappear anytime soon either—even with the new 2002 law that was suppose to reform federal campaign-finance. Even though "soft money" (unlimited donations to national political parties) will be prohibited, significant loopholes are left so that contributions will simply be shifted in other ways to support party-affiliated candidates. For example, large, particularly partisan special interest groups (e.g., NRA, NEA) that have a strong affinity toward either the Republican or Democratic Party will instead receive this freed-up money (through large and unlimited contributions). In turn, they can do the work of the political parties by getting out the message for like-minded, party candidates.

Furthermore, this law doesn't affect contributions to state and local parties, which also could be used for supporting their respective candidates. Moreover, the amount of "hard money" (individual donations directly to federal candidates) actually was allowed to increase from $1000 to $2000. In essence, the new law really only addresses the vehicle mechanism for the receipt of contributions—rather than the contributions themselves.

Shifting Facades of Corporations

It is necessary for corporations to constantly change their public personas in order to get what they want (or a particular, desired result). As was just discussed, if it is in its own interest, a corporation will ride piggyback as the government implements public agendas and policies. Conversely, if the executives of a corporation feel that the government is responding to public opinion or a "whistleblower" about some activity of theirs, they cry that it is an invasion of their privacy. For example, if a decision or action (that is carried out through corporate implementation) should happen to have social or environmental ramifications, they become defensive and claim that it is an internal matter that is being dealt with appropriately by their own investigators. Therefore, on the one hand, when a law or policy is convenient or beneficial to them, then they are quick to jump and take a ride on the government's back. Conversely, if it happens to be detrimental to them, then they do not demonstrate any reciprocity for allowing the government to jump on the corporation's back.

A similar version of these "public" (Dr. Jekyll) versus "private" (Mr. Hyde) behavior patterns is seen when the corporation uses the balance sheet as an excuse. This method is used when a major corporation is in financial trouble and needs a "bailout" from the government. The corporation suddenly thinks that it should be viewed as a public institution deserving of and expecting sympathy, because it considers itself "a noble service organization providing the community with employment and a product which has long been part of the American tradition and should be treated with respect...and obviously deserves a handout."[6] But, this treatment is obviously a double-standard when small businesses fail for whatever reason, they do not have the clout to receive any substantial handout. Whatever happened to the notion of free market competition?

On the other hand, what happens when a corporation is already making steady profits from operations and suddenly decides that it needs to realize even more profits? It quickly takes on the persona of a private business and will take exception to any government or public scrutiny of its affairs. If it decides to close a U.S. plant and move the work across the border to Mexico or some other Third World country (where labor is cheaper), the corporation is quick to assert that it has no obligation to the public to keep Americans employed. It will then use any of the following excuses: (a) we're entitled to make a buck (b) the labor force has to be expendable for the corporation's economic survival (c) governmental rules and regulations are too intrusive.

Philip Slater described the gist of how many large corporations operate (and receive a form of "corporate welfare") in his book, *A Dream Deferred: America's Discontent And The Search For A New Democratic Ideal*: "Corporations have never paid their own way. As a group, they are reminiscent of the proverbial spoiled teenager: they take whatever they want without paying, expect everyone to clean up after them, have a million excuses when caught in wrongdoing ('You didn't *tell* me I couldn't'), and when asked to take responsibility for their actions will expend more energy (and money—on lawyers, lobbyists, and misleading advertising) arguing and dragging their feet, than they would have spent had they simply gone ahead and cleaned up their corporate room.

Exxon's handling of its massive oil spill in Alaska is a case in point...Exxon spent millions on public relations 'damage control' that might have been applied to the cleanup (not to mention the money spent trying to block enactment of the structural requirements affecting tanker construction that would have prevented the spill)...corporations seem to feel that the world owes them not just a living but a handsome profit as well."[7]

Cost/Benefit Psychology

The paramount goal of the typical corporation is to do anything that will further only its own self-interest—with merely a token, superficial concern for the self-interest of the public, the consumers and its own employees. As we have seen, corporations will tiptoe around the law (or even break it) if they can calculate ahead of time that the cost/benefit ratio of the outcome will maximize their own gain. For example, "corporations routinely steal the inventions of individual patent-holders, knowing that there is no way the cost of their wrongdoing can ever catch up with the money to be made from ripping off a good innovation."[8] Morality is conveniently pushed aside while "playing-to-win" becomes the all-encompassing motivation.

A similar occurrence of this philosophical attitude took place when U.S. companies sold sophisticated, computer satellite technology to China, even though such technology would have applications in strengthening China's own weapon systems. Ironically, such weapons could very well be used against our own nation sometime in the future—all because the temptation of increasing the bottom line of corporate profits overrode any conscientious moral concerns.

This cost/benefit philosophy is also applicable if and when the corporation is charged with being irresponsible in regards to worker health and safety. The large profit margin that a chemical company can make with its customers more than counteracts any loss that may be forthcoming from a lawsuit from any mere employee(s), who may have been "contaminated" or acquired a chronic (or deadly) illness while processing a particular chemical that the company manufactures. Even if the executives in the company have confidential knowledge that one particular chemical is hazardous to produce (and may affect a small group of their total workforce), they realize that any damage settlement is just a pittance of the profit that they can make from the production of that one chemical.

Moreover, plant managers or foremen in such a company may use other employees in their workforce to convince any accuser not to even file a lawsuit. They may use the excuse that all of their jobs are expendable if any employees "make waves." Similarly, let's say an explosion occurs in the plant or a railcar derails and a chemical cloud is released in the surrounding area of the small town. Oftentimes, this small town is simply a "company" town in that a large proportion of families are dependent on the company for their own livelihood. So, by the time that, the news media arrive there, the company's public relations people have worked their "smooth magic" on how the townspeople should react—generally meaning to play down the severity of any effects of such an explosion.

Thus, when any response from the townspeople finally materializes on your television screen, the only words (in effect) that you'll hear from an exemplary employee are: "Yeah I have a slight burning in my throat and chest and my eyes are teary, but it's no worse than if I had a bad cold—you don't have to worry about us here, we'll be O.K." (as the viewer sees a huge, mushrooming toxic cloud forming in the background from delayed explosions still taking place from the accident.)

Oil and chemical companies are notorious for removing themselves and their collective consciences from any such wrongdoing and/or exploitation that their actions cause (personally or environmentally). Their huge corporate profits and the smiling faces of their stockholders are dependent on it. This is the ultimate in corporate greed…where extreme advantage is taken (or excessive hardship created) on others all for the sake of excessive profits.

Molding the Employee and Consumer

Industry has been responsible for proliferating the philosophy that the guiding framework for every individual motivation in society should be realized from jobs, money and goods purchased. The more work we do, allows us to make more money, so that we may buy an ever-increasing abundance of goods. Industry has conditioned us to use these functions in order to define ourselves totally—to the extent, that if it were not for these criteria, few of us would have any personal identities whatsoever. Our goal in life becomes the collection of more and more "stuff" (borrowing a term here from comedian, George Carlin)—goods that we don't need or even really enjoy. So, we have encountered here ***Paradox #4***. In essence, we are on a non-stop treadmill. We must continue to produce-distribute-buy to the point of extraneous overconsumption—like some kind of farm animal that has become bloated from eating too much (all for the sake of economic stability, even if the production of the stuff is merely superfluous). In such a situation, we become the servants, not the masters, of material production.

So, today it is not unusual to see such items as "Louie, The Large-Mouth Bass" for sale as a mail order item advertised on television (or similar items in stores as well). Basically, what you get here is a mechanically-in-motion, talking and singing fish on a plaque…I guess to be used for those times when there's nobody else around to talk and sing with. Otherwise, what would possess someone to buy something like this? O.K., it is a novel item for the obsessed fisherman who simply cannot live long periods of time without being around fish (even a facsimile of one). But, wouldn't the novelty wear off after you had heard the fish sing its entire repertoire of songs and jokes a few times? The real question though here is: What other stuff will companies think up next, that we simply do not need?

One could go so far as to imply that companies are looking for every conceivable market (no matter how unlikely) to sell goods to. One past television commercial comes to mind, where a guy is literally free-flying in the air with a goose, all the while pouring soda pop down the goose's gullet. What should we make of this commercial? Should we conclude that the "human market" is so oversaturated, that this company is trying to sell pop to the "goose market" now?

It is truly humorous to visualize a bunch of executives meeting around a table in a boardroom for the purpose of acknowledging that the "goose market" for soda drinks is wide open—while unabashedly agreeing with each other to go after it. One executive may be explaining: "The word is that Research & Development has found that geese have an 'acquired taste' for soda pop. In fact, the geese have been following the technicians around the lab—ever since they received several, measured dosages of the pop from them."...So, the message is buy and consume it anyway that you can—even if you have to pour it down some bird or animal's throat...Which begs the question: Have we entirely lost all of our "marbles"?

There is no "decent" (optimal) level of consumption—rather progress and growth demand that consumption must increase without end. Therefore, our economic health becomes dependent on either duplication or continual innovation. We must perpetually: (a) Keep buying the same product over and over again. For example, the guy who has a half dozen shavers in his drawer at home, even though he only needs one. Or similarly, the guy who has a dozen watches (one of which tells the time in every world time zone, even though the wearer has never been out of the United States). (b) Make existing products obsolete preferably as soon as possible. But, this notion does not address the fact that our problem is not that we have too few material items—but rather that we have too little time to even use the items that we already have. (c) Constantly improve quality or the "new and improved game," where a person is suppose to replace a totally good, practical product with a new and improved version. A good example to cite would be the purchasing of a new car to replace your still reliable one. Also, examples like CDs, HDTV and DVDs are all really only upgrades from the original innovations of stereo records, television and video cassettes, respectively. In other words, we could get by without them and the quality of our lives would not be any worse off because of it. Admittedly, they're better quality but still part of the "new and improved game," a mere upgrade in technology that was already in place. The point to be made here is that our individual, personal compulsions to continually upgrade our material possessions may very well be simply a habitual practice that emanates more from a societal norm than anything else. (d) Invent completely new products.

So, industry presses for two somewhat dichotomous dogmas: keep buying what we already have ("more is better") while at the same time promoting the doctrine of obsolescence. But, this overall concept is more complex than it appears on the surface. This monolithic, economic notion (that is so pervasive and dominant in our culture) shapes how we as individual citizens view our own world, and it narrowly confines how each of us envisions life's alternatives. Even though life should consist of infinite variety, we choose instead to quantify everything that is supposedly "valuable" to the extent that "the only real value can be 'more,' and growth...the only acceptable sign of progress or of doing well. "[9]

Today, each of us has completely entwined his or her identity with what job you do, economically. One's existing job and how you can "better" yourself by making more money is expected to be the highest societal goal for each of us. It defines you as a person and quantifies (in dollar terms) how "valuable" you may be in performing your ever-relevant, purchasing-power duty. How valuable you are depends on just how much money you can "cough up"? (As if you were a cartoon character's head on a "Pez" candy dispenser, whose mouth opened and yielded another payout every time society said, "It's time for you to do your part and make another purchase." Maybe it is not a coincidence that Pez candies are in the shape of mini gold bullion bars).

Of course, this philosophy implies that our lives are no better than a bunch of busy worker bees (i.e., I've done my part financially, now I can die off—or at least temporarily "buzz" off until society needs me again, economically). The purchaser becomes the equivalent of nothing more than a "Pavlovian conditioned" laboratory mouse...with a piece of cheese being thrust out at you, when it is time for you to salivate again.

But, industry's overemphasis on our economic well-being has been at a high (and still growing) cost; that is, to health, relationships, contentment and *overall* well-being (including self-esteem and self-approval). We are in a vicious cycle where we keep sacrificing these things which can make a difference in bettering ourselves as people—for those things which, for the most part, really no longer do (material stuff). Personal growth has been pushed aside by economic growth. It's ironic that the only time that we are willing to project into the future is in regards to what else—but economic productivity and consumption (e.g., where do you see yourself being, financially, in five years from now?)

Personal gain is still seen by most of us in an economic light. The satisfaction of one's "inner personhood" is generally left on a "back burner," even though many of us sense a longing for something that is inwardly missing. For the most part, our current economic structure does not afford an employee the "luxury" to resolve a dilemma such as: Should I work more hours at the company to improve my chances for a promotion or should I come home at the normal time in order to spend more time with my child? The corporate world teaches us all—that you better choose the former way if you want to continue to even work for this company (let alone get a promotion). The message is "Hey, that's a no-brainer; decision made; do you have a problem with that?"

Furthermore, many companies expect us to be mobile, if we want to rise on the corporate ladder. One must be willing to travel overnight (including weekends) for the company—the more prestigious the position that you have, the greater likelihood that you will have to spend more weeks away from home. Even worse, on a corporate whim, you can also expect to uproot your entire family and relocate to different geographic areas throughout the country (or internationally) depending on where the company thinks that you are needed most. In short, you end up getting transferred around the world like an express delivery package. If this occurrence happens often enough, the individual becomes a "portable human resource" (possibly more inanimate than human) for the corporation—a mere cog in a continually moving and expanding economic "machine." And through all of this displacement, the company expects your utmost loyalty, first and foremost (although don't expect it to happen vice-versa). Unfortunately, too much of this routine plays havoc on family relationships, social ties, self-concept, and the spirit for freedom and individuality. In essence, one's personhood is sacrificed for the sake of the corporate well-being.

Consumer Advertising

One can define advertising as simply the psychological creation of "needs" (that in actually, are merely "wants"). ***Paradox #5:*** The value of advertising (from industry's point of view) is that it creates in our minds that "wants" (the non-essential things that gratify our desires) are really "needs" (the essential things for our survival and growth) that we cannot live without. And, advertisers perform this task by making all of us feel perpetually dissatisfied with ourselves and/or our possessions that we currently have. They instill anxiety within us so that we will act on it with the "appropriate" behavior (i.e., going out and buying whatever it is that they are advertising). These "ads serve to deflect discontent with the system into discontent with the self, and then bolster the system by implying that this discontent can be remedied by buying the appropriate products." [10] The important thing to the advertisers is that these "wants" become insatiable and, ultimately, infinite.

For example, advertisers make us apprehensive about whether: our teeth are white enough; our hair is becoming too gray; our faces becoming too wrinkled; our clothes reflect the latest fashion; our cars have the most up-to-date features; our houses should be "made-over" (or upgraded); our pets are being given the "correct" food for their specific age; our gardens are receiving the proper nutrient balance for maximum yield…etc. etc. etc. The point is that these are all "wants" that aren't necessary, but the advertisers convince us that we "need" them as much as the air that we breathe or the water that we drink.

Advertisers are also especially ingenious in how they remold the value of important national figures on their historic dates. In the process, they discount the very nature of any historic significance by promoting their items that they are selling. It literally makes you think twice of what exactly you are giving remembrance to on that date, in the first place?

For example, for the amount and type of advertising that retail department store chains do during Lincoln and Washington's birthdays—it's surprising that some younger kids don't think that these two leaders were actually former department store Presidents, and that's the reason why we are celebrating. After all, how many times have we seen theatrically-dressed look-alikes of these two Presidents come on the screen and make a pitch for buying just about every conceivable item imaginable?

Similarly, advertisers not only do it for historic dates, but noteworthy events as well. How many times have we heard a pitch something like this: "It's Olympic time again, and you know what that means—it's your opportunity to reap 'gold-medal' savings at your local car dealerships." Now wouldn't something like this ad make the Ancient Greeks feel proud of how the original intention of the true spirit of respectful competition and worldly fellowship and goodwill of the Games has gotten turned around?

Thus, advertising has become a major cultural intruder for re-engineering our psyches. It manipulates us unrelentingly (and often dishonestly) so that we will continue to consume simply for the sake of consumption itself. Again, it proliferates the notion that the "economic" self is the one distinguishing characteristic (from the many each of us has) that is all important and which should be most apparent (or visible). "If you are relatively happy with your life, if you enjoy spending time with your children…if you enjoy nature…if you enjoy living simply, if you sense no need to compete with your friends or neighbors—*what good are you economically?*"[11] "The economy grows but the human spirit, seduced into losing its way, is diminished."[12] By appealing to fears, advertisers have "sold the American people a way of living, fast of tempo and focused on private consumption."[13] How much is too much? No amount is too much. It's not a matter that people shouldn't feel good about material items (in a general and practical way), but shouldn't there be some sense for limitation—at some point, diminishing returns? "Only when we are clear about what we need and what we want can we begin to pare away the excess and find…our capacity to participate wholeheartedly and enthusiastically in life."[14]

Furthermore, advertising tends to seduce the consumer and creates desire and envy in his or her personal character. These feelings occur before *and* after the purchase of the particular item that the ad is seeking for you to buy. This desire and envy become so strong in some of us that the inanimate object acquires almost human/emotional characteristics, and the advertisements do nothing to hide the promulgation of such feelings. Automobile commercials especially instill such responses with catch-phrases such as: "*Crazy* 'Bout A Ford Truck" or "Chevrolet; The *Heartbeat* of America" or "The *Family* of Automobiles from Mitsubishi" (or a more recent commercial for a particular model—"No matter how humble you are on the outside, deep down on the inside you're saying, '*I'm better than you are*'.")

And, people's behaviors actually exemplify this fact. Such is the case when a BMW automobile owner has a license plate that reads, LUV BMW…or a gentleman tells his date to be on the lookout for he and "Mercedes" (as in Benz) at about 7 P.M…or when people request in their wills that they are to be buried in the driver's seat of their "adoring" automobile, where each spent so much time (and who now cannot fathom of parting with in the afterlife).

Furthermore, advertisers have no inhibitions in denigrating the good memories that we have of deceased people in promoting sales of their items. A most appropriate example was the use of the marvelous dance talents of Fred Astaire to help sell the "Dirt Devil" vacuum cleaner. With the help of computer-aided design, the consumer was presented with a "mystical" image of Mr. Astaire joyously sweeping the floor instead of sweeping Ginger Rogers off her feet. This enactment epitomizes total disregard for the man and the originally-intended purpose of his creative artistry.

While advertising has an effect on all of us, our most important concern should be how it molds children. Advertisers are relentless in trying to reach them wherever they may be (and whatever they are doing) at any given time. They also "use" them in promoting their products (e.g., sponsoring children's events; marketing program-related items on the very children's television show that they are watching; as walking "human" billboards where apparel is used to promote a company's product).

The epitome of how advertisers have abused their children-directed marketing tool is demonstrated by the competitiveness for market share of the sneaker business between Nike and Adidas. They actually compete with each other in order to find students who are outstanding basketball players at the *elementary* school level who can be used for future promotions. At the high school level, they convince the school's coaches (and ultimately the students) to wear their particular apparel line, so that each school can be categorized as a "Team Nike" or "Team Adidas" school, respectively. In turn, there is an implied conveyance that life is really about "exclusive prestige," and this message (no matter how wrong it might be) becomes imprinted on impressionable teenagers' minds.

There is another way that advertisers use children. Some companies supply teaching materials that somehow relate to their own products. A candy company sends out material on geography to elementary schools, where students learn to locate major cities that coincidentally happen to correspond to where its manufacturing plants are situated throughout the country. A fast-food chain is promoted in a reading program where kindergarten students fill in the blank with the one missing menu selection that is listed in a particular sentence—and which can be found at its fast-food establishments. The rationale being that (since the experience of eating out at their fast-food restaurant) is probably one of the few impressionable moments from their young lives which they have had in the real world, such "reminiscent identification" should keep the children's attention on the corporate name as well as the classroom lesson.

Since many school districts are financially-challenged to provide extra aids for teachers in order to make the curricula more interesting, some teachers feel inclined to make use of the corporate aids, even though they are "soft-selling" the particular product in the process. Moreover, these materials generally are more up-to-date than the textbooks and are, therefore, more topical in emphasizing a school lesson.

Finally, there was Whittle Communications' Channel One, the in-school daily news program that included paid commercials from the producer's corporate clients. The company's Chairman defended the inclusion of youth-oriented product ads between news stories as: "the price schools must bear for up-to-the-minute news and state-of-the-art technology."[15] But, that begs the question: Why should students and teachers have to "bear any price" for the purposeful intrusion of an optional (and certainly questionable) type of learning advanced by corporate self-interests? It would be time better spent, if teachers would explain to their students how the advertising industry manipulates them for its own selfish purposes. How "the unguarded paths of visual imagery...bypass the critical faculties of consumers...[which] facilitates a kind of persuasion different from that of rational discourse."[16]

Crunching the Workforce

Starting in the 1980s, Corporate America has been letting go (as well as letting down) productive employees of a previously loyal workforce. There are mixed reasons (i.e., reorganization, downsizing and re-engineering) for their actions, but, nonetheless, all of their motives are calculated and purposeful.

It started with the practice of "mergermania," an out-of-control "locomotive" that picked up steam as more and more corporate officers realized the profitable financial benefits that could be accrued through such buyouts or fusions. This syndrome separated the financial system from the areas of production and, in turn, made profit an end in itself.

This strategy allowed the "upper-crust" corporate executives to profit strictly from the result of financial manipulations. Production became a tool of finance, not vice-versa. Money was directly converted into more money without even producing any commodities. It was enhanced even further by reducing, displacing and/or converting the workforce (e.g., many of the no-longer-needed, higher-paying jobs in sales, management and administration into lower-paying service jobs).

So, today you have a situation where companies (almost proudly) proclaim that they have job openings. But, there is little mention that they are mostly in the lower-paying service categories. Furthermore, the corporate world is responsible for playing hocus-pocus with the workplace as well as the workforce—placing them on a string like a yo-yo that can be reeled in and reeled out at anytime.

Companies would counter by arguing that they are hiring recent college graduates at good salaries. Well, yes they are—but these type of salaries are mostly reserved for the graduates in the very competitive fields of computer systems, engineering and science (and much less so for other majors). But, you can be assured that once these graduates get to be 45 to 50 years old, their corporate usefulness as employees along with their ever-increasing higher salaries will be seen as expendable—and the corporations will start the whole cycle over again. Today, corporations see a good employee's work span as 25 years instead of 45 years.

Moreover, the fact that many companies still do not use the foresight to show a genuine concern for their established employees (through full benefits; keeping them employed; or helping them find similar jobs in other companies if they must be let go)—is not only bad for their companies, but bad for the country. In the long run, it is truly in the best interests of companies to "take care" of their employees, because they will, in turn, receive dedicated, productive, innovative and mentally/emotionally secure workers. In addition, the companies could be contributing to the positive upbringing of secure and happy children for the next generation of workers (i.e., by providing professional on-site child care, which would allow employees better "peace of mind"). This point cannot be overstated, because if this country needs anything, it is "socially responsible" people. The money that companies outlay for such "human needs" is a small cost, when it is compared to the immeasurable assets (human and financial) that the company (as well as the country) would reap in return.

The sad thing is that it is a comparatively small financial expenditure for companies to give all of their workers full and extended benefits—when one considers the large expenditures put out for all the write-offs, that they are so used to taking for bad decisionmaking in other corporate sectors. Workers would automatically become more productive for companies that portray such "worthwhile" images. The only loss to the stockholders' profits would be a slight downward "blip" when considering the larger picture of the company's whole earnings cycle. Once the stock market easily discounted these added employee costs, its only slightly altered stock price could, once again, resume a natural upward or downward trend based on the company's projected earnings.

Furthermore, when a company lays off workers, a non-monetary corporate cost is often overlooked—"corporate memory."[17] This term can be defined as "the unique business experience that has been accumulated over the years by a particular employee, and that specifically relates to the everyday smooth functioning of the company." "Corporate memory" loss is visible in many forms. An engineer may have an unique or innovative perspective on a product design project. Service staffs can offer critical technical support. Office support can correspond; complete quotations; or settle claims faster—all of which increases customer satisfaction. Trained and experienced sales representatives have the depth to understand the product line; the selling aspect; as well as the "human factor" of a variety of customary clients. These type of personal assets are not easily replaced, and their absence will eventually cost a company financial profits in the long-run. Much is sacrificed "if no one is left to know the experiences that exist or what their content means to current decisions."[18]

The downsizing phenomenon further encourages the corporate practice of hiring part-time workers, temporary staffers and independent contractors/subcontractors. It has been predicted that as much as 35 percent of the U.S. workforce will be contingent workers sometime within the first decade of the 21st century.[19] This trend can only lead to a further deterioration of the feelings of loyalty; security; and sense of significance among the remaining full-time employees. Companies reason that this course of action is necessary, because of global competition and the need for flexibility because of volatile business conditions and market cycles. This assertion may very well be true, but "one by one, the tangible and intangible bonds that once defined work in America are giving way."[20]

The present (and future) typical corporate motto is going to be: "No long-term commitments of any kind." In the tug-a-war with employees, many companies claim that in order to compete that they can no longer offer many of its workers: pensions, health insurance, promotions based on performance, costly training programs and/or paid vacations. Our country's *human* capital is being discounted, and something in the bond between corporation and the workforce is already starting "to give" (and most likely will get worse). The trend to hire contingent workers is a long-term strategy by management to be able to cut employee benefits, because these "account for nearly 45 percent of the total reimbursement for time worked by permanent, full-time employees."[21] This procedure is a great way to save lots of money without it being "psychologically" reflected in the basic hourly wage for work *performed* by the worker.

Contingent workers are being used virtually in every industry, and they cut across all occupational levels including: corporate professionals in computer systems, human resource and financial service departments as well as scientists in the research & development areas. So, every sector of the corporation is being effected: office, management, manufacturing, technical and distribution. Even the federal government, has joined the bandwagon to a lesser, but increasing, extent.

Companies are also using outsourcing (or subcontracting) to supply goods and services in the completion of products or on custom-made projects. It is not an atypical occurrence to hear where a skilled laborer is being laid off from a large company in order to reduce costs—only to be hired by a subcontractor to work on the very project (that was actually outsourced by his former employer) at less than half of his previous wage. Furthermore, all of these corporate practices tend to drive down (or at least keep stagnant) the wages of the remaining full-time workers, who are understandably fearful of losing their own jobs in the same manner.

But, they too are at risk in a different way. The reduced, full-time workforce has to make up for the loss of its former fellow workers by wearing several "hats" on the job, with increased responsibilities for often the same pay and no personnel support. Consequently, the company's operations and integrity are at further risk by causing its workers to be susceptible to "burnout, turnover, absenteeism and lowered productivity."[22] The onset of these stress-induced characteristics are further precipitated by corporate use of video cameras to monitor employee performance, and by using computers to measure how quickly an employee carries out a particular job function (and whether there is room for improvement).

In review, we can see that the "psychological contract"[23] between employer and full-time employee has been compromised to such an extent, that it is very possible that it has caused a permanent schism in the relationship—one which will not be able to be easily bridged by either side, but especially by the workers of future generations.

Given these set of circumstances, competent employees in the corporation have no alternative but to devote the bulk of their personal resources on doing whatever it takes to build their own careers—even to the point where it becomes only self-serving compared to any needs or priorities that the company may have. In essence, self-interest has replaced loyalty on both sides—and, this barrier of concrete is starting to set into place, whereby it will become immovably hard. So, we have arrived at *Paradox #6*: How can a company demand loyalty of others, while demonstrating no loyalty itself? One of the biggest complaints by companies today is that they cannot find workers who are committed, motivated and willing to make sacrifices. Yet, we all can very well see that the companies themselves are largely responsible for creating this lack of positive work ethics among workers in general—whether they be currently employed or looking for work.

Re-engineering

We must also add the ever-present factor of "re-engineering" to the growing list of worker job insecurities. This term simply means restructuring entire companies by replacing humans with technology wherever it is feasible. It would include: a computer answering all incoming calls with a menu selection that the caller must use in order to even hope to reach anyone human; or a computer doing large amounts of administrative management or statistical analysis work that used to be done by many levels of workers in multi-departments; or an automated machine or robot doing a myriad of manufacturing tasks previously done by skilled, technical workers. So, the high-tech elimination of jobs affects all workers; white collar and blue collar.

Corporations are basically squashing down the traditional pyramid-shaped hierarchies that (up to now) have been the standard of a typical organization. In effect, the pyramid has become a much flatter shape. Because, in order to remain competitive in the marketplace, companies must be able to respond quicker in their production using every nuance of upgraded technology, while also making their decisionmaking faster and manageable (i.e., with less hierarchical levels). With the acceleration of time and pace which is characteristic of high technology, middle managers do not have the time to coordinate and control the decisions going up and down the corporate ladder. Sophisticated computer technologies can coordinate and implement these functions much faster than employees at many job levels can perform them.

The corresponding result is the creation of "more direct lines of communication between the 'top and bottom' of an organization."[24] Small, decentralized network and team working units can use computers at any location within the company to retrieve and process information and coordinate decisions for any and all projects. Computer-based technologies have allowed "information to be processed horizontally rather vertically, in effect collapsing the traditional corporate pyramid in favor of networks operating along a common plane."[25]

Large discount chains are using information technology that bypasses any need for their own warehousing of items. Information from point-of-sale scanners can be transmitted directly to suppliers, who then can ship items in the desired quantities. This procedure allows the discounter to eliminate the need for hiring many of its own clerical and warehousing jobs, which would have simply been repetitive, wasted work. Similarly, auto dealers may choose to punch in on their computers a particular customer's automobile options, so that the production plant can make more automobiles virtually "custom-made." In this way, the dealer can keep customer loyalty, while the manufacturing plant can keep lower inventories and, thereby, reduce its costs.

Given the world market, the key question for all industries (more than at anytime in the past) has become: "How can we find a competitive advantage?" The answer: "Anyway you can." A survivalist mentality (where the only alternative is a win-lose situation) has become intrinsically drilled into every company's philosophy throughout the world. If you cannot keep up, you lose. Because clients will continue to request speed of delivery as well as improved quality control, all companies are being forced to invest in further high-tech solutions—unfortunately, to the detriment of the workforces. This fact will always be so, because the bottom line for companies is increased productivity of goods and services—not for hiring people simply to keep them employed.

Protests from workers will be at best only slightly recompensive—similar to the analogy that you might win small battles in certain circumstances, but still lose the overall war. Because today, there are going to always be some companies in other countries of the world, that are going to be able to find it to their own competitive advantage to take up any slack in production or service that such events might cause. After all, just about anywhere in the world, people are willing to work for a many-fold reduction in wages when compared to Americans. Their seemingly low wages still will entitle them to live happily at a higher standard of living than they are used to—but that we Americans would find unacceptable. The message from every company to every employee in the world will be: "At least you have some job, and that is better than no job." Although this philosophy is rather exploitative in nature, it could unfortunately become more and more true in many of our own futures.

But, we Americans might be the only ones that may have a very hard time of accepting it—when we compare it to the standard of living that we have enjoyed (and gotten used to) in the past. Many of us may simply have to grit and bear it. When you consider that the overall changes from re-engineering still have a potentially long way to go (especially in less developed countries), this is a vision that is hard to swallow.

Almost fifty years ago, Norbert Weiner, the innovator of cybernetics, cautioned of the likely negative consequences of automation technologies. His quote may never be more appropriate to use than our present and upcoming future: "Let us remember that the automatic machine…is the precise economic equivalent of slave labor. Any labor which competes with slave labor must accept the economic consequences of slave labor."[26] America is threatened with an ever-growing underclass "as the new thinking machines relentlessly make their way up the economic pyramid, absorbing more and more skilled jobs and tasks along the way."[27]

One might jump to the conclusion that the high-technology sector will provide more than enough new jobs that were lost in other job levels and categories. This assumption would be premature. The new high-tech information segment will continue to have steady job growth. But, not nearly enough *higher*-paying jobs will be created to compensate for the total loss of former jobs that were individually-productive and beneficial, but were "phased out" nonetheless.

Consequently, we are slowly beginning to see the signs of an emerging two-class system in the U.S. (and for all intents and purposes throughout the world). The upper class would consist largely of professional "knowledge workers" (of information/technological systems) representing 20 percent of the workforce.[28] This percentage could be expected to increase slightly over a period of time. Everyone else (above the poverty line) would virtually be lumped into one other category, many of whom would provide functions/support and general services to and for the knowledge sector.

Every Administration and Congress always push for training programs that will help such displaced workers, so that these workers (and the country) can compete in the competitive, technologically-oriented world of work. But, the government is overly optimistic in its assessment of how meaningful such implementations can be, because the momentum has perpetually changed for every sector of the economy to always automate wherever and whenever possible.

Paradox #7: Something cannot contract and expand at the same time. One cannot simply have it both ways. Note that we are not talking here about all jobs—rather a more select group of jobs (that allow workers to readily afford the cost of living, so that they can lead at least a minimally-comfortable life). Since the motive for creating a high-tech society is to become more competitive and profitable (i.e., "leaner and meaner")—the result is going to be a smaller class of selective workers.

Even if we could retrain the large numbers of workers for high-tech jobs, there will not be enough room (or need) for them all in this "leaner and meaner" marketplace. Furthermore, "the gap in educational levels between those needing jobs and the kind of high-tech jobs available is so wide that no retraining program could hope to adequately upgrade the educational performance of workers to match the kind of limited professional employment opportunities that exist."[29] In short, for any number of possible reasons, not everyone has the capability to think "technologically" to the degree needed for daily competent job performance.

Moreover, the government sector cannot come to the rescue for the creation of these jobs. All levels of government are trying to cut programs. The rule of government is to downsize the number of bureaucrats. Its calling is to eliminate any overlap of functions and waste completely, and automate wherever possible. So, the government would not be able to be substantially counted on except for a few, select (and limited) job programs.

Another consideration that needs to be pondered upon is how all of these labor-saving, technological advances may eventually affect the economy as a whole over a period of time. We are eliminating higher-paying jobs, while creating lower-paying service jobs as substitutes. Therefore, in the not-so-distant future, the government is going to have to be watchful for any general failure among the public to generate the necessary purchasing power, so that the economy does not take a precipitous dip. This conceptualization could happen, if this characteristic pattern of elimination/formation of jobs continues.

Critics of this notion (of reduced purchasing power) argue that, new products and services of the future will provide abundant opportunities and jobs for displaced workers. But, this criticism can be, in turn, counteracted with the answer that these future products will be manufactured in highly automated fashions, while any new services are sure to be more entrepreneurial in nature and, thereby, not require "excess" employees.

Other critics assert that "new global markets will stimulate pent-up consumer demand."[30] But, this argument has two shortcomings. First, this new consumer demand might not be so strong, when one considers the fact that workers in Third World countries who will be technologically displaced (and accordingly lose a significant amount of purchasing power and demand), will be far greater in numbers than the United States. Second, because of tremendous global competition, American goods and services are going to have to be "globally priced"—meaning lower costs (including muzzling workers' wages) and smaller corporate profits overall. It would seem that the optimists' viewpoint of unending global demand and purchasing power has to be tempered quite a bit for it to reflect a more likely realistic scenario.

Chapter 3

EGO, GREED & SOCIETY

In order to put some perspective on how we as a society have reached our out-of-control need for consumption and insatiable accumulation of material goods, we must first note what the original meaning of the term, work ethic, implied. Historically, social and economic advancement depended on individual initiative that was put forth by the "self-made" man. He embodied the habits of industriousness, success built on moderate increments, self-discipline and avoidance of debt. "He lived for the future, shunning self-indulgence in favor of patient, painstaking accumulation...[which would eventually lead to] an abundant source of profits."[1] Furthermore, "a godly man worked diligently at his calling not so much in order to accumulate personal wealth as to add to the comfort and convenience of the community."[2]

But today, the very nature of "free enterprise" has changed so dramatically and permanently, that this way of success is much harder to achieve for the following reasons:

(1) The ability of the "self-made" man to compete with the capital-rich corporation is much more difficult, if not impossible. A perfect, yet basic, example would be the "Mom & Pop" store trying to compete with one of the discount mass merchandisers. Because of the comparative scale of operation, the retail price that the latter charges its customers, may (at times) be close to the wholesale price that the former pays just to buy it. This situation has become evident in the towns and smaller cities across all of America, where the buildings on "Main Street" have a plethora of out-of-business or "for sale" signs in the windows.

(2) Destruction of sense of community is the corresponding result—which totally negates the "work ethic" premise of the "self-made man

working for the comfort and convenience of the community." The business and social town center no longer exists, and its existence instead has been transferred to the act of impersonally talking to others while waiting in check-out lines of the mass merchandisers somewhere on the outskirts of town.
(3) The global, multinational corporations and their huge network of subsidiaries can manufacture any consumer, commercial or industrial good desired. The only thing left for the "self-made" man is in the small niche or "special order" markets, and even here the subsidiaries of the larger corporations often branch out to catch these markets. The result: "Big Brother" has left no stone unturned.
(4) Mega-mergers of large companies squeeze out "the excess human capital" (caught in between the fusion process) and makes for stiffer competition. As alluded to in the previous chapter, we are talking thousands of workers pushed out with each merger.
(5) The ever-present, historic (although currently slower) inflationary pressure.
(6) Market advertising (by credit card and loan companies) that makes indebtedness appear incredibly blasé. Therefore, many would-be entrepreneurs may unwittingly carry too much personal or business start-up debt, which can sink them in the cruel and unforgiving vagaries of economic competition.

Given these set of circumstances, an individual's future has become uncertain and threatened. The will to win over your competition (anyway that you can) has taken center stage. The mentality is that if you don't do "it" to him now, he'll end up doing "it" to you later. So, in order to become successful, it has become an accepted practice to exploit others in order to create the "winning image" for getting ahead in the game. In essence, the attainment of success has become life itself.

"A profound shift in our sense of time transforms work habits, values and the definition of success. Self-preservation replaces self-improvement as the goal of earthly existence."[3] Correspondingly, following close on the heels of this philosophy, is the notion that the acquisition of more "stuff" becomes a societal measure of one's personal success. Moreover, this overemphasis on the immediate "wants" of the individual self has created a lost sense of historical continuity. "To live for the moment is the prevailing passion—to live for yourself, not for your predecessors or posterity. We are fast losing the sense of historical continuity, the sense of belonging to a succession of generations originating in the past and stretching into the future...a waning sense of historical time, an erosion of any strong concern for posterity."[4]

What is missing today in our culture gets back to the crux of the true philosophical intentions of our Founding Fathers. At that time, your value as a person was not based on how much material wealth that you could acquire for yourself, but rather in the amount of individual and family character that one could attain in and for the community. It's ironic that in our society today, we are quick to utter the saying that, "It is the American Way to prosper and acquire more individual wealth" (while actually omitting the words, "at the expense of others"). But, in reality, this country's original principles were not based on the attainment of individual wealth, but rather how the creation of this wealth could be used to better an entire community as well as our nation as a whole. What is missing today is individual civic duty, something that would make us feel better about others as well as ourselves.

Wealth As A Measuring Stick

Our focus especially in the last quarter century has been on the "measuring of ourselves against each other, and against some standard of living we continually strive to surpass...As in a television game show, the only real purpose is to try to have the most when the final buzzer sounds."[5] We have become awashed in ego and greed (as well as their corresponding excesses), while the building of individual character, meaning, and values in our lives have become low priorities. As individuals, we have simply become flaunters of our own misperceived value of our material wealth. What has become important is that you try to keep up (with the Joneses) anyway that you can or, otherwise, you could become one of the "downtrodden losers" in a game that only has winners and losers.

The popularity of past, game shows like, "You Want To Be A Millionaire" as well as "Greed: The Multi-Million Dollar Challenge," are perfect examples of this concept. These shows were seemingly harmless enough fun. But, one must question whether there is a deeper implication here about the nature of our society. How far have we sunk whereby we are so thoroughly entertained by contestants on stage epitomizing the lowest common denominator of character, that being, greed. The degree of the portrayal of this characteristic was so conspicuous, that the beings appeared more like one-dimensional, economic entities rather than humans. In fact, one show's mantra was "I feel the need for greed."

It is most interesting to see how the contestants came across (to you the viewer) when they introduced themselves. Each one looked adamantly into the camera and gave you a not-to-be-denied look, and said, for example, "I'm a substitute teacher from Alaska" (and you could almost sense that the contestant wanted to add, "And, I need the money.") To look at them, it was almost as if their eyeballs were actually like spinning slot machine wheels, which instead of stopping on cherries (when the lever was pulled), came up with a pair of dollar signs in their spinning orbs.

Furthermore, it is interesting to note the type of music which was played on both shows. The music almost seemed to equate greed with glorification. On one show, the music was seemingly reminiscent of a choir humming as you arrived at the Gates of Heaven. The other show, had the musical sound of a beating heart, as if each decision being made was a matter of life or death.

With the sweet smell of successful ratings, the networks have now put forth a preponderance of subsequent shows (which we call "reality" shows) that still have the winner-take-all theme, but with added twists. Not only could you receive big money from being the ultimate winner, but if you accomplished this feat through deceptive ways and/or betrayal, the more power to you.

So then, you had "Want to Marry A Millionaire," which characterized the acquiring of supposed, instant wealth as the sole criterion to be used in finding a suitable marriage partner. Only after the show, was it found that both individuals (who were to be married) had not been truthfully forthright in their own characterization of themselves. Then came "Survivor," followed by "Big Brother," then "The Mole"…"Boot Camp"…"Survivor: The Australia Outback"…"Chains of Love"…"Weakest Link"…"Fear Factor"…"Big Brother 2"…"Lost"…"The

Amazing Race"…"Survivor: Africa"…"Mole 2: The Next Betrayal"…"Who Wants To Be A Princess"…"The Chamber"…"The Chair"…"Meet My Folks"…"Dog Eat Dog… "Survivor: Marquesas"… The Glutton Bowl" (where the person who could feed his/her face with the most food in the fastest time, won)…"Survivor: Thailand"…"The Bachelor"…"The Bachelorette"…"Joe Millionaire"…and I'm sure a plethora of others since the writing of this book. Last but not least, we had "Temptation Island," whose premise was to have your loved one placed in situations where he or she would continually be tempted to partake in infidelity…Well, isn't that heartwarming?

All of these shows seemed to have a common thread to them. Each demonstrated the immoral notion that betrayal of others can get you further in life, and, consequently, therefore must be a noble characteristic—even though most of us know differently. In fact, ad spots for two of these shows included quotes from contestants like these: First, "I'll set them up by being nice, and then I'll stab them both in the back." Second, "Yes, I was lying…and I didn't lose any sleep over it."

Nonetheless, let us now get back to the original notion of measuring ourselves against each other, and how it can become even more intensified under the following conditions when: (1) our government warns the public that even when the economy is good, it is fragile, and that continued overconsumption of material goods is needed to avoid any economic downturn and, therefore, any loss of jobs. (2) "a virtually universal consumer indebtedness that, in most times and places, would have signaled crisis…but now [is] (seen as) business as usual."[6] The message becomes that there should be no boundaries on consumer spending. After all, if people are working in an economy that (at least currently) is good—why worry about going into debt even for items that you cannot really afford or let alone need. "Shopaholism" becomes the game, buying consumer goods simply for the sake of consuming, and everyone wants to be a winner. (3) the flaunting of one's importance and wealth becomes the norm (e.g., greater displays of "upperly-mobile" cars made that the standard for all "upstanding" Americans to pursue—if for no other reason, than as a recognition factor).

Meanwhile, any dividing line between "needs" and "wants" has become virtually eliminated. In other words, material items have reached such a high level in our priorities, that they are now seen as fulfilling and giving purpose to our very existence. That is, if I can possess an even more costly, more exclusive, luxury item than I already have, then it is expected that I (as well as others) will see myself as a substantially "better" person. The accumulation and portrayal of wealth is our way of competing for status and power and, ultimately, for feeling superior in comparison to others—although misguidedly so in the long-term of reality. Our continual and consuming desire to acquire such a sense of material, self-importance has resulted in us reeking of a collective smugness.

Meanwhile, the very ideal of the American Dream increasingly becomes ever-more voracious in its wants as we increase our expectations and "materialistic sights." It is interesting to note how our vision of the house with a white picket fence around the yard has now been "upgraded" to the standard goal of a mansion with an eight-foot, high wall surrounding an entire "compound." But through it all, the overwhelming question remains whether such aspirations of the so-called American Dream should be the goal of ours in the first place. Because, although we are constantly trying to meet our materialistic visions—we can often see retrospectively—that such fruitions have not fulfilled many of us nearly enough on each of our individual, internal levels.

The powerful grip of this whole concept is very deceptive, because on the surface material wealth looks like it is the right answer—the right approach. In actuality though, it is insidious in its nature, because it lulls you into a false sense of well-being. Thus, we have created a society based on a "greed mentality," where Americans increasingly feel mistrust, envy, ego and animosity all "rolled up into one." Furthermore, our societal emphasis and promotion of individual indulgence has made our culture one that is less responsible, less cohesive, and certainly less caring.

Material goods create security and insecurity simultaneously (***Paradox #8***)…security by using the faulty rationale that since we have more, therefore, we must be better off personally as well as "better" than other individuals…insecurity by causing us consternation about how to keep (as well as protect) the more that we have, while we try to stay ahead in the "thing game." Thus, the more we accumulate, the more insecure we become. For instance, we compel ourselves to be ever more innovative, in order that we may stay one step ahead of any potential thief. Because of our insecurity, we must continually upgrade our home security systems from the basic to the top-of-the-line "Fort Knox type." With our cars, the security-upgrading continuum started with regular locks...then automatic locks...then the steering wheel "club-lock" holder...then "buzzer & bell" alarm security...then the punching in of coded numbers to enter the car...then electronic gizmos to start your car within a certain personal proximity/radius of it (or conversely to thwart starting the ignition or even being able to turn the steering wheel without your own individual code)...Does not all of this "insecure security" just beg the question: Is a "James Bond-type of secured car" just around the technologically massed-produced corner for all of us who want one?

While we consider wealth and a rising standard of living as progress, our very own public morality and humanity is in decline. With our overemphasis on individual self-aggrandizement, the notion of our social responsibility to others (in their time of need or personal weakness) is becoming lost. Our country was built on humanistic ideals, and we have abandoned them "for a value system of materialism—money, power, prestige, image, conspicuous consumption...Our individual identities are defined by our salaries, our houses, and the cars we drive...We have become so obsessed with the goal of making money that we have lost sight of what living is all about."[7] Yet, what good is a man who is "in the desert with bags of gold but no water."[8] He is merely a dead man, who incidentally happens to be wealthy. This image should be a warning to us—"a warning of the potentially terminal nature of our materialism."[9]

The Inner Emptiness of Self

Almost everywhere today American images overshadow American ideals. What are the costs and individual sacrifices of conforming to such a vision of extravagant expectations? Generally, an inner emptiness and unsatisfied self—that is, gathering riches "on the outside does not necessarily convert into feeling rich on the inside."[10] What is ironic is that even though most of us may conscientiously admit that this assertion is true (to at least some degree), we do not end up demonstrating any changes in our personal behavior patterns in any *actual* way—we simply keep on partaking in "business as usual." In fact, we Americans have become so predictable, that virtually all of our personal motivations and initiatives can easily be expectantly foreseen by simply following the trail that leads to the money.

This craving is like an addict who looks for a "fix" in order to feel alright. Even if an increase in material consumption does not lead to real satisfaction right away, it does not change his/her belief in the behavior, because he/she has had a taste of it already. If society keeps on affirming that "it" is the way to happiness, it must mean that he/she simply needs to try harder in order to realize the maximal attainment of it—(through either acquiring more "stuff" or upgrading it). Therefore, our feelings of emptiness remain shielded, while the deep haunting of whether this stockpiling of material goods is true satisfaction, continues to plague us.

But, a large amount of this false sense of satisfaction stems from the upper class defining what should be the purpose of our strivings, our pursuits—our definition of the American Dream. The people in the upper class have always "sought to instill in their subordinates the capacity to experience material deprivation as guilt, while deceiving themselves that their own material interests coincide with those of mankind as a whole."[11] They have always conveyed that what is "important" is that you must continually move up (God forbid, you should flounder or go down) on the economic scale—that there is no other measure for defining your own being, that accomplishment is solely based on material rewards as an end all. That is, progress is considered a continual upgrading of: job, house, car, vacation spot, and circle of friends.

And, this brings us to **Paradox #9**: life versus lifestyle. The "conspicuously wealthy" deceive us into thinking that these two concepts are one and the same—and of course, we all should realize (on a much deeper human level than we do) that they are not synonymous. The truthfulness of this paradox was wonderfully portrayed by Laurence Shames in his book, *The Hunger For More*, when he summarized a 1987 cartoon by Edward Koren in the New Yorker:

"A youngish man in shorts, sneakers, and visor cap is leaning back against his convertible sports car. At his side is a tennis racquet and a can of balls. In the passenger seat, a woman wearing sunglasses and a big straw hat gives forth a broad and self-contented smile. A palm tree and what appears to be a luxury high-rise loom in the background; in the distance, boats are going by. The fellow is talking to another racquet-toting couple in sunglasses, and his face is slightly troubled—though less troubled than it ought to be, considering what he is saying: 'I despise my life, but I'm in love with my life style.'"[12]

Because Shames analysis of this scenario (couldn't be stated any better) and is so perfect in describing the very crux of the point that I am trying to make, I will continue quoting his thoughts about it.

So, this was "...the conflict, almost never openly acknowledged and perhaps seldom even recognized, between a well-accoutered and seemingly 'successful' image, and a self that was not the least bit satisfied thereby. Unhappiness seeped in from the edges where lifestyle left off—and lifestyle always left off somewhere. When it did, it threw a person back onto the sort of inner resources that too often had gone undeveloped...That's when life itself would rear up and demand to be recognized, awful in its unembellishment and as jarring as a sudden face in a nighttime window.

In the war between life and lifestyle, lifestyle's strategy was to stave off that recognition as long as possible. The trick was to keep life so well dressed and entertained, so encrusted with nice things, that it would cease to know itself—or would even come to despise itself—without them. Lifestyle advanced by substituting false needs for true ones, and it conquered, finally, by making of itself not a set of chosen pleasures but an addiction."[13]

More succinctly, Americans tend to define their self-worth by the symbolic image that is conveyed from their net worth. Our single-minded quest to acquire material goods along with our longing to impress others, compromises our inner sense of meaning, purpose and values. The result: Even with all of our material trappings, deep-down, we are not really happy with ourselves as individuals. In essence, we Americans have become "too cool" for our own good. Under such circumstances, instead of demonstrating our individual characters, people become objects themselves. Your value is determined from your "taste," which justifies a particular item's price. "Not just style but stateliness of person is presumed to be made manifest by a Ralph Lauren blazer...[Any relevance of a] conversation [people might have while dining out] becomes merely a part of the ambience of the restaurants they frequent...The pen they write with is taken to be more revealing than what they might scrawl."[14]

But, are these dreams as worthwhile, as we are led to believe, or are they simply superfluous "fluff" —that should (and can) be magically removed from our minds, if we have the willpower to do it? Because although we think that the goal of attaining this "fluff" will make our lives better, the truth of any such insinuation is more often (than not) simply all in our minds. So you find today, that some people are beginning to rethink this blind pursuit of material wealth. Because of the increasing need to spend a large portion of their financial resources on the basic needs of living, people are finding it harder to match their lives with their overbearing, materialistic dreams, where much more income is needed for "discretionary" items.

And with this admission, a small minority is starting to have the foresight to re-evaluate the significance of this maxim—that just maybe the pursuit of what is supposedly the American Dream is not what they desire. The people in this group have shattered the chains off this notion and have embodied much more value in the concept of determining their own individual standard of success/purpose/happiness, rather than any external one. The realization is that wealth makes people unhappy because "it gives them too much control over what they experience."[15]

For example, meticulous, detailed plans for a weekend trip or even longer vacation can result in less fun than arrangements that were wrecked (or went haywire) for whatever reason. At first, one might think it is a catastrophe, but then you begin to realize that the fun is in the adventure (or the "winging") itself, which would have never transpired in the first place with the original strait-laced and rigid plan.

Many wealthy people would become very apprehensive, if they weren't able to have down-to-the-minute schedules in a resort-style atmosphere. Heaven forbid that they should have to be made uneasy because they have to sacrifice their normal comfort level for even a moment. But, a few are becoming enlightened, for instance, by taking a vacation "incognito of their richness" by renting an average car and traveling the old state highway routes (and possibly encountering the unexpected) rather than keeping a set timetable on the monotonous freeways. They are able to enjoy the experience of being simple people again, without the ever-present worry about protecting their possessions, and they allow themselves to take in the regional customs and see how the people in the area are really like. They have embodied a "can-do" attitude, and they have come to realize that spontaneity and unpredictability do not have to necessarily equate with personal insecurity. They have come to discover that "joy is an emotion that only occurs when we let go of all watchfulness, all concern about outcomes, and simply let experience flood in and feelings flood out."[16]

Advertising and Society

Nonetheless, the vast majority of us still desire the "fluff" —the luxuries or extras—even though many of us have to go into debt in order to quench our thirst for our "gluttonous consumption." Consequently, we have become a nation of compulsive shoppers, and the advertisers realize this and take advantage of it to the furthest extent possible. Furthermore, the competition among advertisers to make the greatest impression on the consumer has become fierce— even to the point of doing a comparison analysis of a client's product with a competitor's one in the same commercial. This practice used to be inconceivable, now it is almost commonplace.

But, advertisers have to go even beyond merely comparing one product's advantages over another. In order to find new profit avenues for their clients, they have to *create* new consumer "wants" and demands, ones that don't satisfy basic "wants" but rather convey the apparent sense of prestige and prosperity. It elevates the notion of consumption as a way to personal fulfillment as well as the answer for any malaises that you may have—whether it be loneliness, fatigue, boredom, disappointment, "the everyday grind," emptiness, meaningless or sexual dissatisfaction.

The goal of advertising is to convince us that "the idea of the good life as one that adheres to principles that contribute to the greater good should be displaced by the idea of the life that feels good." [17] That is, pursue your hedonistic, indulgent pleasures anyway that you want. Consequently, the message is that we cannot (nor should we) be satisfied with getting "mere" gifts for ourselves or others, but that we must acquire the ones that confer perfect status—or else risk being viewed as less "worthy" (or respectable) in our own or other people's eyes.

The most applicable example is the year-end ballyhoo over "The One In-Style Toy" which becomes a "must purchase" for every child at Christmas. Past examples would include: "The Cabbage Patch Kid," "Tickle Me Elmo," "The Furbie," "Beanie Baby," and "Pokemon." The compulsive need to get these items anyway possible was continually portrayed by the literal fisticuffs and hand-to-hand fighting that were waged by mothers to obtain the limited number of these "most valued" of possessions. The rationale was that the child's happiness was dependent on it, and you would have to be held accountable for justifying a "lesser" toy while answering the question, "Why don't you love me?"

But, the wrong message is conveyed when we promote the notion that the only real gift is when it is the "perfect gift." As long as advertising and society continue to define love in terms of acquisition, a lot of unnecessary strain and pain will be heaped upon the true love relationship between, not only parents and children, but all such relationships in general. It is a matter of "wants" versus "needs" again. We give our children everything *we* think that they *want,* and end up not providing them with what they *need* (and actually really want) the most (i.e., interpersonal love, respect, consideration etc.). Parents need to provide their kids with their "presence" rather than concentrating on providing them with "presents."

This impasse leads us to ask an even more enigmatical question of ourselves. Why do we even instill in our children at a young age (or any age) that the concepts of love and materialism are one and the same? As alluded to in the previous chapter, it may have something to do with the fact that advertising has created a chasm between family life (where customary obligation to family unit and the postponing of instant gratification used to be emphasized) and conventional, public life (that cultivates the notion that personal gratification; consumption; and fashion is "progress" and what is good for you). Advertising "flatters and glorifies youth in the hope of elevating young people to the status of full-fledged consumers in their own right, each with a telephone, a television set and a [stereo] in his own room."[18] We are bringing up our children in such a way that we convey to them (in no subtle terms) that you are successful in this society—only when you have acquired enough personal financial resources, so that you can incorporate a "shop 'til you drop" mentality and personality.

In essence, the nature of advertising has been a factor in transferring the authority over the children from parents to industry for the sake of not only immediate profit—but, to inspire children to have instant gratification motives, so that they will develop the "proper habits" of the good, unresisting, impulsive adult consumers for the future. It allows the concept of "self-perpetuating materialism" to continue to be handed down from generation to generation in an orderly, manageable way without threat. This point goes a long way in explaining how and why we are "socialized" to equate love (of self and others) with materialism. Note that one might want to interchange the term, "indulgent pleasure," for love here, because one would have to question whether love can be defined at all under these circumstances. Yet, that is what we have come to *think* regarding the meaning of this word, nonetheless. When in actuality, all we really want to know is whether we can be loved strictly for ourselves and for whom we are—without all of the material trappings.

In essence, the culture of materialism has alienated each one of us from the true identity and nature of oneself. The true self, generally, has inner restraints that can quiet the desire for the immediate gratification of unfettered urges during the process of self-determination. In an overly materialistic society one is "taught to regard one's self as a mechanical given, [where] we neglect to attend to our true self and become vulnerable to outside voices telling us that we can 'have it all,' and that we should 'do it now.' Persuaded that immediate gratification is a sufficient guide to right desire, we fall easily into the grip of consumerist hedonism—even though traditional morality has always been suspicious of a life of immediate gratification...In a society that truly nourished us, one that fortified the healthy human organism, we would not so readily participate in the shallow consumerism of contemporary America. When one becomes accustomed to a diet of whole foods, junk foods no longer taste so comforting. They taste like junk...When one is getting what one really needs, one does not feel unable to get enough of our countless superfluities."[19]

We try to fulfill our deepest human needs (e.g., love, pride, happiness and joy) through the objects that we buy—whether, for example, it be a bottle of liquor or a special new car. In essence, our societal emphasis on production and consumption has changed the dominant, personal drives of many of us. John Kavanaugh in his book contrasts the differences of our motivating characteristics between the "commodity way of life" versus the "natural way of life":[20]

Commodity Life vs. Natural Life

Marketability of Person *vs.* Intrinsic Value of the Person
Productive Worth of What You Do *vs.* Worth of Who You Are
Compete *vs.* Share
Retain *vs.* Give
Hardness *vs.* Compassion
Replaceability *vs.* Acceptance of Uniqueness
Having *vs.* Being
Doubt *vs.* Trust
Uncommitted Sexuality *vs.* Affection

I would also like to add several of my own:

Speed *vs.* Deliberateness
Mindlessness *vs.* Contemplation
Excessiveness *vs.* Moderation
Individual Indulgence *vs.* Social Responsibility

Two Sides to Success

Success has always been a double-edged sword, although virtually all Americans (through cultural socialization along with self-denial) have never fully admitted it. A blind, obsessive drive for success can literally compel people to lose all perspective in regards to themselves as "healthy" individuals. Yet, in this most competitive of societies, the notion is that success can often only be achieved through a burning, resolute aim to "beat out" everyone at all costs. We "force-feed" the incorporation of success into the individual—rather than incorporating the individual into success at one's own comfortable, personal pace.

Because people have a tendency to choose the former way much more often, there are high prices to be paid by those particular individuals and society in general. Some costs would include: abundant stress, hyper-sensitivity, mistrust of one's associates at work, resistance to a personal set of values in lieu of conforming to the organization's aims that value objects more than people, and a greater susceptibility to a myriad of abuses to self or others.

On the other hand, people in the latter category generally bring to the fray "better-balanced egos which allow them to make 'difficult but rational decisions' about what they truly value."[21] Success comprises a variety of goals and ambitions other than money and/or power as the only criteria. Moreover, these type of people do not see the necessity to be a part of the urban "rat race" in order to achieve it.

They are tired of daily traffic gridlock, in order to get back and forth from their overly competitive, stressful jobs. After a hard day at the office, who wants to be in their car on the freeway (and not moving an inch), and have the unfortunate luck to be stuck behind the one yokel who has decided not to abide by the automobile pollution-control laws. You know the type of guy that I am talking about...The guy who has the plastic chihuahua with the endlessly-bobbing, hinged head in his rear window, and you are forced to watch it (because you have nowhere to go)—even though your head is already spinning like a top from your long day. Meanwhile, his exhaust pipe is belching out huge plumes of white smoke into your face, because he has single-handedly removed every conceivable, pollution-control device from his car, in order to get greater gas mileage.

Thus, a significant number of people are reversing the very trend that originally created the mega-metropolitan areas that we live in today. They no longer are simply contented to move further and further out to the far-reaching suburbs (which are still in the orbit of the urban complex). Instead, they are leaving the urban sprawl completely and settling into rural towns once again. Ultimate goals may take longer to reach, but with a better sense of self and community, such people probably are less prone to abuses along their road to success.

The Individual In the Information Age

Today, as we become more technologically-oriented, we hear a virtual one-sided monologue (especially by the corporations who would profit the most) for the need of ever more high-tech gadgetry to run (as well as control) our lives. And of course, I am all for the great improvements that it has brought about in medical procedures; new-age drugs; safer aviation travel; rapid analysis of huge amounts of data; and the quick capability to communicate with anybody in the world.

But (and this is a big but), do we want (or need) the type of technological advancements that may be helpful (although arguably so), but that don't dramatically improve or benefit our lives? The answer is no and yes. No, we don't need them; but yes, we will continue to have them pushed on us simply because the technology is there—and since it is there, it will be produced and we shall receive (if for no other reason than huge corporate profits).

Once again, we encounter **Paradox #4**—the collection of more stuff that we do not really need, nor want, and most probably will rarely ever use. High-tech, consumer-product companies are making a concerted effort to create a world designed by them for us all to live in. Then, they can *tell us* that we "need" all of their gizmos in order to survive in that world (that they themselves actually created). They are almost insidiously conspiratorial in nature, as was evident in one computer software commercial, which softly and simply stated: "If you do what we say, you'll be that much further ahead." In reality though, they are only creating a dependency of expectant "wants" in us, whereby we will continually need the next higher "upgrade," so that we can retain our "high" in their artificial world. So, keeping this in mind, let us take a look at how all of this high-tech, hocus-pocus stuff affects us as individuals.

The more we allow the Information Age to intrude into our lives, you can expect a corresponding *decrease* in an individual's sense of: identity, purpose, culture, self-sufficiency, psychological reason/sensibility, and even future destiny. On the other hand, you will find *increases* in the following: detachment, isolation, anxiety and boredom simultaneously, disorientation, specialization, and dependence.

Americans today are avalanched with such a huge amount of information from so many innumerable sources of technology, that it causes a "numbing" of our senses. And most often, there is a perception of urgency with this information, which, in turn, speeds up the pace of human interaction and creates a constant demand for immediate response. The result is stimulus overload which produces more anxiety and stress. "We are bored and hyperstimulated at the same time. On [the] one hand, we are weary and resigned to the fact that the future is out of our control; we are anesthetized by our inability to cope. On the other hand, we are restless and fidgety; the more we are bombarded, the more anxious we are to see what happens next."[22]

One example is the ever-increasing information that is released on a celebrity and/or sensational news story that may drag on for days, weeks or months. We are sick of hearing about it, yet we can't get enough of it. Part of the blame needs to be placed on the media themselves, because they have a greater tendency today to create news through the sensationalizing of stories, which are often fueled more by speculation rather than fact. There is a big difference between making you aware of a news story and sensationalizing it to the point that you literally acquire a craving for every detail within your very being. The result is that the viewer is force-fed a news story from umpteen different angles—until he or she does not know which way is up!

Moreover, do the television networks need to create more anxiety than we have already. During the nationwide anthrax scare, did we really need to be shown an anthrax microbe under the microscope—that, was seemingly enlarged to the one-millionth power, and whose picture took up the whole television screen. Of course not, because we knew the microbes were out there. Thank you, but if we wanted to take a course in Microbiology 101, we could have signed up for it at the nearest university. Now was this an example of reporting of the news or sensationalism, with the aim to unnecessarily scare us much more than we needed to be?

When the concept of television newsmagazines first started, they were informative and thought-provoking. But nowadays, many of them have merely become emotional-pandering vehicles for sensationalizing the most extreme stories and case examples—all for the sake of the attainment of network ratings. And, with the current trend of many of the media being gobbled up by a few media conglomerates, an even greater danger potentially exists. That being, a mere handful of media companies acquiring the power to selectively control, filter and mold any news story, so that it will reflect in favor of their own corporate viewpoint as well as securely enhance their own financial self-interests.

Furthermore, with so much information at our fingertips, we lose our sense of identity and individuality. In the Information Age, it is hard to ever feel assured of your own identity (or image), when you are constantly being bombarded by so many new and differing messages of who you should be and how you should be. "This is the frustration, the hollowness, of feeling that we have nothing worthwhile to contribute—the realization that machines, computers and robots, can do the job better than we. Why try to memorize facts when so much more can be stored in a digitized database? Why try to figure out a problem when a computer can do it so much faster?"[23] Hence, technologies weaken our intellectual resolve, because we become accustomed to them spitting out a model answer for us to follow via the high-tech mode of thinking. We forget that individual initiative, imagination and intuition just might present a better (even more useful) way—derived from some uniquely different, qualitative (rather than quantitative) perspective. In essence, we permit information technology to become both a "means" and an "end" in and of itself.

Another relevant point that can be added, here, is that access to an ever-increasing, overabundance of information without any limits, virtually eliminates (or at best counteracts) the regulatory function of the family and religion. Paraphrasing what Neil Postman says in his book, *Technopoly*, "with no rules governing the flow of information...the family has no control over their own children [in regards to what messages and suppositions that they are exposed to]...the purpose of maintaining a balance between the old and new is lost...and religion loses its explanatory power in the moral domain over the concept of 'good versus evil.'" [24]

Therefore, in such a society, we are powerless in preventing children at inappropriate ages from comprehending such topics as: homemade bomb-making; homemade drug-making; catalogs about drug paraphernalia/accessories; instructions on how to disassemble and reassemble a wide range of guns; being sexually taken advantage of by "chat room" stalkers via the Internet; being appealed to by satanic cults; being told where to purchase a wide range of "unwarranted" materials etc. So succinctly, the danger we all face is the real possibility of technology taking control over our individual: mental, emotional, moral, and societal components. Even while trying to control these parts of our lives, technology is, on the other hand, useless in solving the very problems that it actually helps to create—namely, problems such as: lack of self-esteem; anxiety; knowing social right from wrong; lack of inhibition; taking advantage of or trying to control others; and the capability to think independently with "non-statistical" reason etc.

Another way that we are losing our identity is through depersonalization. High-tech expediency compels us to distance ourselves from other people. We play computerized video games by competing against a machine. We plug in portable headsets to listen to music as we walk down the street—effectively allowing us to remain aloof to all passers-by, conversations and happenings around us. We use automated teller and vending machines or use a drive-thru—to do a financial transaction or to pick up fast-food, candy bar, soda or newspaper, so that we don't even have to get out of our cars. Our excuses vary from it is too cold (or too hot) or too far to walk or simply because you don't even have the time to step out of the car. We buy home and personal accessories from cable television or mail order catalogs, because the malls are too crowded, our precious time is too valuable, or its too dark outside and, therefore, fear a crime happening against us. We rent videos and view them at home rather than go out to a movie theater and actually see and laugh with other people. With the proliferation of telemarketing, we screen our calls with Caller ID. In the classrooms, we use long-distance learning systems with a "television" teacher or a computer-generated facsimile. We scan the Internet for knowledge, rather than acquiring it through recollections and reflections. We compel ourselves to stand in front of an electronic message board and moronically read the news aloud to ourselves, one word at a time as though we are in some kind of hypnotic trance. We try to understandably decipher the meaning of our car's convoluted and intricate "satellite-linked navigation system"—instead of asking someone for directions or finding the information by opening up a simple road map. We have become addicted to technology just as we have become addicted to material riches. We have equated "technological innovation with human progress."[25] We have been provided with technological ease and efficiency...but at the loss of ease and efficiency of the mind, body and spirit!

Thus, increasingly we are finding our identity and individuality, not through others, but through machines. So, ironically, technologies may bring us together and give us more contacts—but these are of the superficial variety and actually produce the opposite effect by separating us into isolated fixtures. Their importance in our lives has driven us to de-emphasize the forming of emotional attachments and to diminish the meaning of family and community. In essence, communication has lost its "human" elements and its consideration of time. Today, the individual is much less likely to have the opportunity to fully assimilate, digest and analyze information and, in turn, make discrete, rational decisions. This reality literally produces people who are in a continual state of being dazed, confused, and disoriented. "Our complex society demands such a range of narrow specialists that...they all speak different languages. We cannot talk together; we cannot comprehend what each of the others is doing.

How can we expect to live together in harmony and have a feel for what each of us is about when we cannot understand each other?"[26]

Consequently, we have become mere pawns for the information specialists. If we hear their information enough, we end up doing what they say because, after all, they are "experts," they must know what is good for us. We are simply helpless to think or reason. This notion brings to mind how parents are told of the dire importance of giving their children the fastest "intellectual head-start" over others as is possible. Throw out all the books that discuss previously here-to-fore, standard ways of normal child development and genuine parental love. Rather, you must take advantage of every conceivable way to "intellectualize" your child—well before the stage which is stated on any former age-progression time chart.

So that today, it is more likely that one would see the following wacky scenario occurring: A mother-to-be is laying down on the living room floor with classical music softly playing out of hand-sized, mini speakers—each one epoxied to and strategically placed on either side of her lower abdomen—while the father-to-be is crouched down over her and mindlessly reciting nursery rhymes directly into her belly button, as if it were an ear...

Are we all susceptible to becoming like them? Do they think that today's "yet-unborn" supposedly have some kind of extra mystical quality to them compared to all previous "unborn" from throughout recorded history? The truth is your child is never going to be granted such "privileges" in the real world! So, why lend any anticipation to the catering of such desires before birth?

Another way parents think that they can make their children feel "special" is by giving them a name that is spelled in a very unusual manner. For someone to be able to guess the spelling of the name is like being a contestant at a Spelling Bee, where you are having a nightmarish "off" day. I am going to use "Stephanie" as an example, because I have seen this name spelled so many different ways. Of course, the following are just some of the examples—because the possibilities are infinitely endless. But, this spelling exercise has given me a renewed source of empathy for what the data entry clerks at the Department of Motor Vehicles must go through everyday: ......Stephenie......Stephani......Stephanee......Stepfanee......Stefani....

Steffani…Steffanie…Stepfanie…Stepfani…Stephanni…Stepphanie…Stefphani….. Stepfanye….. Stephany…..Stephaney….. Steffaknee…. Steffunnee…Steffunny…Oh, will someone please help me—"brain lock" is starting to set in, surely to be followed by riga mortis!

Chapter 4

INDIVIDUAL ABUSES

Reasons Why We Abuse

For quite some time now, I have often thought about (and tried to resolve) in my own mind the answer to the question: Why we Americans display such a wide breadth of different abuses that we perpetuate on ourselves and others? It boggles my mind to realize how much negative human energy is lost (emotionally, mentally and physically) through the carrying out of our abuses—energy that instead could have been used in some positive, productive ways.

This energy loss is truly a sad waste, and one that no stated dollar amount could begin to clarify or rectify. We do spend a huge amount of resources on treating the abusers (and their human inadequacies and traumas) and the abusees (from the consequences of the actions as well as their traumas)—directly and indirectly. But, just think about all of the personal/financial resources and hardships that could be saved, if all of these people could be on a "level plain" from the beginning (never having to had experienced the downslide in the first place). Instead, we have to go full circle in order to fully treat them. We first have to retrace all of the negative steps taken by each individual, then reinforce "the positive" in each of them (abuser and abusee) in order to make them whole again.

There seems to be at least three major reasons why there has been a proliferation of individual abuses in this country:
(1) The extreme overcompetitiveness of our society (in many aspects, but especially monetarily) and how that affects individual beings—each one of whom is unique and, yet, is often molded into some mass-produced "thing having standard stock specifications."

(NOTE: I am *not* talking here about "normal" competition, which can be a motivator and a helpful thing for all concerned if used properly. Rather, I am talking about how overcompetition affects people's personality structures and their views of others).

(2) An impersonal society and "broken" families largely contribute to the general desecration of people's innately good characters.

(3) Modern urbanization and the rapid onset (and the accompanying fast pace) of the technological/telecommunication age has permanently appeared without taking into account the human consequences. This course of events has negatively affected each of our "personhoods" (and will continue to do so).

So, before we discuss individual types of abuse, let's first explore these factors that cause them.

1. The Overcompetitiveness of Society

This factor casts the psychological milieu for individuals to become abusive. The emphasis on acquiring the Almighty Dollar *at any cost* and the cultural drive to attain the American Dream, forces one to be categorized as either a success or failure based on that individual's stockpile of money and material items. On the other hand, less tangible achievements and acts of "humanism" (e.g., kindness and thoughtfulness) are rarely recognized or are quickly glossed over. If they are acknowledged, it is seen as a pleasant surprise (at best) or an aberration (at worse).

In today's society, although we may assert that our value system includes a wide range of values—for all intents and purposes, we still see the "value" criterion of money as what differentiates one as a success or failure. ***Paradox #10***: "Internally" you could see yourself as a success (not based on the money factor), while "externally" you could be viewed by others as a failure (based on the money factor)—and, in turn, suffer the social consequences.

By using money as the sole criterion, can we categorize someone who happens not to accumulate a "respectable" level of it as a failure? In order that we are not seen by others as failures, are we all supposed to base our behaviors on finding a competitive advantage—all for the sake of money? "Does anyone get points for the intrinsic value of what he or she *tried* to do? Is it taken into consideration that some paths are simply harder than others?...[while] overlooking the role of luck, of favors, of biases pro or con, ignoring virtually every aspect of context."[1]

Economic overcompetitiveness becomes destructive when it becomes the guiding dimension in our lives and is employed as *the* determinant for attaining fulfillment and individual self-worth. Under such circumstances, our entire society becomes based on trying to get ahead of others. Subsequently, we are all repeatedly made to feel inadequate. We are continually uncomfortable because we never feel economically contented, even though we live more affluently than any other people in the world. And yet, we forever seek more of what we *think* will make us fulfilled. This continual striving for a goal that is always just out-of-reach (and which we feel can be corrected by just being more competitive), creates stress and feelings of failure which, in turn, leads to a climate ripe for abuse. It pervades people from all walks of life and from all socioeconomic classes.

For example, a janitor may be anxious and frustrated that he can barely meet the material necessities of life. On the other hand, the high-powered lawyer has no problem achieving that level, but is possibly manically-frustrated that he doesn't have the financial resources to buy that dreamy, super-powered, red sportscar (or a yacht that he would probably only go out on once or twice a year anyway). The standards in which we live our lives are all relative, yet they can affect us all in the same way. The age-old saying, "Men [and women] live lives of quiet desperation" would certainly be applicable here.

This stress turns into abuse when we feel that we have to blame someone or something for our "perceived" (not necessarily actual) inadequacies. Our "perceived" shame makes us feel compelled to place the blame somewhere in order to avoid seeming weak or flawed. Moreover, we can turn it "inward" with the result that we abuse ourselves, or turn it "outward" and abuse others.

Our overcompetitive society constantly instills in us the notion that we can always do better (i.e., that better is not the best and, therefore, is not good enough). When we don't reach ever-higher goals for ourselves, we are made to feel *unnecessarily* inadequate. Then, the will to abuse becomes a very, very difficult motivation to avoid, indeed. It is similar to dangling a carrot on a rope in front of a rabbit and pulling it further and further away just as the rabbit repeatedly approaches it. And in essence, that is truly a needless creation of insensitive frustration (or one might even say, tyrannical meanness).

This overcompetitiveness to achieve also carries over into one's personal/social life. For many of us, even pleasure or play can assimilate into the same achievement standards of work. The simple "go with the flow" good feelings that are experienced in pleasure or play are severely compromised when some artificial measure of achievement is used. "The measurement of sexual 'performance,' the insistence that sexual satisfaction depends on proper 'technique,' and the widespread belief that it can be 'achieved' only after coordinated effort, practice, and study all testify to the invasion of play by the rhetoric of achievement."[2]

Another example would be losing a key point in a friendly tennis match. You may continue to berate yourself for losing the point by comparing yourself to a well-known tennis star and say," why couldn't I have done it like he would have." Whatever happened to the notion that you can learn from your mistakes and simply admit to yourself: "*I* will do better next time"—without any comparison to some professional player.

A final example that relates to "assertiveness training" is apropos here. Some people misuse this procedure to obtain a competitive advantage, so that they can emotionally manipulate and shape relationships in a social (or work) situation. Instead of learning this program for defending yourself against manipulation, it can be used in reverse as an offensive weapon to get other people to do what you want, and thereby increase your "status." Used in this fashion, it becomes a form of psychological abuse. "Americans have not really become more sociable and cooperative...they have merely become more adept at exploiting the conventions of interpersonal relations for their own benefit...a struggle for power."[3]

In summing up, instead of displaying so many types of over-competitiveness, we might all be better off if we could learn to accept the fact that we already enjoy affluence from merely being a competitive society. If we could keep affluence and achievement in perspective, we all could balance our lives in other ways, that would make them personally richer (and certainly less abusive). On the other hand, by overdoing competitiveness, a personal toll is exacted on many of us that results in a condition of "diminishing returns."

It could be said that overcompetitiveness is like a train with all of the negative character traits (e.g., dishonesty, greed, selfishness, jealousy) in the locomotive as the driving force—while all the positive human values (e.g., integrity, trust, consideration) are relegated to the caboose, where they are least effective and used too little and too late as a last resort, when all else has failed. As an illustration, just take a look at the CEOs from the major cigarette manufacturers who perjured themselves in front of a Congressional committee. They said that nicotine was not addictive; that they were not increasing nicotine levels in cigarettes in order to enhance current/new smokers' dependency. Only when contradictory memoranda from within their own companies were made public, did they then take the kinder, gentler, forgiving approach. By admitting their wrongdoings, they then tried to make financial restitution by setting up a fund for smokers' health claims.

Similarly, after the Firestone Tire fiasco, the company implemented a marketing campaign asserting, "our #1 priority is your trust." Yet, trust cannot be truly conveyed through the mere use of the word itself. Rather, it can only be demonstrated through one's responsible actions or performance, and which is contingent upon being done before the fact (rather than after the fact).

2. An Impersonal Society & "Broken" Families Largely Contribute to the General Desecration of People's Innately Good Characters.

Our society's compulsion for overcompetitiveness has kept "people obsessed with their jobs and with personal advancement, at the expense of feelings for others…[and] the effects on the family are devastating, since it destroys the ethos of kindness and care on which loving families depend."[4] The large decrease in the amount of quantity/quality (and leisure) time spent by parents with their children has created a vacuum that is ripe to being susceptible to a variety of individual abuses (for *both* the parents and the children). In addition, one must factor in the negative effects that divorce and/or one parent households have on everyone involved in contributing to potential abuses.

We must keep in mind that no society in history has ever tried to operate without building upon the family as its most fundamental institution. Therefore, we are presently traveling in uncharted territory when we experiment with the nature of a healthy, two-parent family structure without first developing some kind of definitive and tested substitute—rather than some hodge-podge mode of family togetherness. The insecurities that this fact creates in family members' minds and emotional make-ups can inevitably lead to abuses in the quest of finding individual security and happiness.

Meanwhile, the "culture of childhood" is constantly being compromised. Many parents are being forced to "see parenting largely as an investment of their precious time, [and] may end up viewing children as objects to be improved rather than individuals to be nurtured at their own pace."[5] In some cases, children's schedules are resembling those of their parents in complexity. After school and extra-curricular activities, some youngsters are having to come home and take care of even younger siblings. Such added responsibilities as well as the pressure from parents for rapid achievements by their children (in school and personally) are causing depression and abusive tendencies in them at ever younger ages. In essence, they are not having the time to be children.

Similarly, parents are having to accept and adjust to the increased pace of a hectic work/family schedule, which only worsens as their number of on-the-job weekly work hours keeps on increasing (so that family financial ends can be met). **Paradox #11:** Parents' time and energy are being pulled in two directions, virtually a no-win situation. If they don't work harder to support the family, then they lose financially. If they don't spend time to care for their children, then the whole family loses psychologically and emotionally. Any joys and pleasures literally become limited by the 24-hour-a-day clock. Consequently, parents are becoming more susceptible to their own disabilities and abuses such as: mental/physical breakdowns, high blood pressure and heart disease, personality disorders, anxiety fits, alcohol, drugs, and taking their anger and frustration out on their children or by simply neglecting them.

Of course, these effects can only have a negative influence on the children. The appearance that parents may at least seem to prize their careers or material possessions more than their children at times can only be devastating to the latter's psychological nature. And, if the parents are drunk, under the influence of drugs (including prescriptions) or physically/verbally abusive during the small amounts of time that the children do see them, then you have the makings of a broken/dysfunctional family—where the members don't know or care what the others are doing, and lose sight of how to cope.

Under these frustrating and hostile circumstances, the children are going to be susceptible to both: (1) exhibiting extreme behavior or using vices in order to try to receive the parental attention and recognition, that they so much need (if neglected) (2) out of anger, adopting the same abuses that mirror their parents, while grappling to find their own personal identities. This type of abuse, where it becomes cyclical within the family, is probably the most unfortunate type of all. That's because, it is affecting children who most probably had innately favorable characters to begin with.

This erosion of identity with the family and its moral code reflects the reasoning why individuals withdraw "feelings and commitments from others to 'number one.'"[6] Under these alienated circumstances, an individual's unrestrained self-interest can become destructive, and as a result, cultivate the abuse of self or others.

Hence, an individual decreasingly turns to his family and others for identity, purpose and moral resolve. Instead, one's sense of self becomes increasingly dependent on: (1) images and impressions from the mass media. A couple of simple examples would be television shows like *Beavis & Butthead* and *South Park*, where misguided humor is found in other people's misfortunes through storylines that have absolutely no moral message to them. (2) other "lost" peers (3) the narcissistic attitudes (especially found in T.V. commercials) of our society's materialistic culture (as evident by the number of teens who now "hang out" together in our plethora of shopping malls after school). Therefore, an individual is drawing less and less on a family-oriented direction (and its restrained perspective) for gaining his/her own unique self-concept, personality, values and beliefs. Instead, that individual is becoming overly dependent on a culture-oriented direction, which today promotes the self-centered/self-indulgent philosophy that you are #1 regardless of who you have to take advantage of or step on in the process.

Charles Derber in his book, *Money, Murder and the American Dream,* used the term, "wilding," to describe these manifestations of "degraded individualism" and the obsessive need for influence and control. "Wilding" can be portrayed in a spectrum of different ways and extremes for different motives (e.g., greed, lust or for getting attention or respect). And generally, these are basically "good" people who are "snapping" (or at least before they "snap"). For instance, some guy is cut off by another driver on the freeway. In order to recoup this loss of individual space and "regain his respect," he floors the accelerator and catches up with the "trespasser" just so he can utter obscenities at him (or even worse, shoot him). This "road rage" is on the rise as more people become individually frustrated with their own lives. Another example would be the postal worker who "snaps" because he received one-too-many orders from his supervisor (seen as a loss of his autonomy).

This self-aggrandizing behavior can surface on wider, more public dimensions of society, too. The deregulation of the economy in the 1980's "established the environment for the extreme economic individualism that spawned such wilding calamities as the Savings and Loan crisis. Degraded individualism in politics is reflected in the explosion of government corruption, including [in the past] the spectacular looting of the Department of Housing and Urban Development and the Department of Defense."[7]

How can we expect individuals to find their way and demonstrate moral character (e.g., trust)—when our own government, institutions and, increasingly, families are arrogantly abandoning such traits. We are slowly experiencing societal deterioration by dismantling our roots, ties and traditions. "Lost values are what it's all about; a broken sense of belonging; an abandoned sense of place; a mutilated sense of self."[8]

3. Modern urbanization and the rapid onset of the technological/telecommunication age.

Over the years, people have been forced to try to deal with the congestion, crowding, tension and confusion of modern urbanization. Presently, we are being asked to cope with the new age of high technology and rapid telecommunication. Even if we find the capability to *mentally* accept both of these momentous tides as they continue to sweep down on us, one must certainly wonder whether we have fully acclimated ourselves *emotionally* to the former yet, let alone whether we will have the capacity to do it in the future for the latter, too?

It is my contention that urbanization and information technology have both overstimulated and overloaded our individual "human infrastructures"[9] to the extent that it can cause us to become abusive. "There is an accelerating urgency to the pace of life...a constant pressure to get things done...with a computer-notebook organizer in our jacket pocket, a personal recorder in our shirt pocket, a cellular phone in our car, a laptop computer on the plane, a fax machine in our office, and a modem in our den, we are [expected to be] constantly productive."[10]

We cannot even drive a car without feeling the need to be productive—or even worse, falling asleep at the wheel because our daily overproductivity has fatigued us. Both of these occurrences have been the cause of many automobile accidents.

It is not that unusual to see a driver who has a cell phone wedged between his shoulder blade and ear, while he has a sandwich in one hand and a soda pop in the other, and who is, consequently, steering the car with the base of his hands. I have even witnessed with my own eyes a man brushing his teeth while driving—and, I might add, swaying back and forth in his lane on the freeway—so that not a single wasted minute would go by him. Moreover, with the way people customize their cars today, he may very well have had a complete plumbing system installed right in the car itself for "spitting and rinsing."

Even when you are stopped at a traffic light, some drivers don't have the patience to remain a single second longer than need-be. For example, let's say that the car opposite you at a red light has his blinker on to make a left turn. A new ploy by some drivers today is to make a left turn in front of you at the exact instance that the light turns green, within the miniscule time frame it takes for you to move your foot from the brake to the accelerator, in order to propel your car forward. Many automobile accidents have occurred for this reason, simply because the motorist had absolutely no patience to follow the etiquette rules of the road.

So, while the original intent of high technology was to ease our pressures for productivity as well as our personal, everyday burdens—the very opposite is actually occurring. Instead of decreasing, our daily stress levels are increasing—directly as a result that "needed" information has become non-stop, fast-moving, and always changing. After all, a major reason for the Technological Age was for us to save more time for ourselves, yet today we seem to have less time than we have ever had. We receive so much information, that we can't even seem to separate the important messages from the unimportant. Nor do we decipher and collate it to the extent that we need to, in order for us to collectively understand it, so that any relevant information may be acted upon.

Subsequently, the human mind has become overworked without rest—something which it is not intended to do. Each of us has abodingly acquired the sense that literally "if you snooze, you lose." The novel term, 24/7 (which of course means 24 hours, seven days a week) is evidence of this fact. This colloquialism came into being mostly as a reference to the fact that a person could get on-line anytime of the day or night, in order to be updated on the latest information, that would be personally necessary and relevant for you to know. All of this is probably one major reason for the high incidence of insomnia in the U.S.—people feel compelled to think even in their sleep.

Therefore, the phenomenon of information technology has profoundly changed our personhoods (i.e., self-images, values, behaviors etc.) to the extent that people now "fall out of grace" with each other more readily and frequently as a result. By using an array of technologies which are at our fingertips, we interact with each other in a more impersonal, yet precise, empirical manner with little tolerance for the other's feelings, judgments, perceptions, rationalizations, inadequacies or failings. Accordingly, many people have become numb with a void of emotional emptiness that is reflected in a lack of patience and sensitivity in the relationships with each other.

The development of meaningful relationships with others needs the crucial element of slow-moving blocks of time, in order for there to be any feeling of a strong or permanent bonding. Only this slow passage of time can allow us to foster the remembrances and sentimentalities that are needed to fully connect with "significant others." In addition, slower-moving blocks of time enable us to maintain a perspective on our lives in regards to overall time and place. In essence, the speed of time and the fast pace of living our personal experiences today, do not permit our human natures to properly reflect or become nostalgic (or sentimental) about ourselves or our relationships with others. Our lives are simply moving and changing too rapidly, in order for there to be the proper nurturing that is needed to ripen such blocks of time.

Furthermore, we must keep in mind that there are two major differences between digital technologies and humans. First, we luckily have the power to think by taking into account our senses, feelings and intuitions. Second, unlike for example, computers, we need rest as well as the time for carefree playfulness in our lives (as is exhibited by all animal species) when relating to others—in order for us to survive emotionally. Moreover, we all have a need to creatively express ourselves (in many capacities), in order to give individual meaning to our lives. In the computer age, where we have become dependent on merely pressing keys on a keyboard to spit out a common digital expressiveness, opportunities to apply our creativities from our own unique perspectives, have become more limited. The further high-technology exiles us from these all-important human needs, the more emotionally empty and stressed out we will become. Consequently, we have (and will continue to) become more ripe for abusing ourselves and others.

Meanwhile, the occurrence of the other phenomenon, urbanization, has constantly assaulted us with such things as urban noise, which results in disquieting our entire psychological and emotional states. Noises such as: "the traffic rumble, emergency vehicles, animals screeching and barking, doors and trash cans slamming, trains and planes, babble of our radio and TV sets, jangling of our telephones and alarm systems, whirring of our computers and air-conditioning units, lawnmowers and power tools, supermarket background music and pervasive rock and rap, the jackhammer and pile-driver...surround us day and night. Our noise pollution adds to the sense of urgency—reinforcing the breakdown between our inner nature and our technological environment."[11]

Moreover, our flight to the suburbs has not lessened any of it. The noises have simply followed us as we have made formerly small, quiet suburbs into extended mini cities. We have "merely spread out the freeways, shopping malls, industrial complexes, condominiums, parking lots and housing tracts in an ever-expanding circle of metropolitan congestion and despair."[12]

So, urbanization and technology has left all of us struggling to maintain some sort of perspective, balance, and cohesion. Donald Wood said it best: "We can plan utopian space colonies, but we cannot manage our terrestrial cities; we can send teams of explorers to the moon, but we cannot control urban traffic jams; we can transplant human hearts and kidneys, but we cannot deliver rudimentary health care to our indigent citizens...we can build huge skyscrapers, mammoth military installations, luxury resort communities, and vast research complexes, but we do not know what to do with the homeless of our inner cities. It is this sense of imbalance that leads to feelings of simultaneous malaise and anxiety...[as] we are drawn deeper and deeper into the...vortex of concrete and computers."[13]

Before (finally getting down to) examining individual abuses, I would like to additionally mention the fact that when abuses are not dealt with on an individual and/or societal level, they can turn into addictions, which are basically obsessive needs to abuse. When abuse occurs to this degree, the abuser becomes fully deadened to the feelings of anger and pain that caused him to originally begin abusing in the first place. The addiction takes control of his total being—to the point that he lives for it (yet all the while denying he has it). At the same time, he needs to control and manipulate others to perpetuate his addiction. In essence, he becomes a mere "inhuman mechanism" for the "alive" addiction.

As you read on about the wide range of different abuses, take a minute to put aside the 101 other things that you probably have on your mind—and really THINK about all the abuses that we perpetuate on ourselves and others. When we abuse, a tremendous amount of negative energy is used up which, instead, could be allocated in positive ways. The key to not abusing is to have the capability to "step outside of yourself" and look inward to see if that's the way you would like to be treated, while also admitting that there is nothing wrong with having failings and inadequacies just like everybody else. Generally though, we instead tend to take an "outward" self-serving approach where an authoritarian viewpoint is taken (i.e., "whatever I'm doing is right and whatever you're doing is wrong").

There is something sorely lacking in the fabric of individuals in our society, when one sees this many types (and depth) of abuse, as well as how widespread they really are. But ultimately, it is within each individual's power to choose a worthwhile alternative, if one has the will to do so. Let us now look at individual abuses, including many (but certainly not all) elements that each involves. I'm simply going to take the more notable abuses one at a time, alphabetically.

Alcohol Abuse

Since this is the first individual abuse that is going to be discussed, I am going to be using alcohol as an example for explaining how and when a person becomes addicted to *any* substance and/or process (e.g., gambling, sex etc.) form of abuse. Therefore, some of the motivational reasons why one would acquire the need to abuse alcohol, could generally be applied to other individual abuses, too. Also, note that alcohol is considered to be a type of "drug," but since it is so widespread, I am going to place it in an individual abuse category of its own.

Abuses generally start out of a person's need to alter his mood, so that he can remain out-of-touch with particular thoughts and feelings that cause deeply-felt pain (including past traumatic events). So, there are both psychological and emotional elements that are involved. Typical character traits of alcoholics include: anger, depression, personal/family conflict, anxiety, guilt, low self-esteem and unfulfilled aspirations. Many turn to alcohol starting early in life to relieve these feelings, because their individual capacities to deal with emotions and problems of living are limited. Alcoholics generally have a low tolerance to suffering or low capability to deal with reality. Alcohol becomes a panacea for all shortcomings and misgivings. "It anesthetizes emotional pain, produces euphoria, aggrandizes the ego, and modifies reality so the drinker does not have to deal with [them]."[14] Eventually, alcohol dependency expands so that it results in dominating the personality completely, and it creates an overall numbness, so that one can escape and avoid painful feelings.

Alcohol abuse that leads to addiction also has a physical component. Over time, the human body adapts itself to becoming actually dependent on the substance to the point that it cannot adequately function without it. Even if the alcoholic acknowledges and understands the devastation that the substance is causing in his life, he becomes helpless in light of his emotional drive and physical need for it. Furthermore, if he can end up being physically treated, he must overcome the pain of withdrawal symptoms. Even then, positive intervention never cures addictions, but, rather may only permanently control them. The body, once used to regular intake of the substance, is always susceptible to the sensation and craving whenever the will is weak, even after rehabilitation.

An alcoholic member in a family has the potential to have a totally negative impact on the family structure. The nonalcoholic spouse has to spend an inordinate amount of time patching up the relationship, while hiding the ever-increasing problem from their children, relatives and friends. He or she becomes a co-dependent by having to cope with the consequences, the excusing of behavior, and the denial of the alcoholism. This process generally occurs when the couple implicitly agrees that the alcoholism is not out-of-hand and can still be controlled.

But, even with all the denial and attempted silence, the children (no matter what age) will acknowledge the realization that the family has a definite problem. The children will discover that every time that they approach the alcoholic family member, it will be like walking on egg shells. They are never sure when the alcoholic might explode in anger and lash out verbally or physically. With this internalized fear always present, there is a creation of a constant atmosphere of distrust, ambivalence, confusion, and sense of unreality. The dilemma of such unresolved problems as well as having to live in such an environment, can often lead the children to feel emotionally abandoned, because the parents' focus is always on the alcohol problem rather than the children. In turn, this fact can create even further isolation between family members to the point of alienation.

If these conditions continue for an extended period of time, the children's emotional dysfunction stemming from fear, anger, and hurt may very well continue into adulthood. This "Adult Children of Alcoholics" syndrome negatively affects their own behavior patterns and relationships with others as adults. "In the alcoholic family the denial of feelings is so prevalent that children never learn how to honestly express emotions. They see the adults in the family walk around smiling on the outside and boiling with rage on the inside...When the children of this family grow up, they will smile when they are angry, look blank when they are hurt, and remain in constant conflict with how they feel on the inside and what they show on the outside."[15]

Under these circumstances, admittedly, it is hard (but not impossible or inevitable) to break such an unhealthy cycle, so that it doesn't automatically continue in the children. Ending the continuation of this cycle is seemingly dependent on three factors. First, the children (as well as the nonalcoholic parent) need to gain an *independent* perspective and insight on the true nature of the alcoholism during its' *earlier* stages (as it is occurring). By acknowledging this awareness, they can seek extensive social supports before the emotional breakdown of everyone involved. In other words, if nonalcoholic family members can independently counteract their own co-dependent denial of the problem (irrespective of the alcoholic's own denial), the ability for all to move forward in a positive direction will be more possible. Of course, you would still show empathy for the alcoholic (so that he knows that someone cares), but you will have a powerful independent perspective to actualize change in the present and the future.

Second, by being psychologically/emotionally open and cathartic about the abuse and experiences that you endured as a child, the less repressed anger you will have when dealing with your own children. In this way, they will have a more likely chance of acquiring healthier emotional structures to build on themselves. This catharsis would not necessarily have to be done in a therapeutic environment, but could be productively done with a significant other (e.g., your own spouse or close friend).

Third, there is some evidence that the alcoholism problem within a family is not necessarily effectual enough (on its own) to continue the unhealthy emotional cycle within the children. Rather, it would seem that the family generally needs a myriad of structural problems that are tearing at its very cohesion, in order for the cycle to continue. In other words, if the family members are nearing a "meltdown" in other major areas, the likelihood for the continuation is increased. So, if the family is disturbed and incongruous on many fronts, attaining a secure foothold on reality is very difficult. On the other hand, if the members look out for each other's social, economic, mental/intellectual, physical and general emotional well-being, then the family has a good chance of overcoming any detrimental effects emanating from the alcoholic. In short, instead of the alcoholism isolating the family—the family must retain its strength and isolate the alcoholism.

Society could also play a bigger role in promoting a caring nature. If the admitted failings and inadequacies of people (and we all have them) could be accepted and de-stigmatized even more by society (than it currently offers), people with problems (including alcohol) would not have to feel so "debilitated." In turn, this would give incentive for making it much easier for people to come forward and realistically deal with their problems.

Animal Abuse

When the incomprehension of things in this fast-paced world get overwhelming for me, I turn my attention to animals (and nature in general) in order to get me back on the right track. Because no matter how screwed up that we humans get in our behavior patterns, the nature of animals is always a refreshing reminder to us of possibly the only remaining example that portrays the normalcy of this world. And, it doesn't have to be some kind of special weekend retreat into the woods—but rather, even a group of birds that reside daily in the immediate surroundings of your neighborhood.

For example, a large group of little house sparrows and chicadees gather to sleep every night in the same three smallish pine trees that are directly across the street from where I live. My belief is that they gather there (especially in the winter) because all the other trees are bare of leaves, and the pine needles give them a sense of security and protection. Well, every morning you could set your clock to the exact time that they all start chirping, and since there are so many of them, it becomes almost real music, which could win a Grammy Award in a natural music category.

The point that I'm trying to make is that I am able to use their music (since there are so many of them) to drown out the artificial noise of cars that are continually passing by (instead of vice-versa). Generally, you can't (and don't) pay any attention to birds' music in the everyday world, because your ears get so used to hearing the overwhelming amount of "artificial" noise that is produced by machines. But, in this case, their numbers are so large, that I have the opportunity to drown out the man-made din—and truly appreciate these natural sounds that allow me to start off with an invigorated frame of mind in the morning.

Therefore, animal abuse is possibly the one type of abuse that saddens me the most. While we humans have the ability to control our own abuses (if we have the will), animals have no real control over (nor can they act upon) the different forms of abuse that they endure from us. We humans (the ones with the "supposedly" big brains) have let the animal kingdom down and, consequently in the process, ourselves as a species as well. I am in never-ending amazement and wonder of how wild animals cope and adjust—let alone survive and prosper—as we humans push them further and further out into harsher and harsher environs. For example, I think we have all seen how squirrels adjust to crossing a busy street by having to do a tightrope act along a telephone wire (above the street itself)—in order to avoid taking a chance of being run over by a car.

In addition, we have plowed down so many trees within our big-city, metropolitan areas, that birds have to use retailers' neon signs in shopping centers to build their nests. So, it is not unusual to see a nest built, for example, on the bottom of the top loop of the thick, block letter "B" on a store sign denoting "BAKERY." One can only surmise that developers will not be satisfied until they have cemented the whole country—entirely.

Thus, people often think that animals are invading their territory, while, in actuality, it is just the opposite way. Because of the very congestion that we ourselves have caused in the cities, people are fleeing more and more into areas that previously were woods and forests. Hence, we are having to compete with animals that is (and was) "their territory." So, that when one reads in the newspaper such headlines as: "Jogger mauled by mountain lion" or "coyote kills family pet," we are quick to blame the animal and send a posse after it. On the other hand, ranchers find that if they try to eliminate the coyote as a predator, rodent numbers increase, which causes a different sort of problem for them. It is a rude awakening to some people that we humans actually share the planet with other inhabitants.

Similarly, animal trainers in circuses are bewildered when one of the animals that they handle suddenly goes berserk and goes on a rampage either behind the scenes or during a show. Could it be possible that the reason might be that the animals are caged in a confined space much of the day and shackled at other times—then asked to perform unnatural acts in front of spectators? In addition, some laypeople think that they can control wild animals by making them pets and then can depict them as "status" symbols. Consequently, one may see newspaper headlines like: "Pet python squeezes teen to death" or "pet lion bloodies owner." Do you think that a little common sense could go a long way here?

Then, there are those people that see animals simply as "money-makers" (inanimate objects). An increasing number of dairy farmers/dairy conglomerates are injecting growth hormones into cows, in order to stimulate an increase in the amount of milk produced per cow. This process causes cows' udders to become oversensitive and enlarged and even infected. It is not enough to ask the poor cows to produce milk naturally and normally. Rather, they must do it in an ever-faster manner in order to please some greedy, opportunistic, agri-corporate businesspeople (who have once again demonstrated those insatiable, characteristic wants for speed, productivity and profit). What did the cows ever do to us to deserve such treatment? Meanwhile, many of us end up ingesting residues of these growth hormones (which are possibly carcinogenic) into our bodies through the dairy products that we consume—all for the sake of "excessive cow productivity."

As long as there is a single wild animal still standing anywhere in the world in its natural habitat, and which has economic value in any of its body parts—there will be poachers to kill (or capture) it and unscrupulous merchants to sell whatever is of value. They will only stop when the particular animals have been completely slaughtered out of existence—or because the animals are within the confines of a rigorously guarded wild animal preserve. The following animals are all in peril because they all happen to have a "valuable" part: the rhino for its horn; the elephant for its ivory tusk; the tiger for its genitalia (for people's false notion of them possessing aphrodisiac effects). You could also add the capturing of exotic birds for export to especially this country. All of them, contraband, simply for the sake of profit.

I would also like to comment on the use of animals in research. I'm not going to debate here the pros and cons of using animals in research for upgrading surgical procedures and battling diseases that would ultimately save human lives. This exercise would be a book in and of itself. What I do want to assert is that to use animals in certain types of research, in which results and conclusions would have questionable benefits and applications for humans—especially in situations where other procedures were available—is unconscionable.

The procedure for testing household/consumer products on animals is for the most part unnecessary today, yet many companies still persevere at it. There are better ways to determine the toxicity of a compound or product than by seeing how much an animal can withstand before dying. These types of products are never going to be totally safe anyway, because they are still going to contain some levels of carcinogens and poisons. It is a matter of overkill—confirming already determined conclusions.

One industry which has taken the initiative in the last decade to use alternatives to animal testing has been the cosmetic industry. Some companies test products using cell cultures (even human tissue samples are available), patch tests on volunteers, ultrasound and image analyzers. Furthermore, they are using natural, raw materials; extracts from plants and vegetables; and "animal-derived" (vs. "animal-by-product") ingredients (e.g., beeswax, urea and lanolin) in their actual products, rather than synthetic substances, in order to make them safer.

Finally, there is evidence that about 50% of drugs that are ultimately approved by the Federal Drug Administration on the basis of animal experimentation are later ascertained to cause illness, injury and death in humans.[16] This is "because the physiological differences between humans and animals are so great, substances which have no effect in animals may affect humans. This is because substances are metabolized differently in humans and in animals. For instance, 'cortisone produces birth defects in mice, but not in people, while thalidomide works the other way around.'"[17]

I would like to end this section with the hope that we will think about animals with more respect and appreciation for everything that they do for us (including sacrificing their own lives) for the sake of the human condition and agenda. I just wish we could show more reciprocation for the conditions of their own lives and habitat than we do. Joy Williams, an essayist, summed it up beautifully in an article of hers that appeared in Harper's Magazine:

> "If animals...could speak with the tongues of angels...it is unlikely that they could save themselves from mankind. Their mysterious otherness has not saved them, nor have their beautiful songs and coats and skins and shells, nor have their strengths, their skills, their swiftness, the beauty of their flights. We discover the remarkable intelligence of the whale, the wolf, the elephant—it does not save them, nor does our awareness of the complexity of their lives...We know that they care for their young and teach them, that they play and grieve, that they have memories and a sense of the future for which they sometimes plan. We know about their habits, their migrations, that they have a sense of home, of finding, seeking, returning to home. We know that when they face death, they fear it. We know all these things and it has not saved them from us."[18]

Child Abuse

Child abuse can come in many forms and doesn't always have the physical elements to it that is so often portrayed in the media and commonly believed to be automatically inclusive. Child maltreatment can merely be: (a.) emotional (not providing warmth, love, support and guidance); (b.) psychological (criticizing or insulting); (c.) neglectful of necessities and personal time; (d.) and/or simply incompetent parenting. Actually, there is not a more important factor in how children will ultimately turn out as adults, than how their parents (or guardians) treat and relate to them from birth through adolescence. This fact seems obvious, yet it is surprising how many parents (even well-meaning ones) overlook the crucial nature of this criterion and/or take their children for granted.

Parenting is an awesome and overwhelming responsibility, and many people (who may lack the character traits to be good parents to begin with) don't take this truism into account before having kids. The end result is parental attitudes and behaviors that are bad for the child; bad for the family; and bad for society. Parental confidence, maturity and competence should all be well in place by the time the baby arrives, but (unfortunately) in too many instances they are not. The lack of readiness or willingness for parenting, when it is prematurely thrust upon one, can have long-term adverse effects on the child, because of cues that the child picks up upon when being raised by an unmotivated, uncaring parent. Furthermore, incompetent parenting often promulgates the same character pattern to occur when these children become adults and have their own children, so that it becomes inter-generational in nature and perpetuates the burden onto society.

The biggest deterrent to child abuse is not having children for all the wrong reasons. The following are *not* good enough reasons (by themselves) for having children: (1) to keep the family name going (for personal, business or inheritance reasons) (2) as a way of hoping to keep a bond between "not-so-compatible" spouses (3) need some "thing" to relieve your own boredom with life (4) for making you feel like a "whole" person (5) need someone to take care of you in old age (6) patriotic and economic resources (e.g., more people in the labor force equals a strong America) (7) "mold" a being to compensate for what you missed out on in your life (8) to demonstrate one's fertility...I'm sure there are more reasons, but the point I'm trying to make is basic. There should really only be one reason why people should have children—a *strong, inner* desire and willingness to give them the proper emotional (not just financial) nurturing and foundation that they will need, so that they can become their own unique individuals.

Many young parents don't fully comprehend the importance of especially the first four years of a child's life. These are the years when the input of both the mother and father becomes imprinted on the youngster (through imitation of the parents)—"the parental blueprint or design of love and warmth, of understanding and strength, of beliefs and values, of hopes and expectations, of rebukes and rewards, of teaching by example."[19] In essence, it sets the mold; and one that becomes hard to undue after that crucial early time frame. The child's character traits and personality (whether good or bad) will have been fairly well set in place.

Just as important during this time is the need for commencing physical contact between parent and child… "research shows that it is not merely the parents' loving presence or expressions of affection that affect the mental and physical growth of the child, but the actual experience of being touched and even massaged…Holding, touching, stroking, and carrying an infant all serve to soothe, stimulate and communicate [and foster an alertness] at an age when the tactile sense is the most mature sensory system."[20] Overworked and overstressed parents of today often don't take (or have) the time to do all of these things that make for successful child-raising.

When discussing child abuse, one cannot avoid mentioning the problematic nature of the parents (who still may be trying to find their own identity) as part of the cause. Our wide range of lifestyles (in an already-confusing social environment that we have created for ourselves) discourages a family life that is conducive to being stable and secure. "The unmarried parents, the one-parent family, the alternative-lifestyle family, the family reconfigured by divorce [step family], the foster and adoptive family, all of them…constitute the new ecology of the contemporary family."[21]

In fact, "parental units" change so rapidly these days, that I am sure that right now there is at least one resourceful entrepreneur out there, who is thinking that producing a "Pop-On-A-Face" photo frame might not be such a bad idea. Unlike most photo frames, which come with a pre-packed, entire photo of some couple, this type would have the dressed bodies of a couple—but with only drawn outlines where the faces go—so that one could stick a new face photo (with a thin, magnetic-strip backing) onto the picture on an "as needed basis." This handy item would help enable the children to keep up-to-date when they want an answer to the question, "Who are my parents going to be this week?"—And, who says that there is no truth to the phrase, "that pictures speak a thousand words."...Is it little wonder why children grow up being so confused about themselves and the world around them?

Everyone in society is affected by how all children are parented. If the lack of consideration and respect for others is never demonstrated or taught by the parents, that will consequentially carry over to how the children will behave and interact with others in the larger world. We must all eventually develop a "strength of character [that] we need to control our impulses, to tolerate frustration and to postpone gratification—the essential qualities for life in a civilized society. Our children are not born with these qualities...They learn them, or do not learn them, most indelibly from their parents."[22]

How many times have we all seen out-of-control children (and for that matter parents too) running around wild in a public place? I am always very leery of even making a polite suggestion to the parents, because from my past experience, they have resultantly gone "Neanderthal" on me. In other words, you (yourself) become the victim of the parent's misplaced wrath for even thinking that something is wrong with the behavior of his/her child, let alone his/her own parental disciplinary skills.

I once was sitting at a public event in a reserved seat when a family consisting of a father, mother, daughter and son sat down next to me—with the son sitting closest to me. After a short time, the son started haphazardly swinging and twirling around a small crossbow not far from my face. That's right, he brought a crossbow to a public event (and it wasn't an archery competition)—for what reason I don't know. Well anyway, after a few minutes of enduring such behavior, I began to have some apprehension and could forebodingly visualize the freaky, tabloid-like headlines in my local newspaper's Metro section the next day: "Man Loses Eye From Flying, Self-Willed Projectile."

Therefore, after a short time, I decided to lean over to the father and ask him politely, "Can you please ask your child to stop twirling the crossbow?" Well, with his reaction you would have thought that I had asked him to place his son in jail and throw away the key. The father stands up and points his finger at my face and says, "Don't you ever tell my son what to do!" He probably was thinking of taking my "block" off, but I held my ground and reminded him that I wasn't telling his son—but instead was telling him. This comment seemed to put a little sense back into him, and he reluctantly didn't pursue his case too much longer—probably because there were witnesses around.

Obviously, this is not a good way to teach your children social right from wrong, but it demonstrates my point that acquiring bad character is almost always the fault of the parent, not the child. Now I understand why we are almost all shocked when we happen to meet or see a well-behaved, considerate child. Although such a child should be the norm of society, it seems as though such an example is rather becoming more the exception.

Also, it cannot be overstated the way in which today's fast-paced, complex society has worn people down and has, thusly, affected their quality of parenting. Even if they want to give their children the love and attention that they need, they are finding it more and more difficult. Much of the little free time that they do have is increasingly being spent on: (1) just coping with "everyday" problems of personal/family living. (2) pursuing individual goals that are unrelated to the family. (3) becoming more "monetarily productive" so that they can purchase more luxurious "wants," that they don't really need, but which maintain their public image of wealth and sophistication (e.g., some people demonstrate more concern about the care of their cars than the care of their children). (4) appeasing and soothing their own "inner-child" traumas, unresolved issues and demons that they have had to live with (and attempted to correct) their whole lives (5) expecting their children to take on adult responsibilities (sometimes out of necessity) that can minimize the time that the children have for fulfilling all of their own developmental needs. This concept would also extend to parental expectations that kids should achieve on an adult-like scale (and intensity) at school and in athletics at an ever-earlier age (6) and finally, not even seeing parenting as a valuable, growth-oriented activity itself, but rather merely as a "care-taking" function that can be purchased.

It is noteworthy to mention what studies have shown about the effects that different qualities of day care have on children.

"Jay Belsky, a professor of clinical psychology at Pennsylvania State University, studies the effects of day care. He has discovered a strong correlation between early, extensive, low-quality day care and subsequent aggressive, noncompliant behavior in school-age children...the primary determinant of day care's effect on children is quality, and quality is determined by the level of one-to-one interaction between the care provider and the child...The most important thing to children, be they in day care or the care of their parents, is the way in which they are treated. Children tend to thrive, both emotionally and intellectually, when they are cared for by persons who are emotionally invested in them; when the care they receive is sensitive and responsive to their individual needs and desires; and when the caregivers in question have enduring relationships with the children. This is as true of day care as it is of family care."[23]

Unfortunately, day care centers aren't required to have the two-to-one ratio of children to day-care workers, which is most probably the ratio that is optimally needed in order to provide "quality" day care. Parents don't fully appreciate the fact that "the quality of equipment and the credentials of the staff are not nearly as important as the level of [positive] personal interaction between the caregiver and the child and the stability of [the] relationship."[24]

Most parents can neither afford to hire a good, child-care provider in their own private home, nor send their children to a day-care center where they can get the type of individual attention that they need. So my question to companies and the government is simple. Isn't it worth the cost outlay for the creation of a *high*-quality standard of day care for all who need it? We all in society reap many long-term benefits when these children are given a suitable foundation, so that they may eventually grow into responsible, caring adults.

Finally, we need to promote a policy that would advance the *expectation* of competent parenting. At the very minimum, one could require a parental life education program. Young couples' participation in such a program would hopefully make them realize ahead of time about the enormous responsibilities involved in child-rearing. Their need to learn and understand this subject matter is more important than any academic course that they could be otherwise taught. Some states have already taken steps to push this concept further. Wisconsin and Hawaii have already passed laws that would require parents to support their children's children. One may only conjecture whether this is the wave of the future, where more and more states hold parents responsible for their behavior toward their own children as well as their children's behavior.

Communication Abuse

Given the nature and dramatic changes that have occurred within today's society (and which I have been describing and discussing throughout this book), it should not be surprising that much of how we communicate with each other is often reduced to either the "impersonal" or "the lowest common denominator" forms. We have an obsession about quickly receiving either feedback of facts or visual and/or audio stimuli, that will sate our continual and instantaneous self-indulgent/self-gratification impulses and wants. We have accustomed ourselves to communicating, almost robotically, in sound-bites (or snippets). We listen for the first key word and then often tune ourselves out to anything else (including non-verbal communication)—not realizing that there might be an important qualifier to the original statement at the end of the sentence. In short, the speed of our culture has created within us an attention span of mere nanoseconds.

For example, the impersonal acquiring of "just the facts" is evident in the frustration that we all encounter when we call a large company. We have to settle by communicating with an object (a computer) and the reciting of its "menu of options," in which generally the last option that is offered is to actually talk to a live customer service representative. And heaven help you, if you decide to choose the option to wait to talk to a service representative, because you are going to have to wait on the phone for as long as a half hour for one. All the while, you are going to be forced to listen to recorded music of, for instance, a piano repeatedly playing the theme song from the movie, *Forrest Gump*, over and over again—until you will not be able to extricate the music out of your head for at least two weeks thereafter.

On the other hand (if you choose the computer option), you will have to punch in an endless amount of numbers on your touch-tone keypad such as: account number; zip code; social security number; telephone number (including area code); date of birth; PIN numbers; date of bill or statement in question; extension number of appropriate department; a particular number for whether you want your instructions in English or some other language; what state you are calling from; your mother's maiden name (that is on record) for security purposes; multiple-choice questions of a company survey so that it can better gauge who its "average" caller is, so that its "service-related" employees may better serve your needs etc. etc. etc. And of course, if at any time you accidentally punch in any incorrect numbers, the computer's voice berates you—and as punishment, it starts you back at the beginning of the menu.

If after all of this digital input, you can still remember the original purpose of your call, you should most certainly be given some type of reward—which the computer does by connecting you to yet another computer, the appropriate person's voice mail. Through this whole process, you have not talked to even one live human being. The end result: you could literally be on the phone for a half hour and not have accomplished a single thing—and then (on top of that) waste another half hour, in order to calm down from your sheer frustration. So, in regards to the phone, one could rightly state that we don't get talk when we want it (e.g., computer menus), and we get talk when we don't want it (e.g., telemarketers).

Even when you are able to reach a live person in order to obtain information from them, your chances seem about 50-50 of getting the following response: "I can't help you, our computers have come down with a 'virus,' and they will be off-line for the rest of the day (and might be out tomorrow as well)"...Is it my imagination or are we interchangeably using words which would normally be applicable to humans only (i.e., virus) and applying them to technological innovations and vice-versa? Are we slowly becoming assimilated to be one and the same?

Another case in point about phone calls is the plethora of wrong-number calls that one receives. I have gotten so many, that I sometimes simply play along with the caller, as if I am the person that he is actually calling. Sometimes callers will automatically assume that they have reached the correct person, and they don't even give you a chance to respond.

Here's a sample situation of receiving a call from a person who is an employee (for instance, in a mid to large-sized company), and who thinks he has reached a particular co-worker within the same company: "Frank, this is Bill. I'm going to the deli. What do you want for lunch?" Well, I figure that as long as ol' Bill is nice enough to be taking lunch orders, he might as well take ol' Steve's. So, I respond, "Get me a turkey on whole wheat with mayo." Meanwhile, a half hour later when Bill returns, the *real* Frank is disappointed and reluctantly has to settle for the turkey, instead of the pastrami on rye with mustard that he would have really preferred.

All fun aside (at least momentarily), the point I'm trying to make here is that in our frantic-paced lives that we lead, we hasten to move along or get things done as fast as possible. The result is that we have a tendency to talk *at* people (as if they were objects), rather than *with* them (as individuals). The mix-up in the above example could have easily been avoided if Bill (at the start of the conversation) would have simply asked, "Is this Frank?" Communication is talk-listen...listen-talk...not just talk-talk...(or in this case, assume nothing and take a moment to inquire).

Let's move onto language, where I would like to describe some examples of how we have the tendency to become accustomed to the use of foul language in our everyday lives. I have sometimes eaten at a particular restaurant that resembles an old schooner and which has a pirate theme to its decor. They used to have a talking parrot that would sit on his perch within a cage outside of the doors to the restaurant. Once you entered, a long corridor would lead to the actual lobby of the restaurant. Well, over a span of time, a couple of vulgar "wise-guys" must have gotten to this parrot in order to teach him some words that would expand his buccaneer-like vocabulary. Eventually, a part of his verbal repertoire started to include some "profane one-liners with a twist," that he would suddenly throw in with some of his normal phrases. So, unassuming patrons would be walking along and "out of the clear blue" might suddenly hear a saying with an obscene word in it.

The majority of the arriving patrons may have found this language display amusing. Some others probably stood there speechless and in total bewilderment, wondering whether to seek out the services of a hearing specialist, first thing the next morning. Well, needless to say, over time this type of behavior by the bird sealed his fate. Eventually, the nonchalant and unrelenting parrot had to be permanently extricated from the restaurant grounds—all the while babbling obscenities (that he had learned a little too well), as he and his cage were carted off to most probably the parrot ward of a bird insane asylum.

Another example was a non-trashy, network television talk show and which answers the question why people will tune out if you directly insult their propriety enough. An up-and-coming actress sits down on a talk show set, and within 30 seconds after mentioning her film, she starts discussing a traumatic "peeing experience" that she had at the film location in a Mexican jungle. [By the way, doesn't anybody use the word, urinate, anymore?] Nonetheless, the cast and crew seemingly did not even have an outhouse and had to relieve themselves in the same way that a wild animal would. After about a minute of this description, I switched the channel. Just to play it safe, I gave it an extra long three minutes before I switched back. Lo and behold, you guessed it, she was still talking about the peeing experience—except now the conversation was taking on the characteristics of a saga, because she had expanded the story to include the explaining of the little nuances of it all. I won't get into the details, but it ended up that she spent virtually her whole allotted time talking only about this one subject. This is crudeness simply for the sake of being crude. Is the describing of a person's bodily functions on national television suppose to pass as entertainment?

It is no different than some guy getting up from his chair in a restaurant and asking the waiter in a loud, brusque manner, so that everybody at the surrounding tables can hear him: "Hey dude, where's the room with the peeing trough?" Are our cultural customs reverting back to those that were characteristic of the Middle Ages—a period of history when people had virtually no inhibitions on their behavior?

Also, one could obviously make a case that such an uninhibited behavior pattern even affected former President Clinton. Which of the following pair of words should never have to appear in print (or be uttered) in the same sentence—and if they do, means that the Founding Fathers are turning over in their graves?

(a) President-------Foreign Policy
(b) President-------Domestic Policy
(c) President-------Congress
(d) President-------Constitution
(e) President-------Genitalia

Where does one draw the line? Well, one can be fairly certain that when the words, President and genitalia, have to appear in the same sentence, the line has been crossed. The Presidency was not Mr. Clinton's to do with as he pleased. He was merely a *temporary* holder of the Office, only one of many who had passed through it throughout our country's history—no more, no less. When he was elected, the American people expected him to responsibly uphold the Office with dignity and honor, irregardless of how good a policymaker that he may or may not have been. If a President loses character, the public mindset can often lose confidence in his judgment or poise. Aristotle once said that character of a leader is "the most effective means of persuasion he possesses."[25] If President Clinton had personal problems, he should have sought help, but shouldn't have used the Office so openly and blatantly (without any discretion) to have affairs and get away with lying to the American people. After he left Office, how he wanted to conduct his personal life was up to him. But, as long as he was our representative in the Highest Office, it should not have been his choice.

Finally, before leaving the topic of communication abuse, I would like to make a few comments about Jerry Springer and shows like his. His show perpetuates the proliferation of abuse (which is shamefully already near epidemic levels in this country), while giving credence to the notion that the way to resolve abuse and conflict is through even more abuse and conflict. Springer would certainly plead innocence and then defend his show on the assumption that he is merely trying to depict the abuses that go on in society as the indignities that they are.

This would be an interesting premise, but it would be a false one. You cannot vilify abuse by tolerating and even justifying more abuse. It is like trying to define a word by using the very word itself in the definition. Or, it is like him turning a blind eye to abuse and saying, "I'll (subjectively) know abuse when I see it"—but until then, let the warring factions commence their battle for the self-indulgent pleasures of the Roman Coliseum audience. No, there is only one reason for Springer's show and that is to profit on the misery and reconciliation of others, so that he is able to buy even more expensive stogies.

Drug Abuse

A major factor in whether a person ever starts the practice of taking drugs (let alone abusing them) is what kind of internal control system that person has developed up to that point (usually adolescence). Internal control elements would include: (a.) degrees of independent-mindedness and self-control especially if (and when) relating to a drug-user peer group (b.) frustration and stress tolerance levels when in everyday social situations (c.) a positive (yet not egotistical) perception of oneself (d.) ability to reach practical & reasonable goal achievements; and (e) resisting pattern of alienated and/or deviant behavior from "basic conventional mores."

In addition, if one also has a strong foundation in his external control system, the likelihood of ever beginning with drugs is remote. External control elements would include: (a) effective (yet reasonable) parental discipline and supervision (b) consistency of moral training and development (c) parental acceptance and appreciation of the child for his/her individual identity and worth (d) learning to discover new experiences and excitement through hobbies or extracurricular activities and (e) the general avoiding of other societal temptations (especially law-breaking ones). It is especially relevant to have a strong internal control system, which can often compensate in the case of a weaker external control system. But, preferably the less mismatching between the two systems, the better.

Also, it should be noted, that excessive use of over-the-counter as well as prescription drugs and medications can stem from the overall lack of personal control mechanisms. Depending on the circumstances, such drug dependencies are no less dangerous in many respects, although the reasons for acquiring them may sometimes be different. Even the seemingly innocent practice of the habitual use of antacids after every meal could be in response to the psychological intolerance to even minor stomach acidity. In turn, being denied "a fix" for this minor acidity might be seen by the user as causing a "withdrawal symptom," that can only be relieved (or dealt with) in his mind and body through the "popping of a substance" (in this case, an antacid tablet). Therefore, the abusing of any drug or even minor medication can be problematic (at best) and dangerous (at worst). One must realize that "the line between illegal and legal drugs is a historical accident based primarily upon emotion rather than science."[26]

Drug abuse (illegal or legal) like any other abuse, whether it be a substance or process (e.g., overeating, gambling), is a way of avoiding emotional pain and coming to terms with one's personal failings and inadequacies—by blurring, altering or postponing the face of reality. I cannot stress this point enough, because it is the emotional component that is the catalyst that starts such behavior. The physical element and consequences only come later, at a time when the whole abusive behavior is harder to control.

As the societal expectations and realities for individuals become more demanding, the susceptibility for people to abuse can often increase significantly. Moreover, as society becomes more complex, the greater is the likelihood that new subcultures do develop, that see themselves as increasingly "fragmented" from society in general. These groups may use a form of mind control (including psychological intimidation) as an abuse, so that their "altered states of reality" will look normal and acceptable to their own members. An excellent example of this notion was the Heaven's Gate cult, which ended up committing collective suicide.

All of this aside, when you get down to the crux of the matter, I firmly believe that this country is continuing to chase after (and trying to alleviate) the "symptoms" of drug abuse, rather than strongly emphasizing a reduction in the "root causes" of drug abuse. This myopic plan reduces supply without really addressing and alleviating demand. It overlooks the fact that the individual is doing drugs, because that individual's problems are not being dealt with in the first place. America's "Tough On Drugs" policy does not address whatsoever peoples' inabilities to deal (let alone cope) with their problems.

The point is that if we gave our kids the time and provided enough societal resources to help them with their everyday problems before they ever decided to turn to drugs to begin with—the need to combat a national drug problem (after the fact) could be reduced significantly. Of course, it is understandable why the government does not go after the "root causes" with more venom—because this avenue is much harder and more costly to do.

All of the following are "symptoms," and comparatively are like cutting off the top of a weed—they will only regenerate again, because you didn't (or weren't able) to get to the "roots" in the ground.

>   Drugs themselves —SYMPTOM
>   Drug lords —SYMPTOM
>   Drug dealers —SYMPTOM
>   Crime that is caused by those trying
>   to support a drug habit—SYMPTOM
>   Colombian farmers growing coca plants to make
>   a living in order to survive—SYMPTOM
>   Children acting as lookouts for drug dealers
>   in urban housing projects—SYMPTOM

The real problem is the ever-increasing multitude of people that are having a hard time coping with the severe emotional stresses in their lives—within an atmosphere of an impersonal society and undependable families. But, how can one go about changing the negative, alienated focus of a teen on drugs, who maybe hasn't seen his father in years, and whose mother neglects him at best? That is a very, very tough question to answer, and it is hard to fathom how such teens cope. But, one could start by looking at how the mental health system is set up in this country (and which I will devote a whole section to in the next chapter).

While we will forego that discussion temporarily, it should be asserted that a clear and more distinct differentiation should be made between how we handle the dealers versus the takers of drugs. We should continue to put a stranglehold on the former, but should "loosen the rope" as well as show more compassion for the latter. The abuse or addiction to drugs is a disease, and it should be seen as less of a law enforcement problem (because much crime can be seen as an outgrowth of taking drugs)---and more as an illness that can be overcome with individualized treatment, if society has the determined will to see it that way (and do something about it). Empathy, care, and the discovery of the intrinsic worthiness of the abuser/addict should be the order of the day—not intolerance, disrespect, and condemnation.

Elder Abuse

Elder mistreatment is on the increase, as family members are finding it harder to cope and handle circumstances within their own everyday lives, while simultaneously having to face the fact that their parents need more care in their old age. Elder abuses generally fall under one of four categories: (a) physical (including slapping &, bruising) (b) psychological (including humiliation and threats) (c) financial (including illegal or improper use of funds) (d) neglect (including failure of caretaker obligations and also self-neglect by the elder).

It seems that the explanations for elder abuse stem from the interrelationship between two factors. First, the unaccustomed/unhealthy dependency between the "perpetrator and the victim." Second, the helplessness of the victim because of frailty, disability or impairment. We all live our whole lives feeling relatively free and independent, and when it comes time to have to compromise those rights (via this type of relationship), everyone involved has a tendency to balk. A nursing home attendant may lose his or her cool when the same patient has summoned (or complained) about something for the umpteenth time that day. In turn, the attendant may handle the patient, roughly, feed him improperly, start leaving him unattended, not provide enough stimulation or simply restrain him.

Meanwhile, family members may have unrealistic expectations or misunderstandings regarding care giving on their part. They may not fully comprehend or accept the elder's dependency on them for getting dressed, fed and/or going to the bathroom. The relationship becomes frustrating, irritating and frictional. In these cases, the abuse can become physical and/or psychological. Furthermore, because the elder becomes the submissive one in the relationship (because of frailty or impairment), the family members (whether consciously or unconsciously) may take advantage of the elder because of the obvious inequality of power.

On the other hand, the "independence factor" can be held onto just as doggedly from the point of view of the elderly. They try to maintain dignity and insist on remaining independent, while denying that they are under any hardship, so that they won't be a burden to anyone (especially to any children). They see independence as "the major factor determining the quality of their lives in old age."[27]

But, while they may put on a good front of not needing any assistance, there are other occurrences (in addition to physical impairments) that can negatively affect them psychologically and emotionally. There are many losses that may accompany old age: children move away; spouses and friends die; decreased sense of expectations; inability to identify with a changing world around them (both individually and socially). These factors can take their toll on self-esteem and self-confidence to the point where the elderly begin to neglect themselves, and then supportive services may be called in, which will compromise the elders' autonomy. So, there is always this crucial balancing act that must be considered between what is best for the elder's personal safety and well-being versus the choice for independent functioning.

Another type of abuse that is increasingly being perpetuated upon the elderly would be under the broad range category of financial bilking (which is estimated at $40 billion a year).[28] Oftentimes, it is a family member who is the culprit. If a lone child gets the elder to sign a power of attorney, all assets may be transferred to the child's name. A worst-case example is where a child took all of the assets and moved to another state, thereby abandoning all responsibility for the elder. There have been other instances where family members (who stand to inherit from a will) have used very sparing and inadequate amounts of the assets for the actual care of the elder, while holding onto the vast majority of the assets for their own futures.

Finally, there are a variety of elderly scams that are advanced by pitchmen. There are a couple reasons why these cons select the elderly. First, many elderly are searching for purpose and for the ability to be meaningful to someone else. Therefore, they are susceptible to confusing exploitation for friendship. A con man can start the relationship very innocently through simply a conversation or a chance meeting and build up the elder's confidence, trust, and importance. The older person starts to feel grateful for any advice or service rendered and/or chores & errands that the scam artist might start performing. Suddenly, the senior feels indebted and becomes vulnerable to an unknowing fraudulent scheme that his "friend" might put forward. The elder then parts with his money as a token of gratitude for kindnesses received.

Second, seniors are looking for activity to fill their many empty hours. By entering sweepstakes by mail and taking telemarketers' phone calls (whereby they are sold deals and "guaranteed" profits from investments), they become easy marks to become victims of fraud. They may not be capable of reading the fine print of what exactly they are entering—or not fully understand or be confused by fast talk—and, in turn, naively consent to the purchase of something. This is especially the case where they must buy something in order to collect a "prize" (which is always something much less valuable than the purchase itself).

Furthermore, once you buy something from a scam artist, your name is sold to other scammers who then see you as an easy victim for other propositions. But, even when seniors get "burned," they often will not make any formal complaints about their victimization. They have qualms that their mental competence will be questioned by family members or social service agencies, and that, therefore, their independence could once again be jeopardized.

Relationship Abuse

With the breakdown of many families and other contributing societal issues, many people today feel compelled (like never before) to seek and find acceptance and kinship with a "significant" other. But, to find the "right" one is further hindered by two societal factors:

(1) the overly strong emphasis and encouragement of couplehood at any cost, even if the two people are not as compatible as they should be in order to form a happy and satisfying union. (2) the complexities and excessive stimuli (that are found in the fast-paced, informational world of today) have created ever-changing individual wants and expectations. Increasingly, the trend toward "individual fulfillment" is taking precedence over any reality of "couple fulfillment." Therefore, relationships have become fleeting and people have a tendency to fall out of favoritism and substantively differ with each other much faster than ever before. So that, literally, one can start a relationship or get married to a seemingly compatible person and within one or two years hardly recognize that the other person and you have any common ground whatsoever. The end result is that there are many couples trying to stay in-balance even though their personalities, attitudes, likes and dislikes potentially may be changing at near lightning speed. The outcome is that statistically at least 50% of couples are rudely awakened to the fact that the distress in their relationships has suddenly become equivalent to—getting teeth pulled out without any anesthesia or being stuck in the behind with a porcupine.

Our own perceived personal images as well as society (in general) are changing so rapidly from a proliferation of overstimulated wants and expectations, that they are literally changing our characters. Many people are having the tendency to silently ask themselves the question: What benefit is this other person for improving *me?* The ability to, instead, accept a natural complementing of each other, does not seem to be as readily taken into account. Christopher Lasch alluded to this trend in his book: "The prevailing social conditions [has] brought out narcissistic personality traits that [are] present, in varying degrees, in everyone—a certain protective shallowness, a fear of binding commitments, a willingness to pull up roots whenever the need [arises], a desire to keep one's options open, a dislike of depending on anyone, an incapacity for loyalty or gratitude."[29]

One could say that whatever avenue advances one's self-interest the most, that is the one that is taken without much (if any) remorse for anybody else that may be involved. In essence, in more and more instances, social relationships are becoming commercialized (admittedly, sometimes out of protective necessity). People are more frequently needing guaranteed "warranties" and service contracts from people that they interact with in their lives, just as they expect from new products that they purchase. People can no longer assume or trust that —lovers, families, co-workers, doctors, insurance agents, teachers, and even "frozen embryo" biotech labs (which sell reproductive eggs and sperm like they were commodities to the highest bidder) etc. — will ultimately (in good conscience) do what is best for them—once the money and/or any exploitation factors are brought in as criteria. "Increasingly [people] feel the need to be able to hold others legally accountable...to have a club to wield to ensure that they are getting what they pay for out of their social relations."[30]

Furthermore, we have linked monetary expectations with love in such a tight bundle, that we often view the elements of money and love almost interchangeably. For instance, a lover may smile when given a "gem-karat" ring as a gift, but in her mind is disappointed because she was expecting a "rock." Or, a husband may receive 50 shares of stock for his birthday, but is wondering why his wife couldn't have put out enough money for 100 shares.

So, even though objects can be symbolic ways of showing love, more of us are seeing them as replacing actual ways of love itself. The rationale becomes, "Why didn't you buy me a nicer_____(fill in the blank), don't you love me?" In today's world, should we conclude that love (an inner feeling) is really a tangible item? It appears that is the way it is becoming more and more.

Also, as the world has become more complex, people enter into relationships by bringing more mental/emotional "baggage" (including former relationships); different expectations; stress; and even personal neuroses. A mental mistake that happens in some relationships is the disillusionment that may result by expecting too much from it or by visualizing the other as more than he or she really is. For example, a common premise is that we can change the other into something that *we* visualize and that will, correspondingly, make *us* happy. But, while a relationship can complement your being, it cannot replace your being. It can "add to your happiness, but it cannot create a sense of self-worth or well-being where there was none before."[31]

Similarly, both partners must each balance the crucial variables of logic and emotion in order to have a contented relationship.

Otherwise, if one is too logical in the relationship, that person can tend to be too rigid, aloof, factual, and distant in showing the thoughts and feelings of one's inner being (and thereby naive to tone and implicit meaning). On the other hand, there is a danger of being too emotional as well, in that one can become too dependent, giddy, uncontrollably capricious, and jump to conclusions too quickly. So, in order to have a mature relationship, both participants should have an integration of logic and emotion somewhere in the wide, middle span of the "bell curve" — rather than on the more extreme areas of it. Of course, if *both* partners are on one side of the curve or the other, one could foresee a possibly satisfying (yet limiting) relationship as a result. But, most people have varying degrees of both logic and emotion in their personality structures.

Another major mistake that a couple makes when forming into a relationship is not "checking their individual egos and vanities at the front door before entering." Similarly, if each comes in with their own (often uncompromising) agenda, unfortunately, their respective agendas won't always have enough common ground in order for them to remain compatible. So, if either one comes in with the attitude—I'm right, and you're simply wrong—the objectivity, respect and tolerance that we all deserve and need in any type of healthy relationship will be trampled.

Other major behavioral faux pas include: unconstructive criticism, self-serving lying, lecturing, condescendingly directing/ordering, ignoring, nagging, blaming, judging, manipulating, intimidating, character attacking, belittling, boasting when you were right and reiterating when the other was wrong. These are all negative ways of relating and, in excess, can only lead to ultimate trouble. Although most of these seem obvious, it is surprising how many of us continue to repeat such self-defeating, behavior patterns. Even though you may be a couple in a relationship, you still are two separate individuals. Because of this fact, the keys to bridging the gap are sensible, healthy, communicational interactions (and considerate expression of feelings)—even more important than romance and sex. True intimacy is built from respectful communication, mutual understanding of feelings, and the acceptance of our own and the other's vulnerabilities.

Still another major factor that today is not always taken into account (yet is obvious) is the behavioral differences between men and women. Regardless of what some of the more ardent feminists would have you think, there are important differences in behavior patterns and how each sex meaningfully perceives and reasons about the realities of life. For instance, there seems to be an almost innate need for men to go off to be alone in their little "cave," in order to determine how best to solve a problem at hand. On the other hand, women often seem to have more of a need to share thoughts about the problem in a conversation with a close friend or two. Each sex needs to realize that the other must have the personal time and opportunity to carry out these "behavioral rituals." Understanding and acknowledging such differences can go a long way to attaining a mutual satisfying relationship.

Spousal/Sexual Abuse

Whenever the negative behavioral patterns that were listed above become overly excessive (or chronic) and/or have elements of physicality (i.e., slapping, hitting, kicking, punching), then the concept of marital conflict leads on into the realm of spousal abuse. And, the abuser and abusee will also add into the mix any destructive patterns that each remembers from his/her parents' marriage while they were growing up. Then, you have the potential makings of repeating the behavior pattern where each reverts to the role that they saw their same-sex parent play out. William Betcher in his book discusses how these early experiences can detrimentally affect a child's own marriage later in life:

> "Our beliefs about how husbands and wives should relate, our expectations of rights and responsibilities, our vision of what a marriage should be, lie in our earliest experiences of growing up. How we were cared for, what we witnessed, heard, felt, or imagined about our parents and their marriage formed our fundamental outlook. We are not aware of much of this. It remains in our unconscious memory partly because we don't have verbal access to many early impressions. It stays hidden

partly because all families have some unspoken agreements and selective perceptions that a child may very well sense but never express in words. But what we absorbed about our family and about our parents' marriages will affect us deeply throughout our lives."[32]

One possibility is that (unless the hurt is resolved) the daughter of the physical abuse victim (if the victim is the female) will grow up fearing closeness and intimacy (no matter how much she might crave them) in future relationships/marriage, because her belief may be that trying to attain them may cause more pain than the effort is worth. Another possibility is she may become verbally or physically abusive herself in her relationships—as a way to try to resolve her anger from what she witnessed as a child. But, the most likely scenario is that she will play the role of "martyr" in trying to resolve her past traumas. Her hope is that by "replaying the story with a different script," she can attain a happier ending than either a past, failed relationship that she had of her own or the marriage that her mother had. This often is the case, even if she senses that her new, potential mate may be trouble, and the same hurtful pattern could conceivably occur again. "Unfortunately, repeating relationships don't break patterns. People do."[33] Chasing after approval (that was denied to you in the past) and trying to right a past wrong (personal or familial) can be powerful, psychological drives in one's quest to feel "whole," irregardless of any futility or length of time that it might take to acquire them.

On the other hand, the son of the physical abuser (if the abuser is the male) is just as affected by unresolved childhood memories and issues, and may repeat the physical abusiveness of his father and/or take his frustrations out for having a neglectful, unloving mother. Moreover, such a man may also presently find that his career has not lived up to his expectations. He may beat his wife because he cannot actually beat the ones who really were the cause of his provocation, namely, those at work. Similarly, his marriage might not measure up to his fantasies of what wedded bliss should be like. He may feel that, his wife is not what she "ought to" be and does not seem to know her "duty." His rationalization may be that he can make her understand by "knocking" some sense into her.

Anger and frustration cause such a man to see himself as "an oppressor instead of the oppressed. Violence is the expression of the man's impotence...This is a man who feels powerless...and somehow inadequate."[34] Abuse is a release of tension, relief from pain and in the abuser's own mind, "justified" revenge for a past or present hurt. Subconsciously, he may realize that his behavior is wrong, but he denies it or avoids accepting that it is. Consequently, he doesn't end up dealing with the behavior or the problems that he and his wife have in their marriage.

Two other issues that need to be discussed are rape and incest. Contrary to popular notion, both of these occurrences are primarily motivated by the expression of power and anger, rather than out of sexual need. The causal link here is again virtually the same as all the other abuses that have been discussed in this chapter: "from an emotionally weak and insecure individual's inability to handle the stresses and demands of his life."[35]

Groth and Birnbaum in their book explain the motivational cause of rape: "Rape is a complex act that serves a number of retaliatory and compensatory aims in the psychological functioning of the offender. It is an effort to discharge his anger, contempt, and hostility toward women—to hurt, degrade, and humiliate. It is an effort to counteract feelings of vulnerability and inadequacy in himself and to assert his strength and power—to control and exploit...It is symptomatic of personality dysfunction, associated more with conflict and stress than with pleasure and satisfaction. Sexuality is not the only—nor the primary—motive underlying rape. It is, however, the means through which conflicts surrounding issues of anger and power become discharged."[36]

Similarly, incest is where almost always a child is seen as a weak object, whereby an adult can direct his wallowing anger and power through sexual activity. This situation is especially sad because children are dependent on adults in everyday life and expect these adults to treat them responsibly with care and understanding. By the adult breaking this trustworthy pact (for the satisfying of his own emotional needs), the child learns to be suspicious of the personal and sexual motives of other adults in general, and begins to visualize them as selfish and insincere.

Moreover, the child victim of parental incest often cannot confide this "secret" to the other parent (generally the mother) either. The mother, being the wife of the offender, becomes seen by the child as a potentially-jealous rival in a familial "love triangle." Such an unusual situation places a tremendous amount of unnecessary stress and anxiety on the child—a burden so great that it would be difficult enough for a grownup to manage (let alone a child). In essence, incest creates shame, guilt, and anger in the child along with a mistrust of family and future personal relationships with others.

Finally, the increase in breakdowns of the family structure today can only continue to worsen the problem of incest. With the growing isolation and disorganization of a larger family sphere (e.g., relatives), a child of incest doesn't have the feeling of comfort or closeness to relatives, whereby he or she could discuss such troubling incidents. Likewise, the growing rate of divorce can perpetuate abuses of all kinds, if the custodial parent remarries and a new group of people enter into the family. A previously unknown stepfamily can sometimes create a harmful environment, whereby, the child might have to deal with any abuses that these "unfamiliar others" might bring into the new familial relationship.

Suicide

Although suicide may not be considered an abuse in the technical sense, it could be called the "ultimate" abuse, because its outcome is so final. But, if loved ones and society would be more cognizant of its signs and encourage actualization of appropriate treatment, it is an abuse that is possibly the most conducive to being thwarted. This fact is because: (a) it cannot be categorized as a substance or process abuse, where one would either have a dependency or an obsession for continuing the deleterious behavior (b) it is more a state of mind (and therefore easier to change) rather than a behavior pattern that one must slowly and often agonizingly try to break (c) there are many places along the way (before the suicidal stage) where intervention can make a positive change.

It is important to realize that suicide in almost all cases is a gradual process that builds up over time, in which the person in question leaves many clues foretelling his depressed nature. Such a person will repeatedly make statements regarding hopelessness, helplessness and/or worthlessness. But, because these warning signs are intensive and happen over a period of time, they are therefore conducive to helpful intervention before thoughts turn into actions. So, although the suicidal state of mind has intense periods of negative thinking, these periods are by no means constant, but rather intermittent. This fact allows the opportunity for positive change and mood enhancement to take place.

Because of this "coming and going" nature of these intense thoughts and feelings, most suicidal people are often undecided about living or dying right up to the last second. This ambivalent nature is typically portrayed in all three suicide motivational types,[37] but for different reasons:
(1) "the wish to die" stems from trying to escape from some unbearable emotional pain or physical suffering in one's own life (2) "the wish to kill" is where suicide is seen as a way of revenge and inflicting subsequent, guilt/suffering on others through the suicide act itself (3) "wish to be killed" originates from such a person seeking punishment for an unseemly act that he did or some thought that he had or from troubles that he caused others. A perfect example of this last type (that is especially typical in Japan) would be an ambitious or previously successful businessperson killing himself out of a self-imposed view of his being responsible for a business or company ultimately failing. In his mind, he feels that he has dishonored himself and his family and needs to suffer the "repercussions." Once again, this is exemplary of how we (in the fast-paced, industrialized/high-tech world) see ourselves as successes or failures solely based on material economics.

It is noteworthy to further realize that although a potential suicidal crisis has passed, this does not mean that the risk of suicide has been averted. Many actual suicides occur especially within three months after the onset of a period of "seeming improvement" after a suicidal threat or incident. Just because one seems to be in a recovery phase, does not mean he is on his way to a full, healthy attitude and is supposedly no longer sick. Many such people are so focused on their intensive emotional pain, that they acquire a sort of "tunnel vision."

They don't end up calling on past coping experiences in order to help themselves get through any such relapses of suicidal moods.

Furthermore, it should be clarified that suicide is caused by how one's own internal psychological mechanism chooses to view, interpret, and accept the personal realities that occur around him or her. External circumstances (e.g., divorce, disappointments, personal failings, and loss) are not the direct causes, but are instead often the "triggers" for committing the act. If and when these "triggers" occur, it is important that none of us (especially overly sensitive people) become overwhelmed with negative reflections of ourselves. It is crucial to keep things in perspective and retain your confidence that you can and will do better next time (and beyond in the future).

While suicide is not genetic per se, people can seem to inherit "predispositions" to certain psychological illness (such as major depression), which if not treated could ultimately result in a suicidal attempt. People can be susceptible to these mental predispositions, similar to how we've always known that their bodies can be vulnerable to physical ones. Fortunately, chemicals that are out-of-balance in the brain, can be regulated in a more correct manner in order to help us think, feel and behave on a more "even keel" with better reasoning and objectivity. In conjunction with useful therapeutic counseling, lives can turnaround and improve.

On the other hand, the societal taboo of suicide is still seen by many as a moral issue more than a health issue. Even in the face of suicidal danger signs, fear and denial are still common reactions. "Eighty percent of the people who have major depression can be treated successfully with medicine, psychotherapy or a combination of the two…of the people who have depression, only 20% get any treatment, and…fifteen percent of people who have untreated mental illness ultimately will kill themselves."[38]

Work Abuse

This is a most interesting type of abuse in that the very deficiencies and inadequacies that each of the two participants (the company and the employee) are trying to evade actually end up feeding each other. As we have alluded to previously, the downsizing of companies has often led to excessive demands and overworking of the remaining employees. These type of companies have to operate under the extreme pressure of addressing continual and an inordinate number of crises that crop up, simply because of the self-imposed reduced workforce. Extended personal sacrifices become the norm. Most people might (and do) burn out under such circumstances, but for workaholics, it becomes a motivation and a challenge to perpetuate their "fix" of this process-type of addiction.

These companies encourage and seek out the type of workers who will become defined by their job and completely identify themselves with the workplace. Hence, it gives the workaholic the opportunity to endlessly work as long and as hard as he (or she) wants. Simultaneously, it allows him to avoid the conflicts, fears, and feelings of the personal side of his life that (for whatever reason) he considers difficult—and apprehensively dreads to face. It should be noted that in today's modern world, family problems are increasing so intensely, that some people actually see work as a relief, and they can't wait to get on the job. They feel that any problems that they have at work would pale in comparison to the ones that they might have at home. Now, that's a new twist! Nonetheless, the end result is that the company gets what it wants (a willing, unquestioning, over-productive employee), while the employee receives what he wants (time-consuming work in order to escape from a personal life at all costs). The two addictions literally complement (or feed on) each other, and they make a perfect match for the two players involved.

Furthermore, both participants here receive quite a bit of help from our culture, too. As I have already presented earlier, our society promotes overcompetitiveness to the point that it doesn't see workaholism as the abuse that it is. Unlike other abuses, this one is deceptive because the participants can demonstrate just how productive that they are, and in turn deny that they have any addiction, whatsoever. By adding in the societal premise that you can be a "better" person by getting "ahead materialistically," all of it indeed becomes too seductive to one-dimensional individuals. In essence, society itself becomes an abuser by totally denying the existent nature of the disease and its consequential effects. Of course, we are talking about *degree* here—not that regularly satisfying, hard work is bad. On the other hand, society doesn't help any by constantly conveying the idea that the answer to all of one's personal problems is simply ever-greater productivity.

Now, all of this discussion on individual abuses leads us on to the topic of health care in general (and mental health care in particular). Abuse in that system is rampant and out-of-control, and in the long-term future is going to present an even larger problem on many individual levels— regardless of what the politicians and those in the very health care industry itself, actually assert. Because, although the technology of medicine is getting better, the quality of implementing and dispensing health care for many individuals is not.

Chapter 5

HEALTH CARE

The essence of the health care problem in this country is simple to state, but not so simple to solve under the present circumstances. There is plenty of money in the health care system for all professionals who are involved in that field to make a most comfortable (if not lucrative) living. The problem is that the amount in the "coffers" is still not enough to satisfy the major factions' voracious expectations and wants. Generally speaking, these players (i.e., insurers/HMOs, physicians, hospitals, drug companies, and the medical equipment manufacturers) spend too much time trying to find novel self-aggrandizing ways to profit from the system, instead of providing better quality care along with a greater concern for ultimate health care outcomes of the patients. Add to all this, inefficiency and an inhibition to cost-cut in areas that would not appreciably result in reduced care or outcomes, and we, consequently, have ourselves a real problem.

In comparison to other industrialized countries in the world, the U.S. spends astronomically (far and away) the greatest percentage of Gross Domestic Product and the most per capita for health care expenditures. Yet, we finish dead-last (15th)—or we are literally "dead"-first, depending on how you look at it—-in life expectancy, which is really the ultimate determinant of any country's health care system (see table below). Therefore, one can only conclude that it is a fact (not conjecture) that we are doing something wrong, when it comes to the providing of overall health care to the populace at-large.

The main (most likely) reason is because the U.S. is the only industrialized country in the world that still sees the accessibility to equally good medical care, as being dependent on an individual's ability to afford an ever-increasing, profit-driven "market value." Just like everything else in this society, we have even made the dispensing of medical care (to our very own citizens) into a commodity.

TOTAL HEALTH EXPENDITURES OF INDUSTRIALIZED COUNTRIES (2000)

	% of GDP	$ Per Capita	Life Expectancy
United States	13.0	$4631	77.3
Australia	8.3	2211	79.9
Austria	8.0	2162	77.7
Belgium	8.7	2269	78.0
Canada	9.1	2535	79.6
France	9.5	2349	78.9
Germany	10.6	2748	77.6
Greece	8.3	1399	78.6
Italy	8.1	2032	79.1
Japan	7.8	2012	80.8
Netherlands	8.1	2246	78.4
Spain	7.7	1556	78.9
Sweden	8.2	1908	79.6
Switzerland	10.7	3222	79.6
United Kingdom	7.3	1763	77.8

Sources: Organization of Economic Cooperation & Development (OECD), Paris, France.
Life Expectancy Column: U.S. Census Bureau (International Data Base).

This notion was perfectly epitomized in a dark-humored commercial which was advertising a particular company's well-known credit card. It depicted a guy being wheeled in on a gurney into the Emergency Room of a hospital. Within seconds, the ER staff's actions stop completely in a freeze-frame—until the patient's card is swiped through a scanner (right there in the ER) in order to determine whether the card is approved. When it is, the actions of the staff to save the patient, start up again. This commercial was a pointed example which strikingly demonstrated the fact that we live in a country where two-tier health care is practiced—one group that can afford and receive the best health care, and another that cannot.

Consequently, given this fact, it is little wonder why all of the players in the health care-related industry, unceasingly, charge as much as they can get away with—while (in the process) disregarding that their particular products or services are actually human necessities. Something as essential as quality health care (and which we all need at some time) should not be based on what the price of the market can command. Because, those who can easily afford it (i.e., the richer segments of society) will continue to push the market value of it ever higher and higher (and out of the affordable reach of all others)—since they (the minority) have the means to pay whatever it costs in order to obtain the best health care.

Since currently 43 million Americans have no health insurance and at least another 30 to 35 million others are underinsured (most all of these being working people), it is obvious that our overall longevity rates are not higher because we practice different qualities of care in this country. In essence, the U.S. (the richest country in the world) has made top-quality, health care a privilege, rather than a right.

Managed Care

Managed care is the dispensing of medicine through a network of doctors, hospitals, labs and pharmacies. It is typically delivered through the Health Maintenance Organization (HMO). An HMO is often a for-profit, health care association whose enrollees pay a monthly fee which entitles them to receive certain medical services at no additional cost. HMO members receive all of their health care through this established network of health providers. (Oftentimes, if they receive care from a doctor who is not in the network, they must pay for it themselves). Each member picks a primary-care doctor from the particular HMO directory of network physicians that he/she is associated with. The primary-care physician (also known as, the provider) is a general practitioner who coordinates all of a patient's health care.

HMOs have become popular because insurance companies have found that they themselves can save money in comparison to the fee-for-service type of payment plan. But, by placing our health care system on such a profit-driven direction, we have implicitly consented to allow the health insurance industry and its corresponding HMOs to make crucial medical decisions for us. Regrettably, these decisions are frequently based upon cost and the use of a manual of rigid bureaucratic guidelines—and not what is necessarily the best care alternative for the patient in question in his/her particular situational case. Unfortunately, such implementation often results in benefiting the "Organization" and the "Provider" at the expense of the patient (either monetarily, emotionally and/or physically).

I would like to add here, that as a writer, I would be remiss not to call attention to the striking, ironic relationships between: (a) this terminology used for the corresponding participant players in the health care system (b) the potential long-term detrimental path that such a system may be on (where individual choice is lacking) and (c) the symbolic comparison of the bureaucratic, authoritarian system found in George Orwell's, *1984*. In this novel, all individuals' motivations and behaviors were performed strictly for the sake of bettering the "Higher Organization" which, in turn, would be "The Provider" of all individuals' basic needs. We can only wonder if over time, whether this analogy may become uncannily realistic in regards to our overall health care system? With this country's push toward managed care, we may have created an oligopoly that may become more and more insulated and unresponsive to patients' needs and complaints—out of the oligopoly's own need to protect the status quo for the sake of its own financial interests. Hence, the patients would become mere pawns in the overall scheme of things under such circumstances.

Although it is admirable and correct for us to reduce excessive costs in the medical care industry, the concept of the HMO (especially in its present form) is not the most, prudent way. Why? Because the patients (who the industry is supposed to exist for) are not (in many instances) going to receive the best care that they optimally could get and, in turn, will be dissatisfied. Once again, as I have emphasized in this entire book, we have a tendency in this country to see living beings as mere objects, whose supposedly sole purpose for being can be wrapped up in one question: What arbitrary value can we assign to this person, and how can that be used in furthering other people's particular self-serving desires and goals (which are generally monetary in nature)—irregardless of the detrimental effect it may have on that person?

One major problem is that the health insurance lobbyists and their advertisers have convinced the American people (in a calculated, self-serving way) that the health-insurer bureaucracy can run the health care system better than a governmental bureaucracy. In essence, they were able to simply substitute their own bureaucracy (which benefits them) for any potential, single-payer governmental one. This latter one was originally proposed and rejected quite hastily and purposely (with little or no debate), because of the health insurance industry's clout in Washington.

Now, I am not saying that the governmental one (as proposed) was the best either. But one thing is certain, choosing to allow to keep an inefficient, administratively-burdensome, health-insurer industry as a "middleman" in the system is going to add needless costs, big time. **Paradox #12**: In any venture, if the stated goal is to reduce costs, how are you going to achieve it by adding in "middlemen?" "We shovel a fifth of our precious health care dollars into the administrative furnaces of commercial insurance companies, a vast, parasitic bureaucracy that is completely unresponsive to the needs of the nation."[1] Isn't it telling that other industries displace workers when need be, but when it comes to providing the best health care for Americans, we allow the clout of the health insurance conglomerates to dictate policy and keep their needlessly bloated, costly bureaucracy?

Let's take a look at how health care ever reached this point in this country. It is relevant to note, that most of us consumers did not suddenly demand this type of health care. The spiraling out-of-control health care costs along with ever-increasing insurance premiums, have forced major employers to find a way to put a rein on their own overwhelming costs to pay for their employees' health benefits. Enter the HMO, which the insurance companies pushed to the forefront as a delivery system that would limit costs (and lower employer premiums) by reducing "unnecessary and inappropriate" health care. Meanwhile, private physicians could do little to stem the swelling tide of this trend. Therefore, they too had little choice but to sign onto such a plan, in order to assure that they would be guaranteed to have enough patients to stay in practice.

There are many drawbacks to the current type of managed care. One that almost every critic cites is that one of the most popular ways manage care plans (e.g., HMOs) save money is by recruiting and signing up healthy patients, while avoiding taking on the sick (a practice called "cherry-picking"). The rationale is why worry about trying to reduce the costs of hospital stays and drug prescriptions, when you can emphasize signing up members who require neither. HMOs often market their plans in such a way so as to attract healthy people. For example, their advertisements may offer free health club memberships, and we all know that health clubs appeal to active people—not the seriously or chronically ill.

Another drawback is the schizophrenic alliance (or partnership) that the HMO concept compels primary-care physicians and the plan's administrative bureaucrats to form with each other. The bureaucrats become overly-vigilant "gatekeepers" who increasingly suggest to the primary-care doctors what they "woulda, coulda, shoulda" do and not do for their patients. So in essence, there is a far-removed, administrative employee (with a rigid set of guidelines) standing between you and your doctor, interpreting a policy plan of what is "medically necessary and appropriate care"—a phrase that is purposely designed to be ambiguous. The vagueness of this terminology makes any patient's accusation of denial of benefits difficult to defend in court. So beware! Unless a benefit is specifically spelled out, it is sometimes more helpful to know what procedures are not covered (and which you won't be reimbursed for).

HMOs resort to the following antics and tactics in order to cut costs. On the other hand, all of these can negatively affect the quality of patient care, and force patients to battle every step of the way to get the treatment that they want:

(1) monitor and micro-manage primary-care physicians' prescribing and treatment patterns.
(2) encourage doctors to prescribe medicines from the lists of drug manufacturers in which they have contracts with.
(3) expect doctors to follow standard procedures for specific diseases which result in "discounting" each patient's individual situation.
(4) have review departments and panels that determine which test and treatments are "practical" and therefore, should be covered.

(5) if a suggested type of care is deemed too expensive, extensive or experimental, the "gatekeepers" could approve coverage for a less costly, yet older and more basic, conventional treatment—thereby, redefining "medically necessary and appropriate care" on a case-by-case basis.
(6) offer incentives to primary-care doctors not to send their patients to see specialists anymore than is absolutely necessary.
(7) dangerously shorten hospital stays for some types of surgery.
(8) overburden nursing staffs with increased responsibility
(9) increase the amount of administrative paperwork for doctors' office staffs
(10) expect lab technicians to read more tests in a shorter time, which can cause increased incidents of misreading results (e.g., pap smears).
(11) expect the primary care doctor to first approve his patients' visits to any emergency room.

On this last point, how can a patient always seek approval before going to an emergency room? Emergencies can't always be defined so cut-and-dry. One of the first signs of a heart attack is a burning sensation, while for a stroke, it is a sudden, intense headache. But, HMO plans don't deem such symptoms as worthy of a visit to an emergency room. Therefore, if you find out after you get there that (in this particular case) these symptoms were not a matter of life and death, your insurance company could withhold payment. (Note: At the time of this writing, it should be stated that Congress was still nitpicking over a Patients Bill of Rights, and, if passed, could force managed care plans to automatically cover emergency room visits).

Another problem that the health insurers and HMOs have exacerbated is the trend for outpatient (or ambulatory) surgery. "Nearly two-thirds of all U.S. operations have become outpatient, and the numbers are rising."[2] That in itself is not necessarily a bad thing, because new technology (e.g., lasers) has dramatically decreased surgical pain and recovery time. What is reprehensible is that particular operations are being seen by health insurers as being in the outpatient category, even though risk and special, questionable circumstances are not considered for some individual cases. Length of stays are being reduced by insurers with little (if any) medical justification. Sometimes complications can be quite apt to happen such as: significant blood loss, infection, trauma, and the need for injectable narcotic painkillers that are risky to administer at home.

Such early releases from the hospital are strictly cost-driven motivations by the HMOs. In essence, in some cases the insurers are wrongly equating risk-related operations as if they were fast-food take-out. The HMOs "have developed over the years a very sophisticated way of preventing care, delaying care, denying care, [and] retrospectively refusing to pay for care."[3] Cost-slashing is considered first, while quality and access to care are addressed later.

Physicians

In regard to doctors, part of the problem has been of their own making, and part of it originates from the general structure of the health care system itself. Doctors used to nearly always charge patients on a fee-for-service basis. They had a strong monetary incentive to prescribe and provide an overabundance of medical services which weren't necessarily needed. "One study found fee-for-service doctors ordering 50 percent more electrocardiograms and 40 percent more x-rays than salaried doctors"[4] (who practice for HMOs). This fee-for-service practice has often been criticized as a way for physicians merely to "pad" their incomes.

Nowadays, with proponents pushing managed care on America, the pendulum is starting to swing in the complete opposite direction toward salaried physicians. This type of remuneration plan would also include "capitation," whereby the physician would provide medical services to health care plan members for a fixed monthly payment, regardless how many times the members had to use the service in order to see the physician. Needless to say, it is now the doctors turn to be dissatisfied with this system, while the patients are dissatisfied with both systems.

So, we have here ***Paradox #13***. On the one end of the spectrum, we have doctors who obviously preferred the fee-for-service arrangement because the overuse of medical services increased their incomes. On the other end of the continuum, you have health insurers and HMOs strongly advocating a reduction in hospitalizations and referrals, because that will be more lucrative for them. Meanwhile, the patient is in-between being bounced around like a ping-pong ball, and he/she ends up losing either way–financially on the one end, medically on the other end. Isn't it clear that the pendulum should be somewhere in the middle on this issue—where neither economics nor medical care would have to be conceded, and all players could be "relatively" happy? The word for this process is called "compromise" (which evidently is not in many people's vocabulary), because sacrifice is expected of all involved parties in order to allow the "whole" to realistically function. It is a practice that has been used since the dawn of civilization. Why has this concept become so difficult to accept and adhere to in this so-called "new age" of humanity?

Another problem is that there has become such an income disparity between medical specialists and general practitioners, that too many doctors who are coming out of medical school are opting to become specialists. This occurrence is happening at a time when we need primary-care physicians more than ever before, because of the continual push for managed care and HMOs. "But the proportion of practicing physicians who are generalists, now 30 percent, is heading toward 15 percent."[5] Ironically, with everyone being ever-vigilant now to keep costs under control, specialists are not going to be given such free rein to overtest, overtreat, and perform "unnecessary" surgeries.

The past reality where an oversupply of specialists were able to *create* a demand for marginal or questionable treatments and surgeries will most likely only apply to a much smaller group of patients in the future. Those patients would be the ones willing to pay for such procedures, using their own out-of-pocket money. What might have previously been seen as a "need" will be interpreted now as more of a "want" that is optional. Some examples (which if not already limited by health plans) would be: most plastic surgeries; liposuction; sports medicine (because it could be seen as people being more active than they have to be); and illnesses stemming from behavioral choices (like the effects from overeating and yo-yo dieting).

Finally, something must be said regarding how the administering of the health care system has broken down the, heretofore, long-enjoyed bond that once flourished between patient and doctor. In some cases, it has gotten so bad that the relationship could be better described with the word, paranoia, rather than the previously long-standing one, trust, which is a crucial characteristic in any healing process. Because of managed care, doctors are pressed to set more rigidly allotted time for patients' visits, which discourages any depth of discussion of a person's unique health situation. Yet, time is one of the more vital and informative parts of the relationship between the primary-care doctor and patient.

On the other hand, because we live in a much more litigious society today, physicians must be leery of potential malpractice suits by patients. This fact creates doubt and anxiety in the physician's mind and often compels him to practice "defensive" medicine (e.g., ordering more and more tests). In turn, we all end up bearing the consequential rise in overall medical care costs from this reality.

But, the question remains whether such "defensive" medicine will even be allowed to continue under the health insurers/HMOs' edict to contain "unneeded" costs. In addition, you must take into account that managed care has thrust extra paperwork on doctors and often requires telephone communication between them and decision-making, health-insurer bureaucrats on a number of their patients' cases. All of these considerations has to be trying on the morale of most all physicians, too.

Hospitals

Although hospitals in general have conveyed the message that they have cut their costs substantially, one must certainly question whether they have really tried hard enough. Because hospitals compete for doctors to be on their respective staffs, hospitals have always had to demonstrate that they have the "best of everything" (including the latest in expensive medical technology) in order to attract the best doctors. Since this fact creates higher hospital costs, and the doctors are insulated from such increased costs having any negative impact on them, they have no incentive to suggest to the hospital that it should cut such costs.

Therefore, every hospital administration is continually under pressure to improve quality of services and upgrade to the newest in innovative technology, in order to keep staff physicians satisfied. The result is duplication of services and facilities among all hospitals, and correspondingly the underuse of the acquired expensive technological equipment (or in some cases, its unnecessary use in order to pay for itself). Such cost inefficiencies and redundancies end up being added to our hospital bills.

In the 1990s, many hospitals had an overcapacity of hospital beds. In order to cut overall costs, they have been decreasing the number of beds and rooms that will remain operationally in use. But because of this act, consequentially, some ERs are having to close their doors to emergency 911 cases that are coming in on ambulances. There has become such a shortage of rooms for assigning patients who are in ERs, that the turnover cycle of allowing new patients to come into ERs is often delayed. This reality forces ambulance drivers to constantly have to keep updated tabs on the emergency-diversionary status of each hospital as they're driving. Ultimately, the meaning of all of this chaos is that some 911 patients cannot necessarily be rushed to the nearest hospital, at a time when every wasted moment could be the difference between life and death.

A corresponding problem that is creating even more occupancy pressure on ERs is the ever-increasing numbers of uninsured Americans (43 million at last count). They are having to go to ER rooms, because they have nowhere else to receive health care. Therefore, they are using emergency room beds for rather sanguine, non-emergency health concerns. Such usage of ERs can often force paramedic emergencies to be diverted to other hospitals that are further away, and, subsequently, delays the care which is needed by the 911 patient.

But, let's get back now to the original point of our overall lack of cost controls. "Looking at specific illnesses and procedures, [even though] the United States has the shortest hospital stay, often by a wide margin...other countries are all much more successful in containing their health care costs than the United States."[6] The only conclusion that one can arrive at is that U.S. hospitals still have a lot of "fat" in their health care delivery systems that is not being addressed.

Just as doctors do, hospitals also try to *create* a demand for high-profit margin health-care services through different marketing programs. They may publicize the benefits of elective surgeries; advertise how their birthing rooms have all the comforts of home;

promote the availability and need for medical tests (that are really more discretionary choices than needs); administer a range of nutrition and diet programs; extend the hospital's capacity for handling sports medicine and physical therapy ailments; and launch care campaigns for such subjects as: sleep disorders, stress reduction, and breaking personal behavior patterns (e.g., smoking). Such programs can increase hospital admissions, referrals, image and profits. Therefore, hospital planning and strategic thinking are increasingly becoming more of a function of "business" objectives and acquiring market share rather than strictly quality of care. It is understandable that hospitals may want to expand their scope of services, but how about improving the quality and efficiency of its primary hospital care first.

Mental Health

Many of the individual abuses and the consequences of emotional stresses and societal abuse on the general populace could be widely addressed, if we would recognize the need to correct the fact that we have never given much emphasis to prioritizing mental health in this country. Moreover, we have always made access to good mental health care a "privilege" rather than a "right." And it is most unfortunate, that the increasing need of people to seek out and receive therapeutic help (from the greater stresses and pressures of today's fast-paced lifestyles) is coming at a time when everyone (who is involved in reforming health care) is looking for chopping blocks in order to cut costs. Mental health always has been (and will continue to be) near the top of the list to be guillotined. Let's look at why this is so, as well as the subsequent consequences that society as a whole suffers from such a philosophical conviction.

The way that it is set up now, a person cannot consult with an *experienced, competent* therapist on a continuing basis, because it has simply become too costly for your *average* American to be able to afford it. Depending on your area of the country, it can cost anywhere from $100 to $250+ in order to see somebody for a mere 50 minutes.

Therefore, the best that a major portion of the population can settle for is a clinician-therapist-in-training, whose real emphasis oftentimes is on the gaining of one's own professional experience more than any long-term emotional betterment for the client/patient. In fact, many clinics have a six-month maximum period for seeing any one clinician, because the demand has caused long waiting lists and each therapist must move along in his/her training and/or career. In HMOs, your primary-care physician would most likely be expected to treat depression with only medication, even though the consensus is that it is best treated in combination with psychotherapy. Hence, there is a large void that has been created, because there is no middle ground that has been established for most people (who are in need of quality therapy) to stand on.

So, when we turn our television sets on at night or open our paper in the morning, and we see that some kind of horrendous murder/massacre has taken place, we and the media can only sit there and ask, "How did this person's mental situation get so far out-of-hand?" We then become alarmed to discover that when it was thought that this particular person had only a "shingle" missing, in actuality, that person had "half of a roof" missing. This is exemplary of how it has become commonplace for our society to wrongly perceive and rationalize away the signs of the deterioration of a particular person's mental condition and functioning in the real world. Only after catastrophic actions taken by that individual erupt, and (in turn) result in severe consequences, do we then stand up and take notice. So, the lack of *access* to appropriate mental health care is one very large reason why these type of situations continue to occur. Individuals cannot become "whole," if their human needs (including mental and emotional) are not properly met.

Once again, it is a matter of concentrating our efforts on symptoms, and not getting to the root causes. Mental health in our country has become a contradiction. On the one hand, we must keep costs down, while (on the other) we must give a semblance (and in actuality a rather dismal one) that patients are being helped, before letting them out into society again. This acknowledgement takes us to **Paradox #14**: Health insurers see human health as predominantly physical in nature, and almost non-existent as mental—yet it is a common and certain fact that mental/emotional health can often be a major factor in affecting a person's physical well-being. Health insurers can continually fall back on the presumption that there is no visibly cut-and-dry, physically-organic illness affecting any particular policyholder, and thereby are "proven justified" in denying coverage for any so-called mental/emotional "illness."

So, a typical retort that, a policyholder might expect to receive if one were to call up one's health insurer and inquire about being covered for such a thing, would be: "Mental health?...What is mental health? If I'm correct in my assessment of your definition, our insurance company could never afford to cover you for that mumbo-jumbo. You'd have to pay us extra large premiums to be covered for something like that."...This type of rationalization reminds me of how the generations that grew up before World War II trivialized their own traumatic, childhood problems when relating their personal stories later to their own kids: "We didn't believe or have any use for any such people who 'messed with your head'...If we felt 'blue' in the morning, that three-mile walk to school in sub-zero weather would straighten out our mental health." (Translation: don't talk about what is deeply troubling you, just continue doing what you'd normally do everyday—putting "one foot ahead of the other").

It's societal barriers like this one, that forces people not to ask for help when they need it the most. The end result: people who are mentally ill, a significant number of whom may be potentially dangerous to society, are not appropriately and sufficiently treated. Consequently, they continue to walk our streets with no recognizable sign when they just might snap.

Managed care organizations refer to mental health as "behavioral health." This is an euphemistic term that implies that a person's state of mind can easily be adjusted for the better by merely replacing one of the being's malfunctioning "circuit boards" (and zipping him back up)—as if the person were simply a robot. The health care organizations must be knocked out of this type of schizophrenic state. At the same time, they must be reminded that these are the *real* people that they are dealing with—not the cardboard cut-out imitations.

It is noteworthy to point out that this term, behavioral health, acts as a mollifying factor when the health insurers "substitute less intensive and less adequate services than those needed, and shift costs to families, public providers and other care sectors."[7] Even though mental health services have never been well-coordinated, under managed care we can expect even more fragmentation, lack of continuity and large gaps in any overall safety net for the chronic mentally ill.

HMOs do everything in their power to downplay the severity of any mental condition that one may have. They generally set-up an arbitrary maximum standard in the number of visits (often between three and eight sessions) that they themselves subjectively determine can "modify behavior" for any mental/emotional problem. This idea implies "one size fits all" and that every individual must have the strength to solve one's own problems.

HMOs/health insurers also play games using semantics. They often will record phone conversations that they have with the medical specialist. As one doctor remarked: "They catch you on ways you have of talking about the patient. I can say, 'Well he was suicidal. [Their response] 'What do you mean he *was*? That means he doesn't need to be in the hospital.'...The result [is] a complete separation between economic concerns and therapeutic standards, [which] lays bare the worst excesses of our profit-driven drift."[8]

Drug Companies

We live in a society that, while explicitly condemning the taking of illegitimate drugs, implicitly condones the taking of "legitimate" prescription drugs. We allow drug manufacturers to actively promote the premise—that if you have a problem, we have a pill that can alleviate that problem. We have enabled ourselves to believe that there is some over-the-counter or prescription drug or product that will lessen just about any pain, tension or discomfort that one might have. A major reason that many of us have this notion is because of drug companies' extensive advertising to encourage and influence such thoughts. Pharmaceutical manufacturers are now marketing (actually "pimping" may be a better word for their tactics) prescription drugs on television commercials, as if they were just any other consumer household products that you would find in any store. Yet, the fact that people can become dependent (or even addicted) to prescription drugs, is virtually ignored or made to appear inconsequential on these pharmaceutical commercials. In fact, on the commercial for Nexium, you don't even have to ask for the pills by name—because they keep restating that they're purple. How does this differ from an addict on a street corner telling a pusher, "Dude, just give me the little, purple pills!"

The drug manufacturers are so anxious to receive quick profits from this type of ad campaign, that they literally have to spend the entire second half of a one minute commercial, stating a grocery list of possible side effects for different groups of people who may take the medication (so that there will not be any legal ramifications). As a facetious example, but one that will get my point across, let's say a drug manufacturer might have a concern (that the medication may detrimentally affect you) if you have a tendency to experience sudden, uncontrollable urges before or during bedtime. The second half of the commercial may sound something like this:

> "*Women*: If you have been multi-orgasmic at bedtime within the last week or have a general proclivity toward nymphomania, then consult with your doctor before taking this medication.
> *Men*: If you have a strong urge after 9 P.M. to go to an all-night, home improvement center to pick-up materials and start building a patio-deck addition to your house, then only a doctor can tell you whether this medication is right for you.
> *Farmers*: If you have a tendency to wake up in the middle of the night with a compelling desire to start operating farm machinery, then seek advice from your health care provider before taking this medication."

One commercial that would be a cinch to enter the "Drug Advertising Hall of Shame" was the one for Propecia, the pill to treat hair loss in men. One has to strongly question what type of ingredients they are putting in these tablets, because they felt that it was important enough to state: "Women who are or may potentially be pregnant must not handle crushed or broken tablets because of the risk of a specific kind of birth defect." Well, let me tell you something. If a consequence of growing hair is that a "potentially pregnant" wife will be exposed to a certain type of birth defect—then I'd rather shave my head completely bald then concern myself with growing a few extra tuffs of hair.

Similarly, this notion (that there is a substance which can be taken to alleviate any problem that you might have) carries over to non-pharmaceutical companies who cite a "physically-enhanced" reason to buy their product. Such was the case with a gullibly-oriented ad that was marketing a product called, "Joint Fuel." First of all, since when did we humans start making it a habit to ingest "fuel?" Second of all, notice how everything today has to be worded in high-tech terminology. In this case, the name implies that you can fully experience that bionic loosening of all of your tendons and ligaments. Therefore, when you are bodily hoisted on top of the launching pad and fired off directly into outer space, you won't have any tiring of the joints from lack of "fuel"—when you make your bodily trek around the rings of Saturn and then back again!

The point to be made here is that this trend for "the advertising of prescription drugs encourages people to pressure their physicians to prescribe the drugs they [themselves] *want*, rather than the drugs the physician believe they *need*."[9] It is yet another case again of "needs versus wants." After all, the basics of advertising is to *create* a market for a product. Drug manufacturers are just like any other business that advertises, their goal being to maximize profits anyway that they can from the sale of as many product units as possible.

Meanwhile, doctors not only hear what prescriptions their patients want, they also get pressure on the other side by drug manufacturers' salespeople to prescribe their respective company's product line. In such cases, unless the individual physician takes a firm stand for control of his own independent decisionmaking, he may be caught in the middle. Drug companies also promote their name by sponsoring luncheons, seminars and conferences. Moreover, their promotional materials and advertisements that appear in medical journals rarely mention cost. This fact can often leave the doctor at a loss at how comparatively similar prescriptions (with virtually the same merit) may differ (sometimes widely) in cost for the patient. An independently-developed, continually-updated, pharmacological, cost data comparison sheet could go a long way in helping doctors with this problem.

This marketing push by the drug companies can also instill the tendency for doctors to prescribe brand-name drugs over generic drugs. Yet, generic ones have to meet the FDA's strict standards for approval, and therefore have been proven to work as well as higher-priced, brand name ones. This situation of the high cost of brand-name drugs is further aggravated by the fact that manufacturers get patent protection for about twenty years on any totally new drug that they invent. Therefore, they can set the price as high as the market will bear without any concern that another company can market a generic of the same drug for a number of years.

Furthermore, when their original drug patent expires on a particular medication, these companies are now employing the "new and improved" tactic, in order to maintain hold of their market share. They first get a patent on a "new and improved" version of the original drug. Then simultaneously, they convince the public (through marketing) that their "new" version is much more beneficial than any competitors' generic brand of the original formula, that may come out onto the market. The rationale that these brand-name companies are successfully able to take advantage of—is that when a patient's health is at stake, the patient is generally not going to see money as an obstacle to purchase the "best" medication, even if it has to leave him (or her) virtually bankrupt.

So, it is little wonder why year after year, pharmaceutical manufacturers are among the most profitable companies of all industries in the U.S. A typical U.S. company's average profit margin is between 5 to 10%, while the large drug manufacturers have net profit margins from 2 to 5 times as great.

(in millions of $)	2001 Sales	Net Profit	NetProfit Margin %
Bristol-Myers Squibb	19423.	4723.	24.3
Eli Lilly & Co.	11543.	3009.	26.1
Merck & Co.	47716.	7282.	15.3
Pfizer, Inc.	32259.	8350.	25.9
Schering-Plough	9802.	2326.	23.7

Source: Value Line

Looking at these enormous profit margins, the claim (at least by these five drug manufacturers) that the enormously high cost of drugs is needed to cover their corresponding high costs of doing research and testing, simply does not "hold water." Yet typically, pharmaceutical companies spend more on marketing their drugs than developing new ones. Moreover, much of the research dollars goes into simply creating "me-too" drugs (i.e., drugs that are similar to ones that competitors already have on the market, but that offer no real therapeutic advantage despite the manufacturer's claims that they do).

The Future of Health Care

Health care today in the U.S. has been exemplary of how the major factions within the system have made a habit of "passing the buck" back and forth between each other. The result has been that a significant number of people are not getting the optimal care that they need (and which is possible), all in the name of excessive profits. One thing is for sure, in order to have a system in the future that is both efficient and high quality, every one of these players (i.e., health insurers & HMOs, physicians, hospitals, pharmaceutical manufacturers, medical technology suppliers, and even the consumers) is going to have to make some sacrifices and compromises.

Realistic priorities are going to have to be set. For one thing, the system still has too much fat in it. Since the health care industry is labor-intensive (administratively, professionally, and care-giving), in order to lower overall costs, there is possibly going to have to be a significant job reduction (especially administratively). This process may come about automatically, by the fact that consumers are becoming more enlightened on being personally knowledgeable about: health information & awareness (e.g., exercise); prevention; self-care; behavioral lifestyle choices; and environmental dangers. Therefore, medical care demand may decrease somewhat for these reasons alone.

Furthermore, there is becoming a glut of doctors (except primary-care doctors) graduating from medical school, similar to the way lawyers became overabundant years ago. "The total number of doctors keeps increasing, from 334,000 in 1970 to 468,000 in 1980 and 615,000 in 1990 and 653,000 in 1992 [and 808,000 in 2000]...New medical school graduates, about 16,000 a year, are far in excess of replacement and growth needs, and this figure does not consider foreign medical school graduates who are entering practice and now constitute about 20 percent of all practicing physicians."[10] With health insurers and managed-care HMOs becoming ever-vigilant on costs, you are going to have a situation of an overabundance of specialists—who are not going to be able to perform the number of unnecessary procedures that they used to, under the previously popular fee-for-service type of reimbursement.

In addition, because the nature of medicine (new technology and breakthrough-treatment discoveries) is changing rather rapidly, the friction between the consumer's expectations of what they are entitled to and the insurer's expectations of what they are willing to cover, is going to first considerably worsen before it ever starts to get better. "Health care costs are still growing [on average] eight percent a year, or three [to four] times faster than inflation." [11] Some analysts predict that growing costs may consistently reach at least 10% (or over) per year. On top of that, with the managed-care companies' drive for market share behind them (even by 1996, 77% of workers who had health benefits, were in such health coverage programs),[12] they are going to emphasize profit motives even more now.

In turn, as premiums rise, employers are now having to struggle in order to cope. Therefore, more workers are most likely going to face even more restrictive limits on their medical coverage plans. Furthermore, employers generally use low cost (not quality) as the main criterion for choosing a plan. In tandem, large HMOs who have undergone mergers have the best capacity to offer the lowest cost plans, but given their size, they tend to be more bureaucratically distant from their enrollees' concerns, and thus quality suffers even more. Finally, while the employees themselves have not fully felt the pain from past increases in premiums, chances are that they will now. Many employers are going to be forced to pass on at least some of any future cost increases to their employees. HMOs will assuredly keep increasing medical premiums to employers, because they know full well that the employees will pick up the added dollar difference. Why? Because the HMOs know that these employees won't want to leave their families in a medical lurch.

But, concerned employers (especially large-sized ones), who are looking for quality in conjunction with cost considerations, still have some fodder in their cannons to shoot back with. In some cases, they are trying to eliminate the HMO middleman entirely. First, they are negotiating rates for medical services directly from doctor (and hospital) networks. Second, other employers are beginning to band together into a "buying consortium" in order to get larger discounts on their purchasing of health insurance. Third, some are even partaking in types of self-insurance, where they accept degrees of risk themselves, depending on the nature of the different health plans that are chosen by their employees.

Doctors, too, are forming networks of their own (PPMs/PPOs, physician practice management firms/ preferred provider organizations) as alternatives to HMOs. These forms of health-care delivery systems are gradually increasing in popularity (compared to HMOs), because (in these type of networks) the doctors' recommendations are not second-guessed by some bureaucratic "gatekeeper" with a rigid set of conditional-care guidelines. These type of organizations are also trying to counteract the high charges of some hospitals by delivering health care in well-equipped, state-of-the-art clinical settings, where many surgeries and procedures can be performed on an outpatient basis. This practice could eventually force hospitals to actually think about cutting their excess capacity/costs which they still have.

So, logically, it would seem that if there is less money going into administrative costs and excess capacity, the opportunity would be there to significantly reduce patient cost of premium payments. But, although this is a good resolve, it does not necessarily actualize itself into reality. Why? Because there is always the danger that these physician groups might begin to see their own state-of-the-art clinics as opportunities to recommend and perform a number of superfluous or redundant services and, in turn, make more profits of their own.

In such situations, these PPMs/PPOs would have simply swapped the previous costs that were saved from the reduction of administration services and excess capacity, and applied them instead to their own profit margins. For example, under these circumstances, there are increased incentives for doctors to perform more: optional surgeries, medical tests and diagnostic procedures than are actually required or needed. Consequently, under such alternative health care networks, the end result for many consumers is, oftentimes, only a comparatively modest reduction in their health care costs and premiums.

Ultimately, the real question here becomes: Will there ever come a time when the managed-care organizations and the practitioners can consensually agree to forego seeing the health care system as a windfall profit opportunity for their own self-interest, rather than for bettering patient outcomes? Because as you can see, presently, the U.S. health care system has basically become one big, never-ending game—where the consumer seems to lose every time.

Because more Americans are being herded into HMOs (with few viable alternatives), there has become a backlash against HMOs by consumers, because of denial of care as well as reduced quality of overall care (stemming from limited coverage of many plans). Because managed care companies have not been up to the test of providing patients with the best care, there is a gathering of support in Congress (because of constituents' complaints) to compel them to do so through legislation. Although the term, "best care," may be hard to determine and put into law, chances are that at least a "patient bill of rights" will be the minimum that will eventually be consented to by Congress. There have just been too many problems with how the present system of managed care has been restricted and administered. More patients are beginning to feel that some HMOs are not only eliminating the "fat off the beef," but some of "the beef" as well. "Private-sector [managed care] bureaucracies are as good at denying care as governmental ones are bad at providing it."[13] But, in this writer's opinion, any "patient bill of rights" that comes out of Congress will be a compromise to placate the public, and will not end up making much difference in patients' *true* satisfactions. Once again, the power players in Washington will determine policy through their clout.

There has also been some push for HMOs to be held accountable, when malpractice suits are lodged at doctors who are part of the network of physicians of a particular HMO. The position that HMOs have always taken is that they don't practice medicine, they only administer it. But, several times federal appeals courts have ruled that HMO doctors may be considered as representative agents, and that HMOs are involved in medical decisions and subsequent treatment, and therefore is a basis for liability.

Of course, the flip side of the coin is if Congress were to legislate: a "patient bill of rights;" make HMOs liable in malpractice suits; and do away with limiting hospital stays for certain medical procedures etc.—health care costs and insurance premiums would probably skyrocket well above the current yearly percentage increase that we already have. Therefore, if Congress keeps piling on costly coverage requirements that insurance companies need to provide, then we start reverting back to the costly fee-for-service type of insurance, that we originally wanted to avoid. All we are doing on this issue is going around in a full circle. So, we have **Paradox #15:** If our goal is to receive quality health care at an affordable price, and all the factions merely "pass on the buck" and are unwilling to compromise, then it will be impossible to arrive at the desired goal.

Since we have evidently adopted the managed care concept, which has been so adeptly used in denying general patient health care, then we are certainly hurtling toward a stone wall, when it comes to catastrophic health care for the aged and chronically ill under this concept. Most people cannot afford the additional financial burden of long-term-care insurance. With our median age gradually rising in the U.S., that could spell disaster since we have not really taken this fact into account (to the degree that we need to) in projecting overall future health care costs. The current average personal, out-of-pocket cost for nursing-home care is almost $50,000 per year. But, according to the United Seniors Health Cooperative, this figure is expected to rise to the astonishingly, mind-boggling cost of $80,000 per year by only the year of 2010. [14] This figure assumes that our country will be unable to reduce the 8+% projected yearly inflation rate [15] (that the pace of nursing home prices are currently at) all the way through 2010. And the way current situations stand, this figure might not be too far off the mark, unless drastic changes are implemented. Also, you can forget trying to plead poverty. Medicaid doesn't kick in until you have used all of your individual assets, until such time you have only $1500 left.

As an aside, let's take a minute and look at what exactly you can expect to receive for your extravagant $225 per day future cost at your standard, average nursing home facility. Succinctly, basic room and board with no frills or extras. A small room generally the size of a extra large walk-in closet, a small chest and nightstand, a limited-sized sink with no vanity and either a toilet or portable commode. Finally, a simple bed, not even the width of twin size, with sheets so thin, you can see the purposely, dark-colored mattress underneath—

which hides any visible soilage that the previous resident might have left.

As far as food goes, whatever slop one resident gets, every other resident gets. It doesn't matter what special diet you may need to have. If you need no-salt or low-fat diet meals, forget it. Fresh fruit and fresh salad are served as rare exceptions—but for the most part, forget it, they're considered too expensive. Generally, your meals are going to consist of high fat and high carbohydrates—so that you will feel full, but with little, overall nutritional value (e.g., pot pies, chicken with filler in it, hot dog on a bun, etc.). You will also get a lot of non-nutritional types of liquids, so that again you feel full, but not any healthier for it.

Little mental stimulation is given on a daily basis. Many homes don't even have individual televisions in residents' rooms (and some without even air conditioners). And, on top of all of this, you more than likely will have a roommate (whom you may not even be compatible with). Possibly one who may be very much worse off than you and who keeps you up at night with a wheezing cough.

Finally, let me say that the core staff of workers at such homes are generally dedicated, hard-working and well-meaning, but they are overworked with their individual time and energy spread too thinly. They often have to meet the needs of several residents in different rooms at one time. Personnel problems at such homes are generally related to the support staff (rather than the professional staff), because of the turnover rates of such employees. They often can be undependable, negligent, uncaring (e.g., don't help a resident with basic needs, like even brushing one's teeth), steal residents' personal items (if they're not nailed down), and always either misunderstand or downplay the seriousness of the residents' ailments.

Although I dislike having to paint such a bleak picture, unfortunately, this is the reality of your average nursing home of today. It has simply become a repository for old people to enter in order to die—and sadly, to die without dignity. Residents are seen more as numbers than human beings at many of them. As long as the beds are full and the home has maximum occupancy, that's all that each home's administrator cares about. On the surface, they may present themselves as caring about the residents, but the only real bottom line that is of concern to them are profits. They skimp on blankets, sheets, wash clothes, pillows, thick-enough mattresses, and don't even properly fit a resident into a correctly-sized wheelchair. They even know what day that a state inspector will visit them, so that they can add on personnel for that one day, in order to give the appearance that the residents are being well-taken care of. Yet, such visits are infrequent, because states don't have enough inspectors to competently oversee so many nursing homes anyway. With the avalanching numbers of older age seniors expected by 2020, if such standards are what we have to look forward to when we are no longer able to take care of ourselves—then they might as well shoot us all!

But now, let's get back to my original point of cost, again. Care of the aged (e.g., in nursing homes) is heading down the path where our government will simply condone "open season" for allowing a for-profit, health care system to empty out entire savings' accounts of old people, who took their entire lives to accumulate what they have left. So, when the administrator of a nursing home is asked, "How much will that be?" The response may very well be: "Just how much do you have?" (Translated: "Give me all you've got, including the deed to your house and any money that is destined for inheritance.") Even a bank robber doesn't obtain the money and assets that easily!

Nonetheless, since the average stay for an aged person in a nursing home is over three years, than you are looking at approximately $240,000 for your average person (if they cannot afford long-term-care insurance). Paradoxically, if such a person cannot afford this type of insurance, then that individual is certainly not going to be able to afford "out-of-pocket" costs for a nursing home. Furthermore, when considering yearly "real-dollar" percentage cost cuts in Medicare, one will not be able to expect too much help from that program. As it is, Medicare only covers up to a total of 100 days of any individual's stay in a nursing home anyway. Moreover, in the future, the need for nursing-home care will be intensified by the fact that more and more older people are living alone, alienated from broken families and/or uncaring family members.

So, does your average working person at retirement age have a quarter of a million dollars to spend for his or her care (not even taking into account personal wishes to leave any inheritance for children)? Does that person even have $80,000 to cover one year? A typical response might be: "I know that I don't have that amount in my savings account. But, let me check to see if I have 80,000

'George Washington's' under my mattress.''...It is enough to scare even a younger person (who isn't even near retirement age) and give him or her a duodenal ulcer.

Although government possibly should not be involved in the actual providing (or dispensing) of health care per se, eventually it is going to have to acknowledge that it has an obligation not to let its citizens down at a time of their lives that they need the greatest support (i.e., catastrophic illness and nursing home care). After all, what is a nation if it cannot be there for all of its citizens, when they are ailing with few personal resources at hand? Are we merely a block of land where individuals (competing strictly out of their own self-interests) are rewarded for "getting ahead," possibly at the very expense of those others who don't "succeed" because of any number of reasons (many of these reasons most conceivably and circumstantially out of people's control to begin with)? We are the only country in the world that has a "for-profit" health care system. Even in time of others' misery, we motivate ourselves to find a way to make a substantial profit from it. What does that say about our apparent priorities?

Conversely, without any real guarantee of repayment, government can spend billions upon billions of dollars bailing out companies (which got into a bad situation out of their own reckless mismanagement)—all in the name of partisan interests or pork-barrel political reasons. Likewise, we give billions to other countries (many of whom we may consider our enemies), who end up not even using the monies received for the intended purposes. Yet, we are supposed to assume that it can't find the inclination to support and lend peace of mind to its own aged citizens, whose worse mismanagement in their entire lives was that they were late in paying the mortgage one or two months.

By not legislating to protect Americans (especially for future generations) from the costs associated with catastrophic health care—Congress (in its' complacency) has sanctioned an open invitation for the entire healthcare industry to empty the bank accounts of older people. If Congress is unable to get a consensus in order to enact a catastrophic health/nursing home care bill (or at least allow for some appropriate kind of safety net), what are we expected to do with the people who are unfortunate enough to be in such a situation. Are we going to end up having to "Kervokian" more people than we "Heimlich" each year?

Realizations and Suggestions

(1) Under a managed care system, health insurers and their bureaucracy have merely become costly, unproductive "middlemen" who are dispensable. They really serve no purpose anymore in a system where health care can be directly negotiated with doctor groups, hospitals, employers etc. Premiums could be paid into a single-payer, non-profit, national insurance fund—overseen and accountable to an independent board and to the public at-large. We could then constructively use the vast amounts of money (that health insurance companies siphon off in superfluous administrative costs and profits) to instead deliver better health care to America's citizens. Why do we need two bureaucracies to serve one health care system? If we are really serious about having an efficiently-run system, we cannot allow the health insurance lobbyists to have the unrestrained clout that they have on our politicians in Washington.

(2) The concept of "managed care" (and the way it is currently practiced) should be revised. We should manage extraneous care and procedures, not a patient's choice of health care options or doctors. Each person should be able to contractually spell out the specific central elements that individual wants in his or her own health care plan. This notion seems like the only way to know, that what you receive, actually meets your original expectations of coverage. This guidelines-based contracting lends comfortability to the insured for a specific resource level of health care, as well as holding health-care providers accountable when they don't deliver. Therefore, eliminating ambiguous and contractually-cumbersome terminology like, "medically necessary," would be to the long-term betterment of both the patient and health-care provider.

The patient-doctor relationship should be personal and take into account: each individual's set of unique circumstances; particular health care problems; and potential therapeutic impacts. But, a middle ground between undertreatment and overtreatment should be arrived at between the two through conscientious discussion. This procedure could be simplified by using a *physician*-board-consensus manual of what "normal" treatment is considered sufficient for each health problem. Physician board guidelines would certainly take into account quality of care—comparatively more than any "for-profit" insurance guideline manual would. If a patient insisted on being "overtreated" beyond the consensus stated in the manual, extra costs would be paid for by the patient, out-of-pocket. At the same time, this realization would increase the consumer's sensitivity to true costs of potentially redundant medical procedures.

(3) A billing/payment system with one standardized claim form should be instituted. This notion is a "no brainer," and I don't understand why this hasn't been insisted on being implemented by all the health-care system participants. This would cut costs without having any detrimental effect on anybody. Doctors would save on administrative overhead by not having to deal with a different form for every different plan—each of which has different rules for repayment. Furthermore, all claims could be sent electronically (computer-to-computer) to a single, national central clearinghouse or one of several regional ones for quickness and simplicity of resolution.

(4) Hospitals, because of "for-profit" competition among each other for patients and physician staffs, have created duplications of expensive medical technological equipment as well as many of the same redundant services/programs. These two factors along with excess capacity have significantly contributed to overhead costs and, subsequently, patients' hospital bills.

The key word in the medical care industry should be cooperation, not competition. Some hospitals have joined into alliance systems, but often for ease of getting new patient referrals & convenience—than for anything else. Generally, there is still room for improvement regarding reduction of expensive overall costs within each hospital. There is a need in every metropolitan area to "designate individual hospitals within each system [or area] as 'centers of excellence' for specific diseases and conditions."[16] A person may have to drive across to the other side of the metro area for a specific, unique treatment—but his/her overall hospital bill could be noticeably reduced for such inconvenience.

(5) We need to create more lower-cost, yet skilled, nursing facilities to treat patients with chronic illnesses. Many of these patients do not require a full realm of higher-cost hospital services, yet need more than outpatient or in-home care for a number of weeks or months. Thus, the crucial gap for patients in need of quality health care between the two extremes could be filled.

(6) Expectations of patients for receiving better cures and complete wellness programs have increased as medical professionals continue to learn new knowledge and have access to even newer technology. These patients' higher expectations are understandable, but possibly unreasonably hopeful—to the degree of erroneously visualizing their own immortality.

We all feel that we are entitled to the best (often most expensive) health care possible, even in cases when it is questionable that we are receiving any extra benefits for such care. I'm not saying that this is necessarily wrong. I'm just wondering if there is ever a line that we will cross in the future, whereby we will admit that the costs to the overall health-care system is just too prohibitive for all of us to demand a continual, incrementally-small prolonging of life. Although it is hard to accept, death is inevitable.

(7) On the other hand, individuals are trying to take control of their lives through prevention, early detection, and healthier lifestyle choices. These trends cannot be overstated because if we can try to avoid disease from effecting us to begin with, we may stay free of needed treatments and any overall weakening of the functioning bodily systems.

Our increased knowledge of molecular biology and genetics may be a major factor in the future in dealing with costly, life-threatening diseases. By developing vaccines that may prevent severe illnesses from ever devastating the body, as well as delivery systems whereby drugs could be sent to specific, diseased areas of the body with few (if any) side effects—such prevention would go a long way in saving lives and keeping down overwhelming costs at the same time.

We have not fixed the health care system, except with small bits of cosmetic surgery. But, major changes will have to come about (the sooner, the better for all concerned), if it is to remain responsive and viable. One thing is certain though—the system would be advanced if all factions could work together as a whole, rather than for merely furthering each one's own narrow, self-serving agenda.

Chapter 6

GUNS AND CRIME

I (for one) wish that the gun had never been invented. Besides that, I simply do not understand the utter fascination that many Americans have with guns. All of the civilized countries of the world are perplexed by this love affair and toleration that we have for our guns. There are approximately 250 million firearms (about 90 million of these handguns) in circulation in the U.S., and firearm deaths are now over 30,000 yearly.[1] On top of these facts, keep in mind that there are hundreds of thousands of accidental and intentional gun-related injuries each year, as well as countless other times where guns are used to intimidate people. Nonetheless, even in light of these glaring statistics, I have come to the realization that neither side (of those trying to resolve the issue of guns and crime) is completely correct in its respective solution to the problem. So, let's try to sort out all of the propaganda that has been flung at the public from both the anti-gun and pro-gun lobbies, in order that we may try to make some sense of this issue.

The Effect of Gun Controls

Although many of us want to feel that the simple banning of guns (especially handguns) would be a panacea for reducing murder and crime, the real facts just don't confirm that such an idea would actually work. In order for such a concept to have succeeded, Congress would have had to enact such bans many years ago (maybe as early as the end of World War II). After all, handguns in the possession of your average citizen is basically a post-World War II phenomenon. Before that time, only gangsters (for the most part) had handguns in order to protect, their illegitimate dealings—your average citizen did not. But, since then, the proliferation of guns among the general public has been allowed to skyrocket unceasingly—to the point that there are now almost enough guns in circulation to provide every man, woman and child in the U.S. with one.

The unfortunate reality of such numbers would doom any possible legislated restriction of old or new guns from having any *controlling* effect on the criminal element of the population. Felonious predators have themselves often admitted that if handguns in general were ever restricted, they would have many alternative opportunities to obtain handguns illegally. The ways that they could obtain them would be impossible to monitor or regulate, such as: (1) smugglers bringing in guns of manufacturers from other countries (2) bootleg manufacturers in the U.S. itself (3) opportunistic gun traders in the "underground" market (4) registered guns stolen from private individuals in house burglaries (which is a bigger market than you'd think) (5) second-hand handguns purchased from one individual to another (e.g., gun shows) (6) sawing off the barrel of a rifle or shotgun, thusly, not only making such a weapon more concealable, but also as much as four times more deadly—because of a stronger blast and scattering of metal fragments (pellets) with one squeeze of the trigger. Also, pellets (unlike bullets) are less likely to exit the body, thereby creating a higher degree of damage to bodily organs. A quote by one prison inmate is telling as to the effect that gun control would have for the typical armed criminal: "Once I'm outta' the joint, it'll take maybe an hour to get a gun. If you know a junkie, you know where to buy one. Junkies are the residential burglars…[while another inmate stated]: Gun control is cosmetics, a band-aid on a broken leg."[2]

Similarly, while background checks of purchasers of guns does have a small positive impact (and should be continued), overall it only makes a minor dent into deterring the criminal use of handguns. Of all the guns that are acquired for the intent purpose of committing a criminal act, "only about one-half of 1 percent to 2 or 3 percent are personally bought at a retail outlet by a person with an existing criminal record who does not already have another gun."[3] So, although it would potentially keep as many as 3 percent of the guns that are used in crime out of the hands of dangerous people (which is still a significantly meaningful number), it is a percentage that is assuredly below the expectations of what the legislation's framers had originally intended.

Furthermore, even if general gun controls could be made very effective, robbers could most probably change the nature of their crimes which involved a weapon. If they had to use knives instead of guns, they would have to pull more robberies on personal individuals, in order to compensate for a loss of loot from the "bigger score" retail establishments. This change of focus would be the only way that they could maintain their standard of living. Moreover, in order to catch a victim by surprise and so that he wouldn't offer any resistance, an actual attack would have to take place (compared to a mere threat). So, you would see significant rises in muggings and serious injuries especially of the frail, elderly, and any other vulnerable individual.

There is an interesting aside to this whole issue of general gun control and murders. Nine out of the ten least murderous states in the country (ranging from 1.6 to 3.6 murders per 100,000 people) have the least restrictive gun laws in the country.[4] The states are: Maine, North Dakota, New Hampshire, Iowa, Idaho, Montana, Utah, South Dakota, Wyoming, and Vermont. You may recognize that these are states that are noted for smaller cities, simpler lifestyles, and are considered (yet arguably) more stable "family-value-oriented" states. So, it is possible that the complexity, impersonality, and added stress of living in crowded, angst-ridden metropolitan (and even suburban) areas, may very well be more important factors for committing murder than non-restrictive gun laws.

But, although I recognize what would likely be the ineffectualness (and subsequent disappointment) of overly restrictive gun laws, I still do believe that we need to draw the line on access to the ever-more powerful weapons that have been (and will continue) coming onto the market. Otherwise, you proliferate an individual war of one "upmanship," where you start to rationalize that since a criminal can find a way to get his hands on, for example, a bazooka, then I (as a law-abiding citizen) am entitled to my bazooka for my own protection—then, if he can get a howitzer, I want my howitzer—he can get a tank, I want my tank—he can get a surface-to-air missile, I want my surface-to-air missile.

Meanwhile, automatic and assault rifles need to continue to be banned. I also believe that the ban should continue on semi-automatic weapons, which is a type of weapon—whereby each time that you press the trigger, one bullet fires without reloading. They are different from automatics, where squeezing and holding the trigger will fire bullets continually. Thus, since semi-automatics have the potential to cause much unnecessary destructiveness in public situations, they too should continue to be banned.

The Second Amendment

There has been much controversy over the years regarding how the wording of the Second Amendment was intended, and how it should be interpreted. The Amendment as quoted is: "A well regulated Militia being necessary to the security of a free State, the right of the people to keep and bear Arms, shall not be infringed." Needless to say, both sides of the gun issue think that the interpretation of the Amendment justifies their own respective viewpoint. When all is said and done, I personally believe that it is a moot point how one interprets it anyway—given the enormous proliferation and numbers of guns that are in the hands of individuals today, some 200+ years after the fact.

But one thing is for sure, the Amendment was never intended to include handguns. At best, it would have possibly allowed muskets or rifles to be used for the protection of frontierspeople who were living in the wild, and whose closest neighbor might be an enraged bear, rather than a fellow human being. The original Framers could have never (in their wildest imaginations) foreseen such an astounding growth of the country's population—and the corresponding proliferation of all types of firearms (including handguns and the automatic weapons) that we have today. Common sense would dictate, that they would have never intended or allowed such a firearms' threat to exist in regards to the general population.

Thus, it would seem that the intended interpretation was that individuals would have the right to bear arms, only in conjunction with the *necessary* condition whereby a militia would have to be formed. There is no implication that sole, independent individuals would have the personal right to bear their own arms against other people (*anytime* they saw fit)—except in the instance where a whole group would have to be formed in order to protect the freedom of the State. One must keep in mind, that (at that time) there was an uneasiness and distrust that our new national government's standing army would become forcibly tyrannical and oppressive upon the individual rights of the States. This apprehension was especially strong since our countrymen had just won a war from an enemy whose very goal had been exactly that.

Looking at it in a semantic way, if the Framers meant for the Amendment to apply to individuals, there would have never been any need to even include the word, militias. After all, militias are simply individuals (ordinary citizens) composed in a group. If the intention was to allow individuals to bear arms, it would be totally redundant to include the word, militias. That is, if it was alright for individuals to bear arms, it would go without saying that they would also be entitled to bear them in any group composed of individuals.

Crime and Dysfunctional Families

When one takes a brief, comparative look between Japan and the United States on both guns and general crime, there are a few glaringly obvious conclusions that can be determined about how these criteria relate to society and family. The fact that Japan has a very low gun crime rate has more to do with its particular culture than any general gun ban laws. Over the years, Japan has developed into a most amenable society, and therefore its people are accepting of such voluntary social controls, such as obedience and impulse control.

Now, I am not saying that general, unquestioning obedience is a good thing per se. But, on the specific point of obedience to a reciprocal code of conduct between all of a country's citizens, I believe it is something that we all should strive for and learn to do. "In Japan, a person can leave a bag of groceries on the sidewalk outside a store, and come back a half hour later to find it still there."[5] In other words, respect and trust are taken for granted. If a society is ultimately going to be a caring one, these are most important factors. Therefore, guns are not even thought about or needed in Japan, because the concept of having to defend oneself from other fellow citizens holds no meaning or purpose in reality.

In Tokyo, muggings (which often don't even involve a gun) happen at the yearly rate of about only 40 per one million inhabitants, while in New York City the rate has been as high (in the past) as a staggering 11,000 per one million inhabitants. Likewise, the *non*-gun robbery rate in the U.S. is over 60 times that of Japan's.[6] I bring up the glaring difference in these particular statistics for a reason. There is obviously something going on here other than an access or lack of access to guns. The distinguishing influences seem to be learned, social responsibility and family.

In a most aptly named book, *Tragedies of Our Own Making*, Richard Neely (a former Chief Justice of the West Virginia Supreme Court) discusses why his state, although ranked 49th among the states in per capita income, has such a low overall crime rate. What he says on this matter is so profoundly relevant and telling about our culture, and it offers viable explanations of why we have our subsequent social problems.

There are two significant factors about the preponderance of West Virginians that you do not find nearly as overwhelmingly as in other states. (1) Even though divorce and illegitimacy are high in his state, the crucial variable of family structure remains relatively in tact. That is, the children are most often provided genuine care and their concerns are directly met by either immediate or extended family members, who can help the young grow up in a positive way. (2) Although nationally, West Virginians appear "poor" (statistically), they themselves "don't feel particularly poor when they compare themselves to their neighbors, [and therefore unlike other poor who live in large metropolitan areas in the U.S.] aren't caught Up in emotional problems arising from perceived deprivation...'Deprivation' largely has to do with how you think that you are doing in comparison to other people living around you."[7]

That is, West Virginians are seemingly able to keep any lack of material things within a hierarchical perspective of life's virtues and priorities, and (in turn) stay on an even keel. Furthermore, this could very well stem from living in smaller towns and cities (there are no large ones in West Virginia). "Most upper-middle class West Virginians live inside [their] cities and towns...[There are] almost no suburban areas...[Hence,] the interaction among all social classes is much higher in West Virginia than in the urban states."[8] Therefore, people aren't compared to one another to the point that they feel economically deprived.

Finally, keep in mind that this all takes place in a state that has one of the highest rates of gun ownership, and yet at the same time one of the lower homicide rates by firearms. Therefore, it would seem that crime and homicide are not directly caused by poverty or accessibility to guns themselves, but rather a pitiful lack of communal social habits and caring familial attitudes and relationships while "growing up and living in conditions of poverty and [perceived] deprivation."[9]

"Early onset of juvenile delinquency is tied to early disruption of parent-child relations. 'Insecure attachment' by children to parents often predicts future social problems, including aggression, impulsiveness, poor social skills, and low self-control, all of which are associated with criminality...[and] chronic juvenile delinquency is the strongest predictor of adult criminality."[10] Moreover, "more than 70 percent of all juveniles in state reform schools [in the U.S.] come from fatherless homes."[11] "In fact, the relationship between fatherlessness and crime is so strong that, once one considers household structure, [then] race and poverty disappear as predictors of crime in a neighborhood."[12]

Nonetheless, even given this fact, "a good one-parent home is better than an abusive or dysfunctional two-parent home...A household which has [only] one parent, because an abusive spouse was removed, is better off."[13] So, although it is sad to admit it, we have **Paradox #16** (which is really a double, convoluted paradox): A stable, two-parent home is the best way to curb juvenile delinquency and ultimately criminality. But even so, if keeping the two parents together results in abuse (either spousal or child), then in this situation it is better off for all involved to have a good one-parent home. Yet, statistically, the chances are greater that a child will become emotionally dysfunctional in a home that is fatherless. But, if the parent in the one-parent home can "set standards...convey to their children the difference between right and wrong...[and] provide examples of common human decency"[14] when relating to others, then the chances of successfully raising a more emotionally-adjusted child are greater. That is, it is a matter of attitude.

I would like to drive home the point about familial dysfunction by citing an extreme example, yet an applicable one. In the Spring, 1997, in Franklin, New Jersey, a pizza shop owner and an employee were horribly gunned down, while simply delivering a pizza. The two teenagers, Thomas Koskovich and Jayson Vreeland, who were later arrested for the murders, had laid in wait in a remote area near an abandoned house which had been given as the delivery address. It was later determined that there was no real motive (e.g., robbery) for the murders (although it had been methodically planned)—but rather merely a "mixture of alienation and acute boredom."[15] In other words, paraphrasing the prosecutor of the case, it was an irrational act that had no rational answer.

But, looking at Koskovich's (who was the real instigator) family background, one could have seen that he was a ticking time bomb just waiting to go off. As hard as it might be to comprehend, evidently his parents had divorced when he was a child and they simply left him, and "split" town going their separate ways. He ended up living with his grandparents. At age 10, he was cutting cocaine lines for an uncle, who (not so coincidentally) has a long rap sheet himself—and is currently serving ten years time in prison for burglary.

This case obviously demonstrates the effect of irresponsible parenting—and in this instance, actual abandonment by both parents. Under these circumstances, this teen had very little chance of successfully having the ability to sort out all of his problems. Although this is an extreme case, there are many others out there suffering from wide-ranging degrees of dysfunction. In describing the high number of dysfunctional homes, a former jingle from a corn chip television commercial might be very apt: "Don't worry, if we run out—we'll make more."

Violence and Television

The similarities between the storylines on television and the reality of everyday occurrences has become so strongly linked, that it has become a nearly impossible task to distinguish which one imitates the other. For instance, this is the promo that I heard one night on a local station: "Teen murders her mother—details on The News tonight at 11:00 after the network movie, 'The Last Don (Part 2).'" Either way, the link is not coincidental and does not bode well for promoting a responsible society.

The networks say that they are not responsible for what parents let their children watch. Yet, they cannot avoid the fact that many children do learn a variety of "not-so-good" things from their very medium, that may consequentially have an especially detrimental effect on these viewers who are under age eighteen. Although I consider myself a rather open-minded and objective person, I have to admit that over the years, I (myself) have watched what seems like non-edited television shows as well as movies (in theaters), where I sensed that the producer was just off-screen telling the director to get "the body count up" anyway that he knew how—all for the sake of better ratings and bottom-line profits. It didn't seem to matter whether the bodies were rolling around in the throes of sexual passion or laying dead all over the floor with bullet holes in them—just as long as the viewers were given more and more bodies. All of this begs the question: Whether the goal of some programs is to make the viewers so hyped up on gratuitous sex and violence, that they literally cannot live without their vicarious nightly "fix," and therefore must come back for more and more? Is that what it has gotten down to—making our senses so numb and insensitive to it all, that inwardly each of us will simply and easily subdue any remaining, emotional outrage that we may still have towards it?

We should be concerned about the fact that most psychologists agree that all human beings learn behavior (including violence) by observing or imitating others, who they consider as role models or significant people in their lives. "The more prestigious the person modeling aggressive behavior, the more likely it is to be imitated by observers."[16] We learn that if the aggressive act is permitted, tolerated and practical—that it is alright to lose your inhibitions. "What we pay attention to, becomes us, as surely as we become what we eat...When we are bombarded continually with images of violence, brutality, sexual immorality, and betrayals of trust, our minds and spirits suffer."[17]

It does seem to hold true that violence—whether it be on television, movies or video games (which in this last example, the player is given a digitally-enhanced, almost God-like power over his or her "victims")—has an especially strong, detrimental effect on at least one type of child. That category would be those children who have not been well "socialized" by parents or guardians about socially-acceptable behavior and expectations. Seeing violence repeatedly portrayed can dehumanize such unprepared, "raw" kids to the point that violence may tend to be seen as acceptably ordinary behavior to their malleable minds. In essence, the individuals on screen are dehumanized in these viewers' minds. The characters are rendered into merely inanimate objects, that can be kicked around or used in any manner that one sees fit.

Through the repeated use of violent video games, such a child can actually get accustomed (or even addicted) to the macabre thrill of anonymously performing the "task" (of splattering someone's guts all over the place) day after day—until that viewer can eventually see oneself doing it in reality. Such repeated exposure, evidently played a part in both the Columbine school shootings and the sharp-shooting serial killings in the Washington, DC area. Similarly, when there is a portrayal of a person's head being chain-sawed off in a horror movie, the human being (which is portrayed) becomes objectified. Such visualizations can potentially carry over to legitimizing such thoughts and behavior in susceptible viewers. Therefore, the rationale is that if one person can even think of doing something like this, why can't I (the viewer) do something similar?

Meanwhile, for all of the graphic violence to actual people or characters, that is realistically depicted on television and movies, the terrible consequences of such acts are indifferently and rather subjectively edited out. "The cameras quickly cut away from dead and dying bodies. The fast break to the commercial teaches no lesson about the permanency of death or injury."[18] Therefore, it is most likely fair to say that repeated portrayals (and exposure to) violence in tandem with neglectful parenting is especially harmful to a vulnerable segment (yet significant number) of children.

On the other hand, it would seem that for the majority who are able to keep "portrayed" violence in perspective, such exposure to violence may actually be a somewhat beneficial experience. It would seem that such violence allows (especially males) a vicarious way for the expression of repressed anger. Moreover, it may allow all children a way of encountering and overcoming their fears and anxieties over any similar violence that will be found in the real world. Thus, violence in children's stories (e.g., "Little Red Riding Hood") may prepare children (as they get older) for potential realities of violence that may occur to real people in everyday life.

In summary, many children seem to be able to keep "portrayed" violence in perspective, but there is a vulnerable, growing segment of children who are being detrimentally molded by such violence. They see it as an uninhibited sanction and acceptable way to release their own angers and sate their personal desires and wants. So, what is the answer? In this particular case, television and movie executives need to be a little less concerned about furthering their network and studio ratings in this fashion. They need to eliminate their egocentric belief that "the way Hollywood goes, so should America." Instead, it is incumbent upon them to responsibly recognize that violence must be more selectively portrayed, so that viewers can learn from (rather than copy) the behavior. Only in this way, will the larger problem begin to be addressed.

But, it is important to keep in mind that solutions to such problems (with portrayed violence just being one example) need to take on a wider scope to include us all. In order for a free society to properly work, it is necessary that individuals responsibly demonstrate self-imposed restrictions on their own behavior. Otherwise, the pressure mounts (from other segments of the population) for The State to legislate more laws in order to preserve "the good" of the Greater Society. The problem today is that many citizens do not fully comprehend this concept. They feel that freedom sanctions them to do whatever they want (no matter how willy-nilly the behavior), irregardless of how their behavior steps on the rights and freedoms of other fellow citizens. In other words, without these self-imposed restrictions, the comprehensive notion of "living within a civilized society" becomes lost.

Children and Guns

This perspective of responsible citizenship cannot be more applicable, than when it comes to children and guns. We adults need to make a stronger effort to at least restrain our enthusiastic fascination and interest that we have always shown for guns—especially in regards to younger people. Guns should not be seen as sacred things to be revered. Although there are many responsible parents who think that they know their children well enough, it is false reasoning to think that their children will *always* take the necessary precautions when handling or using guns. No matter how mature that you think your youngster may be, a "mature" child can suddenly revert to a "childish" child simply because he or she still is a child. Lacking the years of experience and psychological mentality of a mature adult, a child is more susceptible to letting his "safety-conscious guard" down just at the moment that he may need it most. In his playfulness, he may be less cautious in considering potential problems that may arise in all situations (e.g., like one bullet still in the chamber). So, I don't really understand this rush some adults have to teach their children about guns.

For instance, recently a youngster did not have the psychological wherewithal to cope with negative personal comments that had been directed at him by another child at his school. He just did not have the ability (or desensitivity) to shrug off such comments. That is, he did not have the maturity to reason the particular situation out—instead, he impulsively reacted out of only emotional considerations and, therefore, without much thought to the consequences. The end result was that he allowed the comments to emotionally overwhelm him, and before you knew it, he had gotten a gun from home and exacted revenge for those comments by murdering the other. Was this child psychologically mature enough to have knowledge about guns? Again, this "mature" child had reverted to a "childish" child simply because he still was a child.

And seemingly, almost inevitably, the next day or two the media are interviewing "Gramps" who, while stoically sitting there on his front porch, says "No, I have no regrets teaching him how to be a good shot when he was eight years old (as if there was nothing else better to teach him at that age). If he had not used my son's gun, he would have found another one somewhere else." It is logic like this that forces us all to pay the consequences. Why is it that we push our children to become adults, even before they have lived their childhood?

Societal Costs of Guns and Crime

In today's society, we have reached the point that an innocent person (trying to mind his or her own business) can be shot anywhere, anytime, anyhow, for any reason, while doing anything. In the last decade, there have been well-publicized incidents of people being murdered while doing such simple things as: eating a sandwich in a restaurant; sleeping in one's own car; driving one's own car; pumping gas; changing a tire; walking to or sitting in school; delivering a pizza; working in an office; opening a package; playing on a playground; standing on a street corner; taking a walk; sitting in one's own living room; and accidentally arriving at the wrong address. Moreover, it seems that the motive factors become more and more ambiguous with each murder.

Furthermore, and rather ironically, the innocent people are more and more often building their own little prisons (also known as "secured" residential complexes) for themselves to "live" in, as a way of dealing with their fear of the everyday world. "After all, looked at objectively, the most important function of a prison is to incapacitate criminals so they can't get at us. Therefore, why waste perfectly good and very expensive prisons on criminals when we could live in them ourselves? Good steel doors, fortified walls, armed guards,...a tightly monitored entry gate, and active patrols...can keep the criminals out just as effectively as these security devices can keep them in."[19] Is this anyway to live? It sounds like a prison to me.

And, for those who don't live in such communities, some people today are going to the extreme of upgrading their "protective" animals. In fact a few screwballs today are even keeping lions as property protectors. That's right, they're bringing in King of the Natural Jungle in their hope that he will find comfortability in his new role as King of the Concrete Jungle, too. Forget the German

Shepherd, forget the Rottweiler, forget the Doberman—when you have a roaring lion as your watchdog, one is going to think twice before trying to break in and rob or hurt you. One thing for sure, the criminal is going to lose the natural tendency to call out, "Here kitty, kitty, kitty."

One cannot underestimate this "fear of crime" factor, as well as the damage that is done by allowing handguns in the irresponsible hands of some people with this syndrome. A case in point was Baton Rouge, Louisiana on October 17, 1992. This incident involved a 16 year-old Japanese foreign exchange student, Yoshihiro Hattori, who was going to a pre-Halloween party (with a friend of his) dressed up in a white dinner jacket as the John Travolta character in the movie "Saturday Night Fever." They went up to a house that had holiday decorations on it, and rang the doorbell because they thought that they were at the correct residence. After a short while (when there was no answer) they started back down the walkway. When they reached the driveway, they heard someone at the door, and they turned to see who it was. The woman who came to the door was "startled" (one has got to wonder just how easily does this person get startled?) to see Hattori (and his friend), slammed the door closed as quickly as she had opened it, and told her husband to get his gun. The husband came with his gun, allegedly yelled, "Freeze," and when Hattori failed to stop (his English was not that good), was shot and killed by a .44 magnum. There were no questions asked, no attempt at communication—just blasted away at anything that moved!

Obviously, here was a situation of a person using his gun irresponsibly (and consequentially actually killing someone), without even attempting to contemplate first whether the situation even warranted a gun—which of course it did not. Well, you would think that this would be considered manslaughter, right? Nope, the slayer was acquitted by using "a man's home is his castle" defense. With a verdict like this, it makes you wonder whether anybody in the Louisiana Justice System even went to law school. Regarding the death of Hattori, the then Governor Edwin Edwards could only say that it was "one of those unfortunate things." Well, what was really unfortunate was that he was governor of a state whose justice system didn't work for justice.

The verdict outraged the citizens of Japan to such a degree that they were able to get an astounding 1.6 million signatures on a petition, urging that irresponsible Americans should not have access to guns. Many of them see Americans as out-of-control individuals who "end up ducking responsibility for just about everything."[20] So, Mr. Hattori, who originally left Japan "vertically upright" with good wishes and high hopes of coming to America, had to end up going back to his homeland "horizontally" with not even a twitch in his body—all because he accidentally want to a wrong address!

So, let me get this straight. There are evidently particular areas in this country, where it is O.K. to "blow away" unarmed individuals for no reason and get away with it?

If I'm sitting in my car on my driveway, and somebody taps on my car window, I have the right to blow him away!

If somebody knocks on the door to my house, and I don't like the way he looks, I have the right to blow him away!

If I go out to talk to a landscaper who's working in my yard, and he happens to pick up a hoe as I approach, I have the right to blow him away!

If a teenager accidentally throws a baseball in my yard and he comes to retrieve it, I have the right to blow him away!

If a delivery person rings my doorbell and I am "startled" by him, I have the right to blow him away!

If somebody passes through my yard, I have the right to blow him away!

If a lawn care technician starts spraying my lawn, and I forget that I have contracted with his company to automatically do this job, I have the right to blow him away!

If I'm walking on my driveway to pick up my newspaper, and somebody is walking toward me carrying a long, narrow bag that looks like it may have a rifle in it (but actually only has pool sticks in it), I have the right to blow him away!

If a dog starts "watering" on one of my bushes, I have the right to blow it away!

If any of the above assertions are correct, then I must be living in the wrong society!

Having just described a case where an irresponsible gun owner was psychologically overcommitted to using a handgun, there are other handgun owners who are too psychologically reluctant to use them. But although these type of gun owners cannot visualize themselves actually using a gun because they have "cold feet," they nonetheless have loaded guns in the house that present a different type of irresponsibility. That being, the guns of such owners are more likely to be used accidentally; or in a fit of anger against a loved one; or against themselves by a burglar who might enter the home.

Thus, these examples of gun owners on both sides of the spectrum merely demonstrate, that these types of people should not own guns because they are not responsible enough to own them. Yet, they do own them! Hence, there should be more to owning a gun in this country than merely being able to pass a background check and getting a license, because the safety and health of the public depend on it. You should have to prove that you have the psychological wherewithal to be allowed to own one.

Finally, I want to say that there is much truth in the saying, "What goes around, comes around." Handguns cause fear and paranoia, which in turn causes us to buy our own handguns to counteract that fear and paranoia, which, in turn, causes even more fear and paranoia, and so on. When it reaches the time where you can no longer trust your fellow man, you have no society anymore—at least not a civilized one. In a country that has about 250 million guns in circulation, we are living more in an armed camp than a true society. It is a tragedy to our country's good name, that we have so many homicides and suicides by guns, whereby one could almost categorize "death by gun" as a form of population control. As I discussed before, since gun control will not keep guns in general out of the hands of criminals (and because there are so many guns already in circulation), it is a sad thing to admit that our legacy of guns will go on and on forever (ad infinitum).

What Can Be Done To Lessen The Danger?

(1) The prison time for using a gun in a crime must be higher in all instances—than if no gun was used for the same crime. Also, crimes involving guns would not be able to be plea bargained. Early parole could be possible, but only under stricter conditions and guidelines. This lack of leeway on gun crimes will notify the community of criminals (in no uncertain terms), that these type of crimes will not be tolerated and that the sentences will not be reduced. The explicit message will be that crimes with guns will be seriously dealt with.

(2) We must remove from the streets the small percentage of the worst juvenile delinquents that are responsible for a large percentage of the crime in their age group. Many studies have shown that a mere 6-10% of the worse delinquents are responsible for over half the juvenile crime and over half of the repeat offenses.[21] Either seriously (and sincerely) try to rehabilitate them or lock them up for longer periods of time—but get them off the streets.

(3) Governments should determine what kind of incarceration that they truly want to buy. Correctional budgets are not bottomless pits, which will cover the costs for all criminal offenders in fulfilling their complete prison sentences. Obviously, we want the violent criminals to serve all of their time, so why misallocate crucial, limited resources. Therefore, we must find alternative punishment programs for most of the minor crime offenders who clog our prisons. "Instead of talking only about the size of the budget, or the number of people incarcerated, we should be thinking more about exactly whom we are incarcerating. In situations where incarceration adds little to public safety [such as jailing minor felony class criminals], we should put fewer resources into such incarceration. The savings should be deployed in ways that will maximize the gain in public safety" [by imprisoning the violent and chronic criminals].[22]

Besides, it is much easier and more productively worthwhile to rehabilitate non-violent criminals outside the environment of prisons and away from the violent offenders. Since we have the technology to personally monitor such criminals, let's use it. We could electronically monitor such people by having them wear sensors in more cases (similar to the way animals are tracked and located by scientists in the wild). Also, more innovative residential programs should definitely be created, because minor offenders are more likely to benefit from such help. All in all, we need to be more intelligent in allocating our resources and selectively tough on sentencing—depending on the type of crime.

(4) Try to improve the coping skills of dysfunctional families. I've already talked about the fact that the mental health system needs to be overhauled, so that the families who require its use the most, can have access to some of the best care. Lower the caseloads of both probation officers and social workers by hiring a greater number of such professionals. If you want these people to be able to make a significant difference, they must be able to provide sufficient time (both in quality and quantity), in order to assure that their clients don't "slip through the cracks" in the real world.

Their jobs are already hard enough as is. They have to deal with the unenviable task of making dysfunctional individuals/families (many of whom have socially unacceptable behavior patterns) into functionally "healthy" individuals/families. After all, if we are going to have any chance to permanently reduce serious crime, the professionals working at the one-to-one level, may very well be the most crucial "piece of the puzzle." They must have the time to show, for example, inner-city kids that there are alternatives to the "strife-ridden" neighborhoods in which they live. For instance, there has been some success with programs where juvenile delinquents have been taken out in the country to a farm. There, they have cared for horses and other animals, as a way of not only "doing their time," but to also allow them to see the breadth of life's possibilities.

Such kids must be given the freedom to appreciate the outside world. They must be given the opportunity to realize that the neighborhoods from which they come are merely small parts of a larger world…that there is an assortment of horizons that are available for expanding one's own mind and viewpoint. Sometimes it is necessary to remove oneself from a harsh, unforgiving environment in order to be able to see the potential light of hope and change. If you cannot take the neighborhood from the kid, take the kid from the neighborhood. If you can instill such children with more hope, you can reduce their incentive and need to commit crimes.

Chapter 7

NATURE AND THE ENVIRONMENT

The fact that we humans (as a whole) have never consciously taken into account the environment in a serious manner is evident in the amount and types of litter that can be witnessed along our highways and countryside. The following items are what I myself have personally seen firsthand, and I am sure that you could add others to this list: beer & soda cans/bottles; milk cartons; plastic containers; fast-food, non-biodegradable, styrofoam containers; ketchup/mustard pouches; napkins; cups; plastic forks/knives; bottle caps; straws; toothpicks; plastic bags; gum wrappers; gum stuck to the pavement; consumer product packaging; blowing-in-the-wind newspapers; countless cigarette butts (especially a group of them dumped all in one spot from a car's ashtray); one used surgical latex glove (your guess is as good as mine on this one); used condoms; underwear; one boot with one sock (I'm still trying to figure this one out); plastic diapers; human waste (people urinating in the middle of parking lots in broad daylight); discarded tires and hubcaps; hats; hairpins; hangers; shoestrings; balloons; baseballs; assorted toys; playing cards; business cards; sunglass earpieces; bolts & screws; and horseshoes.

Our sullying of our own living environment (like this) exemplifies self-indulgent, arrogant attitudes that an increasing number of us project onto everything that we do. Why should we care if we sully our environment without heed or conscience? After all, many of us consider ourselves the most valuable inhabitants on the planet, and therefore should be entitled to do whatever that we feel like doing? Well, think again.

Scientific "Progress" vs. the Laws of Nature

(Note: Up to this point, I have been discussing the abuses especially perpetrated by and on us Americans. But, for this chapter and the next one, I am going to widen our scope of analysis to include how all the world's abuse of the planet and "unrestrained progress" affects us all).

Humankind is on the precipice of attempting to become greater than Nature itself. If we try to carry this concept too far, we are doom to fail, because in the long-run "man-made" science is no match for Natural Law. Man has always been known to act upon his decisions before ever fully weighing the pros and cons (and gains and losses) of how each of his decisions affect Nature. This rush to action is generally always done for the sake of "human and economic progress." We continually downplay the potentially harsh consequences and unpredictable outcomes of altering Nature. Yet, it is like opening Pandora's Box—that is, once opened, we must all live with the consequences (whether they be good or bad), and in turn be assured that none of us will ever be the same again.

However, we must keep in mind that decisions or choices always involve value judgments. "[Scientific] knowledge is not likely to remain long in a vacuum."[1] Atomic energy would be a past example and genetic cloning a present one. But, should (or must) all such acquired knowledge reach practical fruition, simply because we have access to it? Who determines such decisions and how are they determined? Is it assured that people will attempt to apply such knowledge for their own advantages and ends, regardless of the consequential ramifications?

Similarly, there is a difference in how the schools of science and the philosophy of Nature arrive at interpreting the real world. The philosophical way is criticized as being "naively imaginative" about any possible effects that science has on Nature and Man. A simple example (yet not a particularly germane one)—but one that we all have an opinion on—would be whether alien beings exist in the real world? The philosophical approach would conclude: "Of course they do. Are we that egotistical to believe that Earth's humans are the only living beings that co-exist with the 'Greater Nature' (The Universe)?"

On the other hand, the scientific approach would counter, "We want actual proof of there being other living beings."

But, the scientific approach lacks in preciseness and definitiveness in its own right. So-called evidence that is collected is often open to differing conclusions based on varying interpretation of the "facts." Conclusions are based on the relativity of ever-changing amounts of what is considered "relevant and not relevant" information. That is, the very same piece of information may be considered relevant by one scientist and irrelevant by another. Thus, fully consensual, uncontroversial conclusions are rarely reached.

Moreover, in most cases, the only actual, agreed-upon conclusion reached is: "More study is needed." The extent to which we use this rationale today has caused a new phrase to come into being, "paralysis by analysis." This term is defined as the overanalyzing of a problem until it actually becomes too late to do anything about that very problem. This syndrome is most commonly used in reference to how we extensively delay comprehensive, environmental solutions—to the point that the negative effects and consequences of such a delay could become irreversible on us as a living species. Accordingly, it could be construed that the "more study is needed" response is merely an excuse of one's unwillingness to accept the fact that there very well might not be any empirical answer after all. "Science is…not [necessarily] ultimate truth."[2]

Conversely, if Nature wants to affect us, it can without first getting our consent. Now, that is the true meaning of "ultimate truth." Therefore, even with all his information and scientific conclusions, Man will lose to Nature in a head-to-head confrontation every time (if Nature whimsically commands to make it so)—guaranteed! The difference is one of "refinement." Man can never reach 100% absolute assuredness, but Nature does have that potential ability.

This fact is the reason why we walk on shaky ground when we automatically come to the conclusion, that we may continue with "unrestrained growth and progress," until it can be proven through measured data that this "unrestrained growth and progress" is actually detrimental to Nature and Man. The lost logic with this notion is that it is generally too late for both Nature and Man, by the time that "conclusive" empirical data is finally collected from such "an experiment." We must not allow the balance of power between

Nature and "unrestrained growth and progress" to tip too much in favor of the latter. Instead of becoming impatient and trying to bend Nature to our purposes, we should (and must) strengthen our symbiotic bond with it. An American Indian belief is very prophetic to note here: Nature will watch over Man, feed and care for him, as long as there is a reciprocal respect by Man towards Nature. In other words, Nature itself is reiterating and affirming an old adage to us: The Earth does not belong to us (humans), but rather we belong to the Earth.

The Relevance of the Geochemical Cycles of Life

In the past, we have never taken into full consideration the needs and the subtle sensitivities of our ecosystems. Consequently, virtually every collective human act has had negative cumulative effects in one form or another on our environment. If we care for the quality of our own lives, we are going to have to stop abusing the delicate balance of the geochemical cycles of Nature. Our interference with these cycles has led to: climate changes; degradation of fresh water sources; agricultural land damage (via erosion and flooding); the proper functioning of forests; disruption of the seasonal cycles of crops (and the soils that they depend on); and the destruction of habitats of other species on both land and water.

We are causing the ecological balance between extremes to falter. Routine and cyclically-predictable climate patterns (which are needed for maximum crop yields) are increasingly giving way to sudden and severe climate changes. Large and changing variations in rainfall are detrimental to each particular area's ecosystem, because each area has adapted over the years to a "normal" amount (and climate pattern) for its own area. Fluctuating extremes of sunshine and temperature have similar negative consequences. Wide shifts in ecosystems' nutrition levels also cause problems (e.g., too much fixed nitrogen in the soil or an overabundant growth of algae in the water). Hence, we are interfering with the sensitive dependency between the essential nutrient cycles and climate (as well as the self-regulating interactions between the two). "The variability of natural environments—their wetness, dryness, chemical composition, temperature, lightness, darkness, and nutrient availability—[strongly] affects...where each kind of life form can exist, its so-called 'ecological niche.'"[3]

We should briefly discuss how our whole environment is crucially related to several key biogeochemical cycles of life, as well as demonstrate how relatively major fluctuations in them can result in disastrous occurrences. For instance, the different varying seasonal rates of photosynthesis (in essence, the process of green plant growth) and respiration have always been kept at a fairly established balance between carbon dioxide and oxygen in the atmosphere. In this way, the carbon cycle of life can remain stable and seasonally consistent throughout the year. But if through Man's actions, the *optimal* mixture of the elements (i.e., oxygen, carbon dioxide, water, sunlight or energy, and temperature) are adversely affected, the quantity and quality of the plant life are likewise changed in a negative way.

By excessive burning of fossil fuels and the unprecedented rapidity of deforestation, the carbon dioxide levels in the atmosphere increase faster than the remaining plant life (after deforestation) can photosynthesize it out. Furthermore, this imbalance (in the oxygen-carbon dioxide mix) aggravates the situation even more by trapping additional heat inside the Earth's atmosphere (the "greenhouse effect"). In addition, our gradual destruction of the ozone layer, which shields plants (and animals) from ultraviolet radiation from the sun, further worsens the equation by baking the plants with too much heat, so that they cannot optimally produce or even survive.

Methane gas is also contributing to the "greenhouse effect." This gas is released when bacteria break down organic matter. Surprisingly, cattle are a major reason for the increase in methane concentration in the atmosphere. There are over 1 billion unassuming cows (seemingly minding their own business) who are languidly grazing on the face of the planet. Yet, the average cow is unrelentingly responsible for the emission of 400 liters of methane gas every day. When you multiply this amount by 1 billion, that's over 50 million metric tons that are annually released into the atmosphere...Now, that is what I call a whole lot of bovine flatulence! Who would have ever thought that the fate (and possibly the very survival) of the human species might forever be linked to the factor of how often the cows of the world stand there and "relieve" themselves from their hind quarters?...Environmentally, the negative effect of this gas is relevant, because although methane is in lesser concentrations than carbon dioxide in the atmosphere, it is 20 times stronger in its ability to block heat trying to exit the atmosphere. Of course, the world would not have the need for excess cattle production, if humans could taper (even somewhat) their "wants" to consume types of food that are higher up on the food chain (such as meats).

A crucial balance of the nitrogen cycle is no less important. A shortage of naturally fixed nitrogen may often take place when crops like wheat and corn (that are known to deplete a lot of nitrogen from the soil without replenishing it) are repeatedly planted in the same place. Without rotating and planting nitrogen-rich crops (e.g., legumes) in-between such single crop harvests, nutrient deficiencies of fixed nitrogen can occur. In turn, the productivity of the land can be significantly diminished.

An obvious answer might be to just use more fertilizer, but this procedure has its drawbacks for the natural environment, too. It is far better for the cycle if lost nutrients are replaced through natural soil regeneration processes (e.g., animal and plant decomposition and composting). But, because the farmers' need to grow abundant quantities of food (for many reasons including financial) is so great, unnatural petrochemical fertilizers are used in large quantities. Unfortunately, this synthetic way of replenishing nitrogen in the soil has negative consequences, and it represents yet another way of how the ever-expanding needs of Man can seriously interfere with the natural cycles of life. "Fertilizer runoff" acidifies rivers and lakes; which contributes to an overabundance of algae and seaweed to grow in the water; which drastically reduces the oxygen in the water; which ends up killing fish and other marine life. Moreover, the release of nitrous oxide in the industrial combustion process of making nitrogen-rich fertilizer (as well as when the fertilizer is applied) are additional factors that further aggravate global warming.

It is rather ironic the strong concern that we continually demonstrate by meticulously washing our individual automobiles with excessive amounts of soapy detergents and manicuring our yards, so that they are completely free of even a single weed. Yet, we show virtually no concern about keeping our greater environment clean and free of harmful quantities of fertilizers, pesticides, and herbicides—

that we irresponsibly dispense over our yards and fields. We seemingly are oblivious to the fact that these excesses ultimately wash down into our streams and rivers, detrimentally affecting us all.

There is one last cycle that I want to briefly mention, which is the sulfur cycle. The main point to make about sulfur is that it is strongly instrumental in increasing the acidity levels of rainwater, surface water and soil. Sulfur dioxide dissolves in water droplets within the air, and with the presence of sunlight (or energy), is then converted into a caustic sulfuric acid (i.e., acid rain)—which is potentially dangerous to all life forms and their ability to survive.

The combined influences of all of these sensitive, interconnected cycles affect our ability to continue to live on this planet. While the critical criterion of climate affects the nutrient cycles—the optimal climate (for the growing of different crops) that a particular area receives is also reciprocally determined by the nutrient cycles. "The variability in climate both geographically (from place to place) and in time (at each place) determines to a considerable extent where and how we can live: what we can grow."[4] The more our human activities interfere with both climate and nutrient cycles, the more we can expect wide variations in the supplies and types of foods that will be able to be grown. With all of our past impositions upon Nature (e.g., pollutants), the question becomes how much more can we detrimentally alter the global climate and nutrient cycles upon which all life depends?

Moreover, Nature has more to do with world economics than one would first think. If there continue to be drastic changes in climate and nutrient cycles, every country's economic activities will be negatively affected in a most serious manner, because every nation will be unable to depend on a consistent (and timely) production of food for its trade and Gross National Product. So, "unlimited growth" economists don't fully take into account that there will be limits—even if they have to be imposed by Nature's laws.

Examples of Man's Abuse of Nature

"Our ecological troubles—air pollution, forest destruction, radioactive wastes, acid rain, resources depletion, the greenhouse effect, oil spills, global warming—all stem from human attempts to meet other needs [and] solve other problems. Our environmental woes are, in virtually every case, either man-made or are seriously compounded by humankind's greed and materialism [through exploitation]." [5] Everything that a healthy ecosystem depends on are dwindling: green plants of the rain forests, life-dependent minerals, crucial topsoils for crops, the protective ozone layer, and the inter-related, biological diversity of all living things.

I am going to cite some specific global examples of environmental degradation that have originated from humankind's excessive need to developmentally exploit for its own short-sighted, self-aggrandizing, out-of-control ends. For instance, a real threat to our maritime waters are from sediment and contaminants that come from washed-down topsoil, fertilizers, pesticides, sewage, and industrial wastes. Unfortunately, coral reefs, which many fish species consider home, are very sensitive to sediment and are starting to die. Because of agricultural runoff, as well as sewage and coastal erosion, the Florida Keys' barrier reef is gradually dying a little more each year from such cumulative effects. Also, marine biologists fear that the coral reef off the coast of Belize will be irreparably harmed, because of the large increase in tourists to that country. A lack of caution by snorkelers and scuba divers is placing the reef in danger, while fishermen are starting to deplete certain fish species that are unique to that area.

In order to provide for tourists, unrestrained development is affecting many places in the Alps. Access roads, railways, cable car lines, and an overabundance of ski runs and lifts have played havoc with the terrain, while increasing the occurrence of mudflows and avalanches. Even in remote Nepal (home of Mount Everest), careless trekkers have discarded trash (including plastic containers, paper products, cans, batteries etc.) along trails, routes, and base camps. This type of litter pollution would be quite avoidable if visitors were simply more conscientious.

Clear-cutting of forests have been occurring in every area of the world. Yet, trees have the unique ability to store carbon, and (which) if we could simply keep them standing (and rooted in the ground), could help us (in a natural way) solve the growing problem of excessive carbon dioxide in the atmosphere. More than half of the prime timberland has been cut in Vancouver Island's formerly-pristine rain forest, and the rest could conceivably be gone within another 25 years or so. Meanwhile, financially-strapped Russia is expanding logging of their immense Siberian forests as one way to help their dismal economy. But, this practice is increasing soil erosion and sending large amounts of silt into fish-filled rivers, and in turn decreasing oxygen levels in the water. In Indonesia, the combination of logging, fires and coal mining have devastated so much forest area that it is unlikely that the forest will be able to regenerate itself. Ethiopia has stripped virtually all of its forests for firewood and farmland. But ironically, this act has allowed so much topsoil to wash away, that some of the land that was cleared for farming can no longer bear crops. Much of Madagascar's rain forests (known for thousands of plant and animal species that are not found anywhere else in the world), have been cut down to make room for farming and ranching, all to the detriment of these unique species. A final example of vast destruction of lands (although in this case not rain forests) would be the overgrazing of cattle and sheep in Australia. Consequently, that country's central arid zone is expanding toward the coast, which is aiding in the extinction of quite a few of that region's mammals.

Finally, something needs to be mentioned about the future, worldwide supplying of energy, in order to meet our expanding human needs. It has been projected that the amount of energy that the world will consume over the next 20 years, will equal all the energy that was consumed by humanity in its entire history. It has also been estimated that the yearly release of carbon dioxide into the atmosphere will triple by 2050 (from 6 billion tons to 20 billion tons per year).[6]

A large cause of this effect will stem from the expectation that huge numbers of people in underdeveloped countries will begin receiving electricity for the first time. This occurrence will be especially strong in China where the government is making a concerted effort to upgrade its population's standard of living. This is evident by China's decision to build a huge, hydroelectric dam on the Yangtze River. Ironically, such a project is ultimately going to displace about a million people and permanently flood over large areas of land, that could have been used for the growing of essential crops. Likewise, mass projects that are underway in India and Chile are expected to have similar effects in those countries as well.

Moreover, many more Chinese are going to be using automobiles (and their gas-combustible engines) to meet their transportation needs. Unfortunately, the two biggest causes of world air pollution are— electrical power generation and transportation—which are both run by fossil fuels. The former accounts for 43% of the total of human-induced carbon dioxide which is released into the atmosphere, while the latter is accountable for 24%.

Consequences of Adverse Environmental Change

There is one glaring statistical projection that dwarfs all others when discussing how environmental changes will affect us all over the next century. The *consensus* among many of the scientists who have been studying the "greenhouse effect" (through years of monitoring and studying computer simulations) is that the temperature on Earth could rise *as much as* 4 to 5 degrees Fahrenheit by the year 2100.[7] [It should be noted here that updated test data (which was prepared by hundreds of scientists for a 2001 report by the Intergovernmental Panel on Climate Change) confirm these experts' earlier scientific projections of such temperature increases by global warming through this century]. This rise is based on the assumption that there are no major changes (positive or negative) in the rate of human emission of greenhouse gases. But, even if the temperature were to increase only half of this projected figure, the environmental and human consequences would still be catastrophic. Because, although at first thought this amount of rise may seem modest, consider the fact that our planet has only warmed some 9 degrees since the last Ice Age, some 18,000 years ago. Taking this fact into account, needless to say, these are very disconcerting statistical projections.

Even though we are beginning to try to reverse this trend of emissions, the fact is that there will be more people from the ever-increasing, world population performing daily tasks that increase greenhouse gases. Thus, as fast as we try to decrease them, the fact that more people will be performing tasks that increase such emissions, will only lead to an overall neutralizing effect, at best. Therefore, in the future, it will be an ongoing challenge to continue any downward trend of overall emissions *in real quantities*.

Hence, if this anticipated temperature increase occurs, a mind-boggling scenario could be created, whereby the consequences would be cataclysmic. Rainfall patterns would be altered in location and concentration levels, flooding some lakes and rivers while drying up others. The warming of climate norms will push northward across the globe. Forests in certain regions will die because they will not be able to keep up with this "migration" of their climate range, that they have become historically accustomed to. For the most part, coastal areas will get more rain while country interiors will get drier from heat waves and droughts. Hurricanes with greater intensity will create even more havoc on coastal environs. Temperature increases at the poles will cause seawater levels to rise, potentially endangering the survival of island nations as well as coastal cities and wetlands preservation in larger countries.

This entire situation will be further aggravated by the depletive effect that is occurring in the atmospheric ozone layer, especially over the Antarctic, and which is contributing to the meltdown of its ice shelf. Moreover, it should be noted that the EPA predicts that the overall *worldwide* depletion of the ozone layer will be 10 to 12 percent by 2010, and as much as 20 percent by 2025.[8] The subsequent increase in ultraviolet radiation would cause fairly severe crop losses. It would also detrimentally affect the photosynthesis of plants (including plankton that all aquatic life depends on) in order to continue the living food chain for all species. Increased ultraviolet radiation will damage the human immune system, and will make us more susceptible to traditional and new infectious diseases.

Meanwhile, at the other pole, the Arctic, the projected estimates of a scientific study (regarding the meltdown of its ice shelf) were announced in November, 2002. The projections are so severe, (that upon hearing them) it literally could take one's breath away. The Arctic ice shelf is currently melting at the astounding rate of 10% for every decade. That being the case, the Arctic pole could be totally melted by 2100.

Finally, as I previously mentioned, the environment will cause disruptions in world economies (especially severe on agriculturally-dominant national economies). It is also going to significantly affect long-term public works' projects such as: hydroelectric power, irrigation, sewer systems, dams, land use, structural designs and energy planning. This fact is so, because the planning of all long-term civil engineering projects are "based on the false assumption that the climatic environment their ancestors have experienced for thousands of years will continue to exist fifty years from now...Present-day buildings, bridges, dams, roads, sewer systems, canals, and machinery of all kinds are designed for climatic stress tolerances that will no longer be applicable fifty to one hundred years from now."[9]

Furthermore, it should be stated that nearly all the *best* potential cropland in the world is already being cultivated. The lands that are left are not: sufficiently rained upon; easily irrigated; or easily cleared. Other areas of land are being lost to: erosion, loss of soil nutrients, acidification and salinization. These effects will only be made worse by the adverse environmental changes that are expected over the next many decades.

Another realization that must be considered is that a very small percentage (about 3%) of the Earth's water is fresh (and most of that in ice caps and glaciers). Water is unevenly and chronically short in many parts of the world, and the result is a major threat to many countries' crucial agriculture production. Moreover, as water supplies have become more limited, demand by the agricultural, industrial and residential sectors have increased. Thus, the competition between cities and rural farmlands will continue to intensify. But, where in the past, cities seemed to have the decided advantage in being allocated more than their fair share—in the future, the need to save croplands from irreversible erosion and drought will end up sending the pendulum in favor of the rural areas instead.

It is quite clear that as the supply of fertile land and irrigation water decrease, while the demand for both increase, the likely result will be an upward rise in grain prices and, subsequently, staple foods. Such a dilemma would eventually be a threat to the economic stability of many countries. Furthermore, if the problems were to become extensive (and not fully addressed), the potential would be high for political instability in at least some (if not many) nations, because obviously everyone must be able to afford basic foodstuffs in order to survive.

Another drawback of global warming and precipitation shifts will be the spreading of previously-limited tropical diseases (i.e., malaria, dengue fever, and yellow fever) to other areas of the world that would have little natural immunity to such diseases. Mosquitoes would carry such diseases especially to higher altitudes in tropical regions, which in the past had little occurrences of such diseases because of their cooler climate. Cities in the highlands that have large urban populations (e.g., Nairobi, Kenya) would be particularly susceptible. Also, drug-resistant disease strains could likely make the case scenario even worse than expected.

Extreme weather patterns, such as dry spells in wet areas or excessive rain or flooding in normally dry spots, can cause disease-carrying pests (e.g., rodents and insects) to flourish. For example, in 1993 a long drought that was followed by heavy rains produced a deadly outbreak of hantavirus in the American Southwest from the tremendous increase of deer mice in the area. In 1994 in India, a long monsoon followed by three consecutive months of heat and drought forced rats into cities, and an outbreak of pneumonic plague was a consequence in one city. Meanwhile, pollutants, ultraviolet radiation, and heat waves all tend to weaken our own human immune systems and, subsequently, our natural resistance to fighting diseases in general.

The increase in water temperatures of the oceans and seas will most likely expand and extend the range of cholera incidences and outbreaks. The cholera bacterium generally enters small marine animals, copepods. As waters warm, algae grow and proliferate as do the copepods, because of their plentiful food source. In turn, these events lead to an increase in cholera. This whole chain of events is exacerbated by humans, when we allow our nitrogen-rich sewage and agricultural fertilizers to be poured or trailed off into the seas.

Environmental change is bound to adversely affect the climate-sensitive habitats of many different species, and, consequently, present a threat to their continuing diversity. Habitats of species are also destroyed when we must alter lands for planting of crops and to expand our suburban sprawl. Some people may ask, "Why do we need all of these species?" Well, the diversity of life is crucial for our own survival, because it: interacts with the atmosphere to regulate climate; to help form soils; cleanses water pollution; and keeps harmful pathogens under control.

Finally, there have been troubling research findings that would suggest that what we are putting into the environment may cause endocrine hormone-disrupting problems in all species along the whole ecological chain (including humans). Before allowing chemicals to be thrown willy-nilly by industrial polluters all over the environment, federal regulatory agencies never thought of testing chemicals for hormone-disrupting effects. This fact could have very well been overlooked by pressure from lobbyists of chemical companies, in order that their products could be fast-tracked to market. Regardless of the reason, it is yet another example of companies being allowed to thrust "unknowns" into our environment before determining certainty of safety. I should point out here, that this is not a situation where, for example, a terminally-ill patient is willing to take a risk in trying some untested experimental drug. Rather, this is a short-sighted, conscious decision to expose an entirely healthy environment (with all kinds of healthy living species in it) to a significantly indeterminant, detrimental risk—all for the sake of expediency and "progress."

The findings of this endocrine-disrupter phenomenon have been brought to the fore mainly by Theo Colborn, a zoologist; Louis Guillette, a wildlife endocrinologist; and Michael Fry, an avian toxicologist. They have found that some chemical pollutants (e.g., pesticides, dioxins, and PCBs or polychlorinated biphenyls) can affect an animal's natural hormones by disrupting them (either by: (a) mimicking (b) blocking or (c) amplifying them). There is much concern because hormone systems are very sensitive, whereby secretions of small amounts into the bloodstream can cause dramatic changes in the body.

In Florida, Guillette has especially noted this effect in the sex hormones of animals such as, alligators and aquatic birds (because of the dumping of pollutants and pesticide runoff into lakes). Somehow this effect was exposing males to an overabundance of some kind of synthetic, estrogen compound or residue in the chemicals themselves, because their genitalia were significantly smaller.

Likewise, Colborn was finding a similar problem in the Great Lakes ecosystem. Bird predators (e.g., eagles) who ate fish in contaminated waters were either failing to reproduce or producing defective offspring. Therefore, the problems were not showing up in the adults who were exposed, but rather in their offspring. Consequently, something had to be happening at the embryonic or fetal level.

Finally, by referring to other studies that had been done by Michael Fry in the early 1980s, the most illusive part of the puzzle was found that would provide the complete answer to the problem. He had been able to replicate in his laboratory an anomaly that he had found with male gulls in DDT (pesticide)-contaminated areas along the California coast. He found some males were ignoring breeding colonies, and (through dissection) had become hermaphrodites. Under controlled laboratory conditions, he later replicated this effect by infusing clean gull eggs with DDT.

It is probably too early to project absolute conclusions on how all of these chemical pollutants are affecting humans, but the data collected so far is very concerning, if not convincing. But, the artificial estrogen, DES, which was prescribed for women as late as the 1960s, may be very telling. Just like the cases of the wildlife described above, this drug appeared to have little effect on the mothers who took it. "But when their daughters reached maturity, many suffered from infertility, had malformed reproductive tracts, or were afflicted with an otherwise exceedingly rare cancer…DES sons showed an increase rate of problems such as…testicular cancer, and reduced sperm counts…synthetic pollutants that virtually all of us now carry in our fatty tissues [and are not excreted] could explain, for instance, why rates of breast and testicular cancer have soared, and why male sperm counts in the industrialized world have plummeted by a startling 50 percent since the dawn of the 'chemical revolution' that began after World War II."[10]

There is an even more recent example, whereby chemical-effect "unknowns" were thrown directly into a healthy environment, and which were actually mandated by our asleep-at-the-wheel government in the Clean Air Act of 1990. To give us cleaner air, it was decided to reformulate gasoline by placing the additive MTBE (Methyl Tertiary Butyl Ether) into it. This decision was sanctioned even though there had virtually been no tests previously performed, in order to determine toxicity levels of this chemical in humans.

Almost a decade later, many wells and aquifers that are used for drinking water have had to be shut down, because of evidence of thousands of areas of contamination across the country. It would seem that many of the gasoline storage tanks have leaked directly into our underground water sources. The problem is further complicated by the fact that the chemical is very soluble in water, yet takes years for it to breakdown. Since nobody knows how to remove the chemical, a technology must now be devised to extract it out of the affected water supplies.

Once again, this is a perfect example of our government demonstrating no holistic foresight, but exhibiting plenty of "patchwork-style," post facto hindsight. In fact, there seems to be an ominous trend on our future horizon, and it focuses on the combination of two precarious elements: (1) Government and industry, throwing all caution to the winds, creating and then, in turn, having to deal with problems which should have never existed in the first place—because of their overinitiative and choosing a path wrought with a lack of reason. (2) A situation that is additionally aggravated and compounded by a significantly large group of overconfident technocrats constantly telling us: "Don't worry, we can come up with the technology to solve any problem that you (or even we) create."

How is it that we can make the same type of mistakes over and over again on so many fronts? Is it in the name of only corporate profits or is it something worse—like our government having a death wish for all of us? It is almost as if the country is on automatic pilot and nobody's at the helm!

Playing Environmental Politics

Even as global warming and other adverse environmental effects continue to occur, we find ourselves having to cleanup for our past environmental mistakes and short-sightedness. Even then, we only address these problems, simply because we are forced to by their obvious visibility. The sites that have received the most publicity are cleaned up in order to placate angry citizens, while less obvious ones are left to fester until nearby residents of those sites make a ruckus.

Thus, the government and industry continually give the public the mainly symbolic and false assurance that things aren't as bad as they seem, while conveying the pretense that all is well. I think that just about every area of the country has experienced this governmental attitude (firsthand at one time or another) regarding cleanup of hazardous wastes—refuse that should never have been disposed there to begin with, if the government would had been vigilant.

Let's take as an example the Superfund that has been allocated for addressing the cleanup of the worst, most critically-urgent sites. The government has designated 1300 sites to have Superfund status. The EPA has fully been cleaning up approximately 300 sites at the rate of about every 10 to 12 years. Unfortunately, it must be noted here that Superfund went bankrupt in March, 2002 with only 800 of the original 1300 sites cleaned up. Therefore, unless Congress continues to appropriate more money for it, the remaining sites (that still need to be cleaned up) will remain dormant.

An additional, disconcerting fact of the matter is that there are another 19,000 sites that the original preliminary assessment by the Environmental Protection Agency indicated "appeared serious" enough to probably be placed on the Superfund list. Thus, if all of these additional 19,000 sites were to be cleaned up under Superfund, the complete job would be finished between the years of 2630 and 2760 (if no more additional sites came on-line between now and then). What can be said about this astronomical number of years that it would take to complete the job?...The only thing one can say: "Keep on cleaning...just, keep on cleaning! And, when the job is completed, will someone tap on my gravestone?"

Moreover, Superfund is literally and figuratively a "bottomless pit" of spending. With so many sites to be cleaned up over such an extended period of time (as well as considering cost overruns), there is no way even the most knowledgeable person could accurately tell you how much it is going to ultimately cost. It is criminal that the regulatory agencies of the government allowed industries to get away with such willful, toxic dumping all of these years. It would have saved us all a tremendous amount of valuable time, money, and heartache.

Some skeptics may ask, "Why not let the toxic pools and barrels of hazardous waste just sit there?" Well, we can't, because the containers eventually rust and then rupture. Hence, the hazardous waste and toxic pools will increasingly enter the water aquifers underground (that many of us are dependent on for our drinking water) as well as seep up through the sewers and foundations of unsuspecting homeowners.

The battles of environmental politics are waged in other ways as well. Every time that the world's nations meet for an environmental conference, the battle lines are set. One of the major obstacles is that currently about 85% of all commercial energy comes from the burning of fossil fuels (i.e., coal, oil, and natural gas) which (as previously mentioned) produces carbon dioxide. Unfortunately, we are dependent on these environmentally-destructive forms of power energy for keeping the pace of all economic production and activity continuing throughout the world. Even though the industrialized countries are trying to get their legislatures to ratify a reduction in their emissions of greenhouse gases by 6 to 8 percent below what the levels were in 1990, this reduction is still not going to be enough to solve our global warming problems in the long-term. Moreover, the coal, oil and gas industries are going to fight any reduction in their markets (or alternatives to their markets, like electric cars), up to the very last moment whereby the world actually runs out of fossil fuels. They simply have too great of a financial self-interest at stake.

In another vein, the industrialized and developing countries are playing politics with each other. The former feel that if the latter don't have to meet similar reduction goals, that the industries in the developing countries will have unfair economic advantages in their production of goods and their ability to create larger numbers of additional jobs. This assertion is probably correct as well as relevant, because by 2030 the developing countries are expected to surpass the industrialized nations in greenhouse gas emissions.

On the other hand, the developing countries feel that they are being pressed to make unrealistic concessions that would stunt their own economic progression. Furthermore, they also feel that the industrialized countries biasly control which environmental issues should ultimately be considered important enough to be addressed by the entire world. For example, their own concerns about fresh-water supplies and the spread of deserts are outweighed by the industrialized nations' concerns over global warming and ozone depletion.

Likewise, the industrialized countries view the cutting down of tropical rain forests as a loss of tremendous biodiversity and a lost opportunity to absorb carbon dioxide to lower the phenomenon of global warming. The developing nations see their forests as potential farmland and as a fuel resource to be used and sold. They cannot understand why they should have limitations (or outright bans) on cutting their tropical rain forests, while the temperate-climate forests of the industrialized countries continue to be cut down and flattened.

Their point is well-taken, but nonetheless we have **Paradox #17**: The notion being, "If you do it, I'll do it." But, if neither of them will do it until the other does it—the end result is that (the larger) "It" doesn't get done...Excuse me for asking, but isn't this similar to the game that we all played in elementary school? Once again, instead of cooperating with each other, we are competing—so that we all end up suffering in the long-run.

By mainly seeing the environment as a relatively short-term economic resource (to be used as we humans see fit) is the epitome of man's abuse on himself. Not only that, but this philosophy becomes a double-edged sword—because we not only diminish critical resources, but (in the process) pollute our very own living environment. We have lost track of what the definition of "sustainable development" really is: "the use of natural, self-renewing resources (air, water, topsoil, trees, minerals) at a rate that does not exceed nature's ability to replenish and cleanse itself."[11]

Conversely, we like to think, that it is our destiny to be able to control Nature for the biggest possible benefits that we can reap for our own human agendas. "[Man] acts on the basis of his own laws, not within the framework of a broader ethic which includes all creation."[12] In our conceit, we believe that we can improve upon Nature's slow, meandering pace by using technologies that are alien to it. Just like everything else we do in this fast-paced world, we also think that we can somehow speed up Nature to meet our overextended human needs and wants—overextensions that we have unfortunately created through our own making. We are unwilling to accept the standard of Nature that has allowed it to develop over millions of years, while (at the same time, and rather contrarily) we see no problem in applying our own human standard to place a harsh rein on its endurance in a span of a mere couple hundred years.

Our economies see Nature in parts rather than in terms of "wholeness." We see the environment almost like something that can be perfectly manufactured whenever we need it, and which can virtually be plopped down—like an artificial backdrop on a Hollywood movie set—at any time or place. We can't seem to comprehend that it is really composed of living, synergetic entities that have important common interdependencies. We view each adverse environmental event as isolated, and we end up compartmentalizing each one separately…"an oil spill on the high seas, the discovery of a toxic waste dump near a schoolyard, infectious wastes washed up on the shore forcing the closing of summer beaches, a smog alert warning senior citizens not to venture outdoors for twenty-four hours."[13] We isolate each incident so that we may avoid having to seriously question the underlying motives or overriding assumptions that make up the belief system of the modern world. Even the "greenhouse effect" and ozone depletion are made to sound less dire than they are. For example, we rationalize away the expanding hole in the ozone layer over Antarctica by falsely assuring ourselves that it is at the bottom of the Earth, far away from populated areas. Any extrapolated meaning for the rest of the world is downplayed and not given much credence.

When we scoop out this or that resource (here and there) or burn down a rain forest in order to create (in the larger scheme of things) a relatively small area of farmland, an ecological effect is perpetuated upon the whole system. Andrew Schmookler states it quite appropriately: "At an accelerating rate, our civilization is breaking apart the network of interconnection and exchange on which all life on earth depends. In our Midas-like ignorance of the nature of life, we sate our lust for wealth while we erode the foundation of our existence. We forget that a creature that defeats its environment destroys itself. 'Winning against' is not part of the [natural] order of life. The idea that existence is a…war of elimination is itself an artifact of the diabolical processes that corrupt our thinking."[14]

We will finally cease with our madness, when we have disoriented Nature to such an extent, that we will be forced to stop—even though it most likely will be too late.

Chapter 8

THE OVERPOPULATION EFFECT

Increasing Populations vs. Limited Resources

In case that you haven't checked lately, there is no shortage of people on the face of our planet. In the table below, especially note the exponential increases in world population over the years that are designated.

Year	Populations (in billions)
1000	0.3
1700	0.6
1860	1.2
1950	2.5
2000	6.0
2050	9.0 (projected)

Source: United Nations' Department of Economic and Social Affairs, Population Division. (For statistics before 1950, see Wood, p. 160).

In the time span of 100 years from 1950 to 2050, the projected population is expected to increase by 260%. After 2050, the expectation is for a slowdown in growth, yet nonetheless still increasing. But, it is this crucial time frame up to 2050 (probably our last "window of opportunity" to positively change the course of history) that I am going to emphasize here—by discussing the potentially irreversible consequences that could blight our world from any such drastic increase in population.

Whether we humans can tightly pull the reins on this projected statistic, so that it doesn't happen in actuality, could very well determine the fate of the survival of humankind as we know it! We simply cannot allow the world's population to grow that amount in a mere 100 year time span, if we are at all concerned about the quality of life (or even life in general). Without dealing with overpopulation, we are merely "treading water" in regards to our long-term survival. All other problems that we try to solve would be similar to a dog trying to catch its own tail, and never quite succeeding at it.

Let's take a look at the consequences of such projected population increases. Obviously, environmental change would be much faster and more widespread and severe (even compared to today's standards). Scarcities of all sorts (especially food) could cause much social disorder and violence (e.g., riots and political coups) similar to what was seen in Indonesia in the Spring of 1998—which in comparative retrospect, will look like a mild disagreement.

Border skirmishes between nations would most likely erupt over rights to water resources. Countries could have enormous power simply because they have the ability to control downstream flow of water of an important river. For example, the large number of dams and irrigation systems that Turkey expects to complete on the Euphrates River, could drastically reduce the amount of water available to Syria, a very water-scarce country. Moreover, such a downstream nation could be especially vulnerable to upstream pollution, so that what water they do get would probably be much more contaminated.

Uneven, global environmental damage could increase the gap between rich and poor nations still further, ultimately ending in violent confrontations. Poorer countries out of necessity may demand a fairer share of the world's resources, while the richer nations use food and other resources as a "weapon" of clout in order to alter a neighboring nation's policies and wishes. Larger numbers of refugees from poorer countries could spill across borders demanding sustainable allotments of resources, while possibly disrupting and eroding relations with differing ethnic and religious groups. Also, conflict could very easily arise with countries that do not do their part or uphold regulations for environmental protection within their boundaries—causing other countries to have to absorb environmental costs for them.

China is a perfect example of a country expanding its economy full throttle in tandem with very little regard to the implications of its environmental degradation (whether it be land, water or air). Because of its huge population and rapid increase in economic progress, China could single-handedly affect environmental factors (e.g., climate change and ozone depletion) more than many of today's industrialized countries combined. In the next quarter century, its coal consumption could as much as triple. Most of the coal being burned is "unwashed," which even worsens the acid rain and global warming effects worldwide.

Although China has environmental laws, they simply aren't enforced because of bribery and "softening" the law/compliance for state-owned companies. Otherwise, many factories and state banks would probably go bankrupt, which would unemploy tens of millions of workers. Therefore, the Chinese Party is in a quandary. Thus, to keep its own legitimacy, the Party must keep the economic expansion going. On the other hand, it would seem that the people might go to the streets in protest, if their environment gets so intolerable that they don't have safe drinking water. "The government knows the environment needs protecting, but it fears the social consequences…it worries that doing the right thing environmentally could be political suicide."[1]

So, China publicly conveys to the world that they see any environmental issues thrust upon them as simply the world's way of wanting to limit China's economic development. In essence, the Chinese are saying to the world, "If our pollution concerns you so much, you'll have to pay for it" (knowing full well that the world cannot do anything about their attitude). They see their economic growth as crucial in maintaining political stability, and therefore they will always give that goal preference.

One thing that everyone in the world is going to have to be concerned about is fossil fuel energy consumption per person, and how that will affect the amounts of carbon dioxide and other greenhouse gases that will be released into the air. It would seem that the industrialized countries are going to have to financially bail out the developing countries on these costs for quite awhile, because the latter simply aren't rich enough to afford it. These costs could be very substantial as the developing countries industrialize and create wide-ranging electrification and transportation programs. For instance, private car ownership in China could go from the present few million to as high as 400 million in 50 years.[2] This projection doesn't even take into account the environmental costs from the massive development projects (e.g., roads) that China would have to first undergo in order to support such an increase.

Many people in poor, developing nations simply can't worry themselves about protecting the environment. Instead, they have to worry about such basic things as where their next meal is going to come from and how they can pay for it. They don't have any inhibitions about clear-cutting a rain forest for planting crops, while selling the wood for income or using some of it for themselves. Likewise, since they have to live in the here and now, they are not going to concern themselves with regulations that would limit the auto exhaust emissions on an older model car that they happen to drive. They are instead going to be concerned about how to keep the cost of driving it as low as possible, so that they can get to work more cheaply, and meanwhile use the savings to help feed their families.

In addition, the industrialized nations' appetite for energy resources has not lessened, so that literally "from every corner of the planet, nature's storehouse is being systematically raided to meet expanding consumption demands."[3] Our country's acquired dependency on oil over decades of use, has caused an inflexibility to any needed change of our economic and political policies, because of special interests and our support of oppressive regimes to attain that oil. The technology of hydrogen cell-powered or electric cars could have been made feasible years ago, if it weren't for the special financial interests of the oil and automobile companies to delay the practical reality of this technology as long as possible. Smaller and naturally-powered cars means less profits for original equipment manufacturers as well as for the aftermarket replacement parts industry, while the labor unions would never have tolerated the subsequent loss of jobs.

Our support of oppressive regimes to attain oil (and, in turn, negate any possibility of the implementation of alternative energy resources) is somewhat more complex. In order to meet our own insatiable appetite for crude oil, we have had to support nepotistic, authoritarian regimes in the Middle East. Our dilemma is that if we don't back such regimes (in order to bolster their economies), chances are great that fanatical, religious extremists would take over their governments—which would be weakened from a loss of incoming revenues from the sale of oil. In other words, in order to keep stable governments in the Middle East, so that their general populations won't become poor and, consequently, riot—as well as for the prevention of religious extremists to take power through anarchy—the U.S. must continue to purchase oil for the sake of international security. The dilemma is resolved by choosing the lesser of two evils. Meanwhile, any potential viability for the use of alternative energies (in order to power cars) is lost in the political process.

When we look at the overall relationship between increasing populations and the exploitation of resources, one thing is for sure—that we simply cannot continue to go at our current pace on both of these factors. Scarcities of critical resources used to appear on a relatively isolated basis. Now, because of our excessive use of our resources, scarcities are popping up on a much more interrelated level. "An agricultural region may, for example, be simultaneously stressed by degraded water and soil, greenhouse-induced changes in rainfall and increased ultraviolet radiation. [Thus,] the total impact of these interacting problems may be much greater than the sum of their separate impacts."[4]

Not only are scarcities developing more quickly, industrial societies (and increasingly developing ones) have gotten used to normal patterns of resource and consumption uses. These scarcities may be harder to address because we have become accustomed to such patterns which stem from our short-term, self-motivated interests. For example, Americans are buying so many large, gas-guzzling vehicles, that statistics for 2002 showed that the combined sales of minivans and SUVs surpassed automobile sales for the first time ever. Essentially, people are opposing the preservation of resources, because they would be forced to do it at the expense of compromising their expected lifestyle. Therefore, we have created and will have to tolerate much more unpredictability and unstableness within the many ecological systems that are so intricately interconnected. If we are going to have a "livable" future, we are going to have to raise our collective human consciousness, so that we can realize all species of life have intrinsic worth (not just one) and are necessarily interdependent.

"The market encourages us to be profligate heirs, counting only the costs of writing the checks and disregarding the value of the account from nature we are rapidly drawing down."[5] Stemming from the market's blindness, we consider everything expensive except Nature. As Wendell Berry writes, "Labor is expensive, time is expensive, money is expensive, but materials—the stuff of creation—are so cheap that we cannot afford to take care of them."[6] For example, when we buy produce in a grocery store, the true cost of a scarce resource (i.e., fresh water for growing it and which has been diverted from an original supply source) is hardly ever reflected in the price.

We are unwilling or unable to accept the facts—"of deserts spreading, of extinctions accelerating, of waters dying, of climate and atmosphere being transformed by careless human activity."[7] This situation can be compared to a pack of wolves wearing down its prey. No single attack kills the prey, but over time the prey's defense systems are worn down to the point of exhaustion and, ultimately, loses the struggle.

While animals have physical limits to their appetites, we humans have unrestrained appetites that can be far more destructive to Nature. For example, even in a country like Mongolia, increases in population have forced it to use the little fertile land (that they have), in order to create unrestrained profits which are needed for the care and well-being of the additional populace. You see, a main export of Mongolia is cashmere, which comes from the fleece of goats. In order to increase profits, the shepherds must increase their number of goats. In turn, these goats then ravish more and more pastureland (that they must eat in order to survive)—which, in turn, creates more useless desert lands, that ultimately cannot be used by either Man or animal.

As a final comparative example, it is noteworthy to point out that even lemmings (those furry, little creatures), unlike us humans, have an intrinsic sense to recognize a severe imbalance between the overpopulation of their species and their required resources. In order to bring this causal relationship back into balance in a particularly overpopulated area (and for the overall survival of the species) many of the group will go off on a mass migration, even though the fate of the vast majority of them is death along the way. In fact, it used to be thought that they would simply go to the edge of the nearest body of water and fling themselves in and purposely drown, but scientists today have found that this isn't the case.

Proliferation of Old and New Diseases

We've all heard the saying, "As long as you have your health, you don't need anything else." Well, if humans don't start changing their motivational and behavioral patterns, this assertion may never have more meaning. That's because, we are seeing resistant bacterial strains of diseases (that doctors thought they had under control) to antibiotics. Also, new diseases are emerging as humans enter previously uninhabitable areas (e.g., tropical rain forests) that have either been occasionally "infiltrated" by some people or totally cleared for all to live.

Some medical experts believe that we are headed down a path where "even minor infections could turn deadly for lack of effective treatment...[because] nearly every disease-causing bacteria known to medicine has developed resistance to at least one antibiotic."[8] A cholera epidemic in Rwanda killed 50,000 people because it involved a bacterial strain that was unresponsive to standard antibiotics. Until relief agencies were able to find an effective alternative medicine, the deadly disease had gotten a long head start. Furthermore, scientists are finding that many resistant bacteria have the ability to pass these resistant genes on to other bacterial species.

For instance, drug-resistant tuberculosis is becoming more common, because some patients do not take the drugs as prescribed. Because treatments often relieve symptoms within a few weeks, patients stop taking the prescribed doses too early because they feel better. By prematurely stopping treatment, the tuberculosis bacteria can mutate; become resistant; and then multiply rapidly. Therefore, any subsequent attack of the disease becomes much harder to treat, and over time the resistant strain may be transmitted to others.

There are other ways that resistant bacteria flourish. In some countries, antibiotics can be obtained over-the-counter. This occurrence allows people to either inappropriately fluctuate their own dosage or gives them the opportunity to take them for something that they shouldn't be taking it for. Another way is when farmers add antibiotics in feed so that their cattle can withstand infections and, therefore, grow larger. When humans eat the meat or drink the milk, the cattle's bacterial resistance to antibiotics may be passed onto our bodies' bacteria.

New, deadly diseases have emerged (and will continue to emerge) as long as we force man-made environmental changes on previously unchanged ecological systems in remote areas. It is not coincidental that diseases like AIDS and Ebola originated from the African rain forests. Whereas mammals (e.g., monkeys and baboons), who had their origins in the rain forests, have developed symbiotic immunities over thousands of years to many of the microbial life forms there, man has not. Therefore, monkeys, baboons, rodents, and insects (e.g., mosquitoes) act as hosts for these diseases, since they don't affect them. So, when humans make new inroads into untouched jungles in order to make room for their own overpopulation, it goes without saying that we are going to suffer the consequences.

Even when we build dams on rivers that wind through rain forests, there can often be an effect. Since the water table rises under such circumstances, this act encourages proliferating numbers of mosquitoes to breed, which in turn transmit diseases to us and even our sheep and cattle. So, the threat of new epidemic infections extend to other animals (as well as plants) that humans depend on for food. New viruses in plants can wipe out entire harvests, especially if the crops are grown outside their natural ecologies. In developing countries, where food is scarce and desperately needed, such a threat as blighted harvests has most severe consequences. Thus, it is most ironic that the very act of clearing the rain forests (in order to plant crops) may very well result in causing the actual decimation of the crops that are planted.

Finally, our seas play a vital role in the planet's ecological balance. Our own sewage, industrial waste, and fertilizer-runoff are creating cesspools especially near our shorelines. It is increasingly likely that potentially dangerous microbes are going to affect our food supplies there as well. We have already had sporadic out-breaks of food poisoning in people from the eating of contaminated shellfish.

It is clear that as we continue to abuse individual ecological systems and the overall environment, we are going to significantly increase the threat of our acquiring new, potentially-deadly diseases—types which we have no understanding as to the cause, let alone a cure. If a disease comes out of the rain forest that is communicable by the air that we breathe, a worldwide epidemic would spread like wildfire, because we live in such a mobile world. We were lucky that the Ebola virus had such a short incubation period and caused death quickly in the relatively unfortunate few who contracted it. Otherwise, the chance for spreading the contagion would had been catastrophic. One can only wonder when our luck will run out. But, the Ebola virus certainly made one thing clear. It underminded our "faith that humans have been liberated from the determinisms of nature and can master nature...[and that] such viruses subvert modern confidence that increased scientific understanding of nature will lead to human mastery over nature."[9]

The Biggest Paradox of All

We in America (especially since the end of World War II) have been conditioned to view ourselves (and the whole of society) in one way—that "the only real value can be 'more,' and growth in some quantity the only acceptable sign of progress or of doing well...[that] if everything is reduced to one number [e.g., GNP], [then] how we are doing can always somehow be added up [and compared]."[10] The fact that there could possibly be better alternatives in how we view ourselves, our society and the world in general have always been quickly and at times even disdainfully rejected. "And so we experience an imperative to grow. The word 'growth' becomes for us synonymous with the good...[and it becomes] very difficult for us to accept any idea of a limit to growth as implying something other than stagnation. Our emphasis on growth leads us to equate contentment with complacency."[11] Our motto becomes that bigger is really better—which in turn justifies our goal that, yes, we really can "have it all."

This philosophy of ever-increasing economic prosperity can succeed in the short-term. But, over the long-run, after you have added in the crucial factor of overpopulation (projected at about 600 million extra people each decade through the year, 2050), such prosperity simply cannot be maintained. In other words, we may be able to get away with it for a *relatively* long period of time—but, we will not have the capability to get away with it for an *indefinitely* long period of time. Indeed, it may well be a severe misperception of such monumental proportions, that it might literally doom us all!

Donald Wood in his book describes how we have looked at things with one-dimensional "tunnel vision," that lacks a true sense of direction:

"Our economic structures have been built...on the assumption that our planetary resources are inexhaustible. Every social enterprise, every political plan, every financial move has been predicated on the ideology that there would always be more—more territory to explore and conquer, more resources to mine and exploit, more trees to cut down, more land to plow, more room to build cities and industries, more products to manufacture and sell, more babies to clothe and feed...year after year.

[In actuality,] This push for economic growth and progress has been the root cause of many of our social and ecological problems...The exploitation of our natural resources, the resulting global pollution, and spiraling worldwide population pressures are all evidence of our dependence on continued linear growth and expansion—with little consideration of our responsibility for future generations."[12]

In effect, we are pursuing a course that will result in "mutating" (and eventually falsifying) one of the key axioms that economics has always been based on—that being, "the more the demand, the greater the supply." While we have always viewed this postulate as a positive thing, it becomes an aberration when the factors of overpopulation growth and environmental degradation are accommodated into the overall equation. That is, with ever-increasing supply in order to meet the demand of an ever-increasing world population, there is a point that is reached where such economic growth actually becomes detrimental to the "whole" (the world) and its "parts" (the participants involved, namely, us). In essence, "diminishing returns" for humanity's long-term survival.

This "mutation" of the norm leads us to **Paradox #18** (the biggest paradox of all): The more materially-productive that we become (which is the goal of virtually every nation), the more that we hasten the demise of the human species (and all other ones) as we know it. In other words, our excessive preoccupation and prioritization of economic growth is eventually going to severely test our own human survivability. We have overemphasized the social value of economic growth to such an extent, that we have lost perspective to the fact that economic survivability is merely "one part of the whole" within the larger reality of our overall survival. The only way unlimited economic growth would work is if we were a species of robotons (who only required a daily oiling of its valves), that had no dependency on obtaining sustenance from the Earth and its atmosphere for the species' very survival. This is the only possible set of circumstances, where we would not have to concern ourselves with whether we have enough space to live; air to breathe; or sufficient water to drink.

An example that the world has lost all sense of perspective and overall human purpose was once epitomized in the Japanese (although it could be applied to any industrialized country in the world) Matsushita (Panasonic) Company's anthem. Their motto conveyed a narrow-minded obsessiveness, and treated economic growth as if it were a living entity:

> "For the building of a new Japan
> Let's put our strength and minds together
> Doing our best to promote production
> Sending our goods to the people of the world
> Endlessly and continuously
> Like a water gushing from a fountain
> GROW INDUSTRY, Grow, Grow, Grow." [13]

This analogy of unlimited economic growth can be equated with the pathology of cancer, where there is a limitless destruction of healthy cells in regard to speed and number. That is, this "unlimited growth syndrome" can only lead to disaster. Therefore, the only conclusion that can be reached: The world is more concerned about its fleeting, short-term economic gain and progress than its long-term, ultimate human survival...How is that for logic?...This conclusion certainly begs our need to redefine the meaning of progress and what would be considered "positive human direction" for the 21st century.

If we are to succeed, it is incumbent upon us to correct the ever-expanding imbalances that are taking place regarding population and the international exploitation of Nature. It is truly baffling that even though the world has known for decades about the risks that we take with overpopulation and degradation of the environment, we continue to do both without hardly the least pause. Why? Because governments don't emphasize the critical need to address such issues. Rather, all countries seem more concerned about upgrading their weapons in order to fight each other—when our worst enemy could very well end up being the future wrath of Nature, that no amount of weaponry would be able to protect us against.

Furthermore, these imbalances will not be easy to resolve, because we have placed ourselves between a "rock and a hard spot." Keeping in mind the likelihood of the expected overpopulation problem over the next half century, here is our dilemma: If we muzzle economic growth in order to allow us to solve our dire environmental problems, tens (or even hundreds) of millions of people could lose their jobs worldwide. On the other hand, if we let unrestrained economic growth and environmental degradation to continue, we could literally be signing the death notices for future generations.

The immediacy of the time factor cannot be overstated, because we literally have our backs against the wall on these issues. Rather inauspiciously, we would probably need an entire generation of time in order to get our populations to "survivable" levels, while simultaneously allowing Nature to cleanse and redevelop itself again. We often say that we care about the future generations, yet we overspend (as well as waste) the very resources that should be destined for these future generations. In short, while we sincerely say one thing, we are subsequently turning right around and insincerely doing another.

The implementation of the correct solution is greatly aggravated by the fact that most countries' leaders, industries, and multinational corporations refuse to fully recognize that the world has limited resources, many of which we are using up quite rapidly. They don't accept the fact that Man and Nature measure progress differently. They turn away from acknowledging the intricately-woven interconnections between economies and ecologies—that for every action we take, there is a reaction by the environment. They only take into account the costs and benefits of "parts" (i.e., market systems), while the "larger whole" deteriorates. Thus, preference is given to the needs and wants of the "parts" at the expense of the "whole."

Once again, the common denominator for everything becomes mere numbers. "The environmental and human toll never shows up on the electronic boards of the international commodities exchanges, or in the neatly stacked rows of numbers printed out on the computer screens in Wall Street investment houses."[14] We never try to determine "Net" National Product compared to "Gross" National Product, because if we were to subtract our real losses (of resources lost from unrestrained economic growth) from our gains, we would not be able to keep our heads so high in the air.

It is disillusioning to see arrogant multinational corporations, run by arrogant CEOs, discount the severity of the environmental situation (e.g., ozone depletion, tearing down of the rain forests etc.), while they continue with "business as usual." They may declare themselves victors in many battles, but Nature always wins the ultimate war, 100% of the time GUARANTEED! One way or the other, we are always shown "that we cannot *afford* maximum profit or power with minimum responsibility"[15]—that the losses of the other participants within "the whole" invariably come back to afflict and haunt the winner.

With the modernization of the world, the reciprocal relationship that we once had with Nature has changed into sheer exploitation on our part. Yet, it is not our inherent human nature that has changed, but rather how the reality of modernization and unlimited economic growth has changed us as people and our view of the natural world.

For instance, we are even slowly beginning to see the signs whereby the administering of our National Parks is becoming a directly-related function of how much financial productivity we can eek out of them. In fact, there has been some talk of allowing corporate sponsors to "privatize" them via outlays of corporate money for their upkeep (a practice which I call the "corporatizing" of

America). Hence, it might not be too far fetched to visualize a time when you may have, for example, Disney's Yellowstone National Park. In such a case, the sponsoring corporation would not only try to recoup their financial outlay, but want to make a profit as well.

So, you could have a situation where visitors would very likely have to put up with the angst of having to view gigantic, helium-filled Mickey Mouse and Donald Duck balloon ears perched on successive mountaintops or peaks—as a subliminal reminder to purchase some "ears" at the concession stand for the kids (and maybe even a pair or two for yourselves as well) before exiting the park. Of course, such additions to a previously pristine landscape would detract from the original reason we came in the first place—the viewing of the park's natural beauty. But, the corporate claim which most likely would be made is—that's the price that we must pay to view **our own** country's National Parks.

We have come to view the world as "just an 'it,' [where] modern societies can treat even living [Nature and] animals as mere mechanisms. Chickens are rendered into egg-laying machines that never get to walk around or to peck the earth, and cows are reduced to four-legged factories for producing milk."[16] Every earthly embodiment becomes broken down into a commodity form. For example, we discount the replaceability of the raw materials that go into making a "marketable finished product," and in the process become uncaringly wasteful of them. Meanwhile, mountains are seen as having value only because there is gold in them, while beautiful, wide-trunk trees are seen merely as floor planks, shutters and picnic tables. Our woods and meadows are seen as simply zoned plots in order to build new suburbs, offices, factories, and retail malls.

When we view Nature as inanimate and destroy its aliveness, we all lose some of our own human qualities as well—because (after all) we are natural beings ourselves. The more that we tend to stray further and further away from our natural selves, the less is our ability to discern our inherently true selves. We have seemingly created ourselves in the image that the market chooses—beings infinitely wanting and craving for more—"consuming resources to satisfy momentary whims…[while] spending the capital of the biosphere."[17]

We have been taught "that greater consumption—material progress—would mean greater personal security. Instead we find ourselves more isolated and less secure—at war with the environment, at odds with our fellow human beings, and without an alternative approach to securing ourselves in the world."[18]

Is Imitation the Sincerest Form of Flattery?

So, contrary to all rational reason, we continue to persist with our addiction for unlimited economic growth and material success. Moreover, we have exported this concept to the world, so that now nearly everyone on the planet strives for such misguided expectations. And now, it is the developing countries that are on the doorstep for their pent-up share of material wants. As they have witnessed all of the material possessions that we have accumulated from our higher standard of living, they now insist on not being denied themselves. And, who can blame them.

We would be mere hypocrites if we were to pass judgment on them by using the philosophy: "Sorry, but the planet cannot afford to let you exploit the world's resources and pollute the biosphere to the same extent that we Americans [and, subsequently, the other industrialized nations] have over the past one hundred years; we have enjoyed an exceedingly comfortable standard of living, it's too bad that it isn't ecologically possible for you to do the same."[19] Thus, we are the ones that let the genie out of the bottle, and now it's very hard (if not impossible) to cajole him to get back in. To stop such a trend now, would be like constructing a papier maché wall across some railroad tracks in an attempt to stop a bullet train. Yet, stopping that trend is the very thing we must do, because our long-term survival depends on it.

In a world that is relatively sparsely populated (or which has small, incremental growth patterns), people's "wants" (or non-essential luxuries) can be attained and incorporated with virtually no detrimental effects on our overall, living systems. On the other hand, in an already densely populated or exponentially-expanding world (which we have today), such strivings ultimately can only lead to devastating consequences. Why? Because once these luxuries are available, we all *want* them. Subsequently, the overproductivity of these "wants" (in conjunction with continually increasing populations) simultaneously create extreme stress on keeping intact our correspondingly fragile, living environmental system.

So now, in many developing countries, the realization of economic growth and the attainment of consumer items that will make the lives of their populaces easier is now necessary just to maintain social and political stability. The U.S. has made personal wealth the standard, and now the developing countries' leaders must make good on their promises of higher standards of living for their peoples—or else suffer the consequences. Therefore, it will be increasingly difficult for leaders in such countries to keep growth and development within a confining enough level, which would take into account the consideration of consequential effects on the environment.

Hence, with the developing countries' firm conviction that they will not let this opportunity for unlimited growth go by the wayside, they are basically saying: "It's time we acquire 'our pound of flesh' (to the same degree that you have), even if it has to kill us all"...How do you like that for logic?...It substantiates what a professor at one of India's universities replied when asked, "What will happen when the overpopulated, undeveloped countries attain industrialization and commercialization?" His potentially telling comment was: "Then you can kiss the world goodbye."

By advocating productiveness and output as the "end of all ends" and equating power with whatever one wills to do, industrialized countries and multinational corporations have made the situation even worse. To get their economic growth up (and to keep competitive costs down), you are going to continue to see a lot of industries within developing countries forsake any degree of environmental protection. The companies that can produce the cheapest-priced products (via ecological irresponsible ways) will have the competitive advantage. They'll be able to get away with these antics because the open market simply does not see the environment as a cost of production. These countries will continue to send delegates to conferences on International Environmental Protection, but for the purpose of either watering down any agreement that would tie their hands (economically) or for voting down any such agreement outright.

Furthermore, these countries and their populations are going to be tolerant of putting up with the pollution found in the air, land, and water—if it is going to translate into more jobs, better pay, and nationalistic progress. For countries like China, "newfound wealth has only whetted its citizens' appetite for more. China's huge population wants to join the global middle class, with everything that entails: cars, air conditioners, closets full of clothes, jet travel."[20]

While the Chinese government has continued to downplay environmental issues, their own people (for many years) have strongly resisted the government's policy for families to have only one child. Even as far back as 1984, China's authorities have been forced to retreat from enforcing this official policy especially in rural China (where about 70 to 75% of the population lives), because of attacks and incidents of social unrest by the peasant farmers. These people see larger families as extra labor to increase family income and as old-age insurance. Also, as the Chinese in general increase their standard of living, the people will see even less reason for the need to have such restrictions. It would seem that the false Maoist notion (that more and more people is a beneficial, nationalistic resource) was allowed to continue too long for the good of their nation and the world.

Finally, one cannot overestimate the goal of multinational corporations to make governmental authority subservient to the interests of them. One could even say that governments have become merely cheerleaders for corporate interests, always taking the role of eternal optimists, in order to maintain citizens' unrealistic hopes for ever-increasing prosperity. This fact will increasingly become a major problem for attaining any future balance in the world's priorities. Multinational corporations are slowly taking control over the world's affairs and are subordinating nations' and citizens' concerns. Corporate interests and their encouragement of greed are what takes center stage in the world today, and they more or less dictate the domestic and foreign policies of an ever-greater number of individual nations. In fact, any particular individual or group would probably have a better chance of getting beamed up by space aliens—than actually convincing any government (or overall society in general) that there are hidden dangers to our overmaterialism, and that we, therefore, must begin reversing course.

With more national interests being based on corporate interests, more and more people in the world are mistakenly beginning to equate prosperity with overall quality of life. But, such a short-sighted view will not sustain us in the long-run, and we will be faced with complex problems regarding life's issues, and even survival itself. It would seem that the entire world "represents the first large-scale attempt to found stability and authority...directly on the achievement of economic production and the satisfaction of needs...[that] the well-being of every individual is thought to be identical with the steady rise of the Gross National Product...The principle of legitimacy for modern society...now consists in a permanently rising level of consumption."[21]

It is unfortunate that the entire world is being sucked into the misguided vacuum—that the desire for more and the attainment of more is better. By actualizing this philosophy, the world is raising the potential for disaster several notches. It wants "to achieve godlike powers without the corresponding godlike wisdom and virtue."[22] It has come to view unlimited economic growth, exploitation, and consumption as a game of "one upmanship," when the sad reality is that it is not a game at all, but one of survival of the human species. We have all bought into the notion that we are the masters of material consumption, rather than the servants. Consequently, our priorities, values, and collective purpose have all taken a turn for the worst. In turn, we will only become more alienated from ourselves, others, and our natural world around us.

Our Lost Sense of Who We Are

We have let unrestrained economic growth and consumption get so far out-of-hand, that we no longer know when to restrain or deny ourselves. We can no longer properly judge when "how much is too much" or where to stop with our self-gratification and indulgence. Yet, it has become (and will continue to be) a growing epidemic throughout the world, because it is the basis of what we are told is considered "progress." In turn, we lose sight of the proper proportional scale between "progress" and our natural selves; our human goals; and our sense of who we really are or want to be. That is, we must emphasize more what we are able to humanly become, without it being within the context of what is good for economic growth and progress.

Our industrial and personal overuse of our resources is not mainly because of the prerogative we so often cite, that being, the euphemistic "free-enterprise" motive. Instead, it is out of our desperation to quickly beat out others (whether it be individuals, nations or other species) for the limited resources, in order to satisfy our own out-of-control, gluttonous self-interests. Therefore, self-serving, individual rights are given more preference than socially responsible rights. In so doing, we have all collectively lost sight of the "whole." Humans feel it is their "right" to control Nature, while at the same time they see no hypocrisy in their refusal to place any limit on their "own nature." Our inordinate infatuation with materialism does not allow us to consider what things truly are valuable, and how fortunate we are to have the things that really do matter within our grasp. People call some luxury, material items priceless. Yet, in the larger scheme of things, these are not priceless. A real example of a priceless item would be when your ship has sunk and you are treading seawater (while desperately trying to stay afloat)—and you agonizingly see one last life preserver floating farther and farther away from you. Now, that is what you call a truly priceless item!

Life in a society that gives an overly high priority to consumption is really about images (which are actually false ones) that you convey to yourself and others. The high-priced items that you buy are supposed to say a lot about you as well as define your identity. But, this practice doesn't really say anything about you in any larger (or "higher") sense, and it results in discouraging you from finding your true identity through self-development and authenticity. We then become dominated by image, while we become estranged from our natural selves. If an individual uses only "appetites, desires, and tastes [as criteria]...A sense of self has to be sought in the parade of images and products; [then in this context] this [type of] culture becomes the main determinant [for one's] morality, beliefs, and purpose."[23]

"We have always been collectors, but it is only in the modern era that our objects have come to possess us...Isolated from others, we surround ourselves with things. They become a surrogate, engaging our time and attention, love and affection, as if they were sentient and capable of responding in some meaningful way to our inner-most needs to communicate and share ourselves."[24] Furthermore, such things can exploit our vulnerabilities. Like an abuse addict, we can literally get "hooked" on an item or (if we should tire of it) may need to obtain newer items in order to continue and reach that same level of "high." But, such addiction is hopeless because it continually directs us away from whom we really are. Moreover, it erodes our contentment and inherent worth as human beings, and subsequently diminishes our capacity to fully participate in life itself.

In our rush to acquire our new "modern attitude," we have lost all sense of values and appreciation for the natural, real world. We have made human nature today a function of economics, not anthropology. For example, we do not care how we have depleted Nature to satisfy our thirst for energy—as long as our cars start; we get light when we turn on a switch; and our homes are always well-heated. As long as modern man continues to excessively use Nature for personal consumption purposes, the less chance he will have of attaining the inner security that he so desperately searches for. "With intricate order an essential characteristic of life, 'anything goes' just does not work in a living system…So long as power flows from the outside in, human life is turned inside out. The systems surrounding us encage the nature within us."[25] We have simply lost our "natural mindset" and replaced it with chaos—whether it be endless commercial messages rattling in our ears or a plethora of attention-getting, retail store signs blinding our eyes.

Donald Wood describes how a society can become unwittingly complacent: "As institutions and people become set in their ways, it becomes more difficult to jolt them into needed change…[resulting in] the unwillingness to consider needed modifications and alterations, an unswerving dedication to maintenance and continuation of the status quo…Our whole economy is driven by a development/growth syndrome that impels us forward with its own money-making institutional momentum [IM]. Materialism has dulled our sensitivities; greed has weakened our sense of community; consumerism has overshadowed our spiritual values. And establishmentism robs us of the ability to challenge the materialistic ethic we have adopted."[26] Unfortunately, even if we started today, it would probably take us a couple of decades (which could very well be too late) to completely wean ourselves away from our ravenous, overmaterialistic natures. It would be similar to someone slowly and painfully freeing oneself from some type of drug addiction.

By overzealously embracing unlimited growth and consumerism, we have become intellectually and emotionally bankrupt. Through exploitation and the corresponding suffering of others, our own egocentricities, and the lack of continuity with all of Nature—we have made ourselves aliens on our own Earth.

Choices And Priorities Determine Our Destiny

Humankind is approaching a critical crossroads, and while there are some nations' leaders reticently acknowledging this fact, you see virtually no nations' governing bodies doing anything practical about the situation—and in most instances denying the severity of any such problem. In this last section, I am going to discuss the consequences that we may all expect, if we do not change our thinking and behavioral patterns regarding the universal abuses that the world perpetuates upon itself. I am also going to note how negative trends (that are now occurring) must be addressed in order for us to have any chance of living in a survivable world.

We still have a "window of opportunity" to turn these trends around, but it is closing ever so rapidly. If we are willing to recognize the signs, the impact that we receive might be able to be withstood. But, if we go on with "business as usual" and are unwilling to recognize the signs, the impact will be like a car full of passengers that is speeding out-of-control as it's heading toward a brick wall (i.e., your fate is upon you faster than you can react). If we wait until the nations of the world really feel the full strength of the pain, it will most likely be too late to do anything about it.

For the sake of all humanity, governments and multinational corporations will hopefully have the will to overcome their short-term interests, in order that they can acquire the needed foresight to prepare us for dealing with the circumstances—before they become direly forbidding problems. But, there are two reasons why this philosophical change will be hard to actualize: (1) because of the inherent, resistant natures of such institutions to change (2) unfortunately, the public has rarely pressed to the forefront an issue (and the solving of that issue), whereby it (itself) must make sacrifices. It has always been people's natures to require that they first see at least some negative consequences of their inaction (and which directly affect them), before agreeing to any such change. That's the very reason why the inherency of this particular problem is so insiduous. One thing is for sure though, we will all have to do our part and make sacrifices, if we are to fully solve this huge, approaching monster of a problem.

As we have seen, humanity's unending assaults upon Nature and the environment, as well as its arrogant attitude that it can control the totality of Nature (for the purpose of fulfilling humanity's own needs and purposes) is a central issue. Humanity incorrectly perceives that it can become the manager (in essence, itself a Higher Being) of its living environment—and subsequently, its own evolution. This delusional schizophrenia of visualizing humanity as an immortal Supreme Being (in which it sees no scenario of any negative consequences coming back to haunt it) is an irrational misperception, and will ultimately be its undoing.

So, let's go over the trends and most likely consequences. Again, keep in mind that every single one of these trends is currently going in the *wrong* direction (if you are considering the criteria of the long-term sustainability and survivability of the human species).

(1) The misperception that technology can get humanity out of any hole that it digs for itself.

There is no certainty that our technical ingenuity can overcome, for example, food scarcities, especially to the degree that it most probably would be needed, if we continue with the rate of our environmental degradation. "Moreover, scientific and technical knowledge must be built incrementally—layer upon layer—and its diffusion into the broader society often takes decades."[27] We are certainly placing "all of our eggs in one basket," if we think that we can do whatever we choose to do to the natural world, while anticipating that technology can correct all of our misdeeds.

For instance, genetic engineers have "designed" fish that can grow four to six times as fast as the natural fish that we are used to eating.

But, do we really want to risk the ingesting of such questionably-safe, genetically-engineered fish on a regular basis? Moreover, one could question how far are we going to take this process of bioengineering, in order to meet our food needs in the future? Will we go as far as redesigning creatures—with our only priority being the efficiency and practically of preparing and ingesting it?

For example, might we take what formerly was a chicken and make it into what simply would be known as a "chickwich?" A new entity simply defined as some living, amorphous-type creature whose wings, feathers and legs (have now been considered rudimentary for its new function, and therefore) have been scientifically, bioengineered "out." On the other hand, whole wheat grains (that would grow into sandwich slices) might be bioengineered "in" between equally-proportional segments of only the juiciest, most succulent layers of chicken breast. One thing is for sure, it would certainly bring a whole new meaning to the term, "pre-prepared chicken sandwich."

Finally, I would like to bring up something that I alluded to in the previous chapter—the chemical-effect "unknowns" of adding MTBE to gasoline—and demonstrate through comparison how the unknown effects of bioengineered corn and potatoes may be just as potentially risky. In both cases, sufficient safety tests and subsequent guidelines have not been provided before allowing each one to come into the marketplace. But, there is one major difference in the two scenarios. In the former one (MTBE), this dangerous substance was going only into the ground, and eventually (over time) reaching into water supplies. In the latter case (i.e., the bioengineered corn and potatoes), potentially-precarious food products are going directly into our bodily systems, without any substantial safety tests of the efficacy of ingesting such substances.

But even if bioengineered foods were found to be safe in and of themselves, it would still be conclusively-indeterminant as to whether it was safe to ingest, for example, boiled corn or heated potatoes that had been bioengineered. An additional question would then be created. Whether any harmful effects would be directly correlated to heating them at different temperatures and for different lengths of time? Altering genes is one thing, but altering genes and applying a heat source to those altered genes opens up even further damaging possibilities. For instance, recent research demonstrated that the heating process of roasting *natural* peanuts causes a substantial increase in allergens. In turn, the ingesting of such peanuts by allergic people can be dangerous. Keep in mind that these research findings were for non-bioengineered-type peanuts.

As a comparative example, most people prepare corn by boiling/microwaving it or apply high heat in preparing potatoes. It is a fact that the application of heat can affect the physical (property) natures of compounds as well as living organisms. Do we really know with certainty whether any properties are being harmfully changed in these foods, when heating processes are applied to such altered, bioengineered food?

Food companies and bioengineering firms have been genetically-altering more and more types of food, without the public's knowledge or consent. So, even if we wanted to choose the more natural way, it would be too late to remove such modifications out of our food. In fact, after considering everything that has been said in this book, one could state that we are slowly becoming a society in which individuals don't have the freedom to choose how (and in which ways) they want their lives to be affected (e.g., bioengineered food, persistent overdevelopment of our living space, administered health care through HMOs etc.).

Moreover, now we are even splicing and cross-breeding genes across totally different lines of species (known as transgenism). For example, we may cross the genes of an insect, plant and/or animal, which (at least currently) may have unknown consequences. Whenever I hear something like this being done, I immediately visualize those bizarre creatures that were depicted in those bad science-fiction, B-movies from the 1950s. I'm sorry, but I can't get out of my head seeing some creature walking around with the body of a man and the head of a fly. Is this a possibility of what could be in store for us? Are such bioengineering firms placing the cart before the horse when they say, "Let the efficacy tests for safety of transgenic cross-breeding eventually catch up with the production and its abundant dissemination?"

But getting back to my original point, being that if we ever reached the point that we would have to depend on bioengineered foods, consider the possible reasons why. It would be because either

(a) extreme depletion of soil and water had left virtually drip-dry prairies or (b) continually-flooded farmlands had been caused by all of the radical climate changes that we had forced onto the environment. If such biotech food is the wave of the future, because of such climate changes, must not one have to question whether the corresponding implications of how we would actually be living, be worthwhile?

So, in some areas of the country, you would have families in their habitats "forking down" bioengineered food, as their roofs were blowing off from the tremendous Dust Bowl windstorms that they were experiencing (similar to what happened during the Great Depression). While in other areas of the country, with floodwaters ceaselessly rising, you would have families "chowing down" while they sat on their rooftops—as a television newsmagazine reporter was rowing out to exclusively interview them.

(2) The technology revolution (although seen as favorable progress for humanity) will actually end up triggering incalculable millions more human workers worldwide to be unemployed, and in turn cause serious social repercussions (that we will call *Paradox #19*). This dilemma is the classic case of an anomaly (whereby a highly-technological world crosses paths simultaneously with an overpopulating one). The outcome is an ominous contradiction of two directional courses, whereby the solving of one problem actually only creates another.

A perfect example would be how farmers (worldwide) would be affected, if bioengineered foods become a common reality? With the advent of biotechnologists growing food that use tissue culture techniques, all purposes for farmers in the planting, cultivating, and harvesting of crops would be eliminated. For instance, biotechnology companies have developed a process to produce vanilla extract through the use of tissue cultures. As many as 100,000 farmers, whose livelihood depends on the vanilla plant would have to find another way to make a living. Keep in mind, most of these farmers are in developing countries where agriculture dominates the economies. Therefore, many of these people have nothing else to fall back on but agriculture, because there is simply nothing else.

Meanwhile, the biotech companies (which acquire the patents on the genetic compositions of the tissue cultures) will get away like bandits. They not only will get rid of all of their competition (the farmers) in one fall swoop, but they won't have to compensate any of the countries for the commercially viable genetic compositions. These cultures will be able to be reproduced over and over again at a lower cost than any farmer could *naturally* produce it. When you take into account, that every crop grown has the potential to be genetically-engineered, the result is that hundreds of millions of farmers could possibly lose their livelihoods.

The technology revolution could displace workers in many types of job categories. Genetically-engineered trees could uproot the timber industry, because they could underprice any timber that is produced via the "extractive" forestry method. Ironically, drilling technology could make natural geothermal energy more feasible, but at the loss of jobs and profits. You could be assured that the oil and coal industries would not stand idly by to see a natural form of energy cut into their profitable, fossil energy-producing bases. In addition, technological improvements that extend the "practical life" of products (such as cars) would save the consumer on replacement costs, but in this particular case, would cut auto industry jobs and wages. Finally, as we talked about in Chapter 2, computers and other digital technologies will displace an ever-increasing number of higher-paying, mental-task-related jobs. Companies' philosophy of profit conservation—that is, getting more productivity for less cost through the implementation of these technologies—will always result in the loss of jobs in order to protect the bottom line. A perfect example of this reality was the West Coast longshoremen strike of 2002. These workers literally put the entire U.S. economy on hold by refusing to unload shipping containers coming in on arriving ships. They were unwilling to accept the fact that the shipping companies wanted to use the latest automated, technological systems for the removal of cargo—and, in turn, displace many of the workers' jobs. In sum, all of the above examples are a portrayal of the classic signs of our future dilemma. Whether we choose to think more in terms of short-term, individual, self-serving benefits (especially in regard to jobs and profits)—or rather, overall long-term, societal benefits?

When one adds up all of these higher-paying types of job losses worldwide, significant fluctuations in unemployment and standards of living among populaces could result in substantial bitterness and violence. Such widespread occurrences would symbolize a historic crossroad. "The new technologies are bringing us into an era of near workerless production at the very moment in world history when population is surging to unprecedented levels. The clash between rising population pressures and falling job opportunities [particularly worldwide, but less so in the U.S.] will shape the geopolitics of the emerging high-tech global economy well into [this 21st] century."[28] The triad combination of technological implementation, multi-nationalism, and overpopulation will strongly test the world's ability to remain civilized.

(3) As the developing nations industrialize, there already are the beginning signs that they are going to wrongly differentiate "wants" as "needs," just like the industrialized countries have done all of these years.

As long as we evidently have chosen the imprudent path to increase our populations, we are going to have to reduce these "wants." We all are going to have to find a "balance" in our determination of just how important our material possessions should be to us. "To find this balance in our everyday lives requires that we understand the difference between our personal 'needs' and our 'wants.' Needs are those things that are essential to our survival and our growth. Wants are those things that are extra—that gratify our psychological desires. For example, we *need* shelter in order to survive. We may *want* a huge house with many extra rooms that are seldom used…We *need* functional clothing. We may *want* frequent changes in clothing style to reflect the latest fashion."[29]

We must enlighten our behavior in order that we (at least) alleviate our addiction for material "wants" (both individual and societal). This obsessive and abusive drive will need to eventually be replaced by sharing of more goods and resources instead of possessing them. The U.S. already gobbles up a hugely disproportionate percentage of the world's resources for its relatively small segment of the overall world population. This fact has created venomous anger and bitterness among the less fortunate populaces in poorer countries. They cannot understand why we must flaunt our material excesses to the rest of the world, when many of them don't even have the rudimentary or basic elements to even survive. Therefore, in order to avoid worldwide strife in the future, our motto will most likely have to become: "Live simply so that others can simply live."

But, this change will be difficult because of **Paradox #20**: The goal of corporations is to sell the greatest number of goods to the greatest number of consumers, so as to make the greatest amount of profits. Since their advertising and pushing of goods feed people's material addictions, then obviously these realities become contradictory—if our necessary goal is to try to lessen our extrication of the world's limited resources. One could assert that corporations compulsively feed on Nature and the human spirit at the same time, in order to maximize their own gain. Finally, and rather ironically, as we have seen in examples throughout this book, that as highly as we value inanimate objects, we live our actual lives as if they were very cheap (i.e., abusing ourselves and others).

(4) Overcompetition among individuals, peoples, nations and corporations are creating too much resistance for our very survival.

Overcompetition at so many different levels creates additional unneeded stresses and abuses. In turn, such conditions make it that much harder to promote situations of cohesion—citizen to citizen as well as human to human. This cohesion will continue to breakdown even further as increasing numbers of people simply attempt to survive from day to day.

Meanwhile, competition for the world's limited resources are creating a "country vs. the world" type of mentality for most nations. This concept is still seen as the norm and shows no sign of abating. If such attitudes continue in the future, the chances of major wars occurring will increase because of each nation's need to possess crucial (yet dwindling) resources for their respective populaces. Unfortunately, cooperation is still seen as something that must be forced on the actual behavior patterns of governments—rather than naturally occurring out of common interests and concerns for each other's well-being.

Finally, the reality of today's global marketplace (i.e., the constant tug-of-war of each nation pushing for the sale of its own respective exports) is going to guarantee (in the not-so-distant future) that no prolonged boom will be able to be expected in any one economy. Continual economic uncertainty will be the norm, where you will find each nation doing whatever it takes to save its own workers' jobs at the expense of other countries' workers. Since the competition will be so intense, more significant up and down cycles will be characteristic of all economies, and countries will be exposed to longer recession cycles than would be expected from historic norms. Correspondingly, the continual and ever-widening fluctuations and differing strengths of each nation's currency, in turn, will negatively affect each country's ability to purchase others' exports.

This situation was most recently evident in Argentina. In this case, the strength of the U.S. dollar had weakened Argentina's currency (the peso) to such a degree, that it had made its exports too expensive for other countries to buy. Accordingly, Argentina's unemployment dramatically increased to unprecedented numbers. In turn, with a much reduced revenue tax base, Argentina decided to default on $140 billion in debt that it owed to other countries. Correspondingly, this realization has caused Argentinians to riot and attempt runs on banks to salvage what they can of their savings and assets—which have been rapidly shrinking because of both the weak peso and the defaulting on the debt.

(5) Religious and national leaders are still either promoting (or at least remaining silent on) the proliferation of world populations.

All such leaders must not only advocate birth control and family planning, but they must also make it a reality by using their religious or political powers and persuasions. They must come to realize that we do not live in Biblical times—where resources were bountiful and the population sparse. Rather, we are living in an age of limited resources, limited space, limited food, and limited jobs that people can survive on! For the survival of the human species, we cannot have it both ways. It seems as if we have forever been told to propagate and prosper to our heart's content, to the point, that now the world has itself a real problem.

We must all do everything that we can to put a hard check on the world's overpopulation problem. Otherwise, all the work that we do is simply "treading water" or patching symptoms (rather than solving root causes). If we choose not to lower our birth rates, Nature will automatically reduce our populations for us in more ugly ways (i.e., through war, famine and disease).

We must also consider what overcrowding does to our individual and collective psychology. People have a tendency to get angry and abusive more easily when they feel that they don't have their "space." They become despairing, cynical, and violent (e.g., ethnic confrontations and wars). Furthermore, our good natures change for the worst when forming an opinion in regards to the "potential and comparable goodness" of our fellow man. We see other nations as competitors—rather than as encompassing citizens of the same species which have more commonalities with each other than differences. We've never fully realized that the only way to make a better world for ourselves—is to work with one another, rather than against one another. "When we meet a stranger on the road today, we react with suspicion, not charity. When a country sees millions of strangers building up on the other side of its national border, it reacts with hostility, not compassion. The correlation between our increasingly crowded planet and our increasingly ill-tempered public disposition cannot be ignored."[30]

We must internally acknowledge the absolute futility of war and stop the lunacy of fighting with each other, both individually and collectively. Because, we are going to need everyone in order to overcome the approaching, monumental struggle that lays ahead for the survival of humankind...It sounds odd doesn't it—the fact that we must stop fighting with each other (because after all, we humans have been fighting each other for so many centuries). In fact, so much so that if we actually were to subsist from fighting with each other, it would feel very strange to us, indeed! We simply would not know how to react. Actually, in many cases, if we took pause to think, I doubt if we would be able to collectively even remember what the original reason or cause (other than strict, unbending hatred) was which instigated the fighting in each specific instance in the first place.

In fact, humans are the only species which fights (without any individual provocation) specifically for the express purpose of destroying other members of its own species (excluding incidental conflicts that arise among all species). Rarely, will other species fight to the death with another member of its own species and, even then, unlike humans, it is not a consciously calculated or conniving effort to eradicate or destroy the other for no conceivably good reason. Where death does occur, it happens as an unfortunate consequence of the heat of the battle (rather than as an intended goal in and of itself). Conversely, the overcompetitiveness of the human species has mentally created in all of us the view that our very own fellow humans are the enemy and, therefore, must be annihilated. Succinctly, unlike other species, we humans have repeatedly demonstrated that we simply cannot comprehend the concept of being kind and peaceful with each other for the betterment of us all.

(6) How and who determines the economic and political power structures throughout the world is negatively affecting us all.

In such cases, populaces are pacified into feeling a false sense of complacency, while the narrow self-interests of the powerful are furthered. In his book, *Illusions of Choice*, Andrew Schmookler's insight is right on target:

…"of all the cultural options apparently available to civilized humankind, only those ways of organizing society that confer sufficient power [seem to] survive. All other options—however harmonious they may be with human needs or with the biosphere—if they make a society vulnerable to predation from surrounding societies, are ultimately swept away.

In addition,…ideas often become prominent, not so much in proportion to their intrinsic merits but in proportion to the wealth of the interests [that] the ideas serve…

It seems that the people who talk about a glorious future of technological marvels are the same ones whose way of conducting business shows little regard for the future…

…It seems that many of the same people who say we cannot limit 'growth,' lest we consign the poor of the world to their impoverishment, forget their concern for the poor in other contexts, where helping the poor runs counter to increasing their own wealth...

[It would seem that]...Our values shape our society, and we therefore get the society we choose. At the same time, our society shapes our values, and it therefore gets the people it chooses."[31]

So, one might say that when it is "all said and done," it gets back to values and priorities. It is noteworthy to mention, that after World War II, the United States could have promoted any value system onto the world. With no inner restraints, we pushed the "more of everything is better" policy full bore. It became a standard for us and for much of the world. Now, the developing countries of today want to bite on it—"hook, line and sinker" too, and it still doesn't seem that anybody has any second thoughts about it. Even though we should see that it is now a short-sighted view, we still unhesitatingly equate progress with unlimited growth and consumption without any reservations.

Both the political and economic leaders still don't (and evidently won't ever) get "it." Without any accountability to the rest of the world, they want to make millions upon millions, and even billions upon billions of dollars. They will go to any extent to accommodate their desires, yet they have no understanding of the larger scheme of things (i.e., human survival, including their own). This is abuse of the most far-reaching kind, because it avoids reasoning about the critical issues of human existence, while lacking any true commitment to the common good. These are the type of people, that if they were handed a lit stick of dynamite, would view it as merely a lit candle in celebration of yet another prosperous year of good fortune and sheer, indescribable magnificence.

So, our approaches to our well-being (as well as to our social problems) continue to be piecemeal and unconnected. In fact, the retention of our very jobs (many of which already exhibit duties that are simply unnecessary and overly redundant) are dependent on continuing to process and solve our society's woes by piecemeal, short-term solutions (rather than holistic, alternative ones). Emphasis is given to special interests rather than collective interests that would enable us to cultivate compromise and cooperation. Meanwhile, underlying causes are not addressed and, therefore, any partial remedies that are offered don't have much effect (or even worse, contribute to the problems themselves). By never taking a holistic approach, the status quo of limited interests is maintained.

Unfortunately, because of the reality of the world today, all six of these trends, which have just been discussed here, will most likely continue in the wrong direction (as opposed to the direction that they all should be headed).

As a civilization, we are going down a very precarious road—one that has many more dangerous pitfalls than would appear on the surface. "If we are not successful in rethinking our priorities, modifying our political and technological and economic attitudes, and adopting a more reasonable and responsible approach to problem-solving and decision-making, we may not be able to sustain our [selves]."[32] Our priorities need to be re-evaluated, because what we do over the first quarter of the 21st century will be crucial. The choices that we make will affect the fates of future generations (possibly for centuries), and, therefore, we cannot afford to make the wrong decisions.

For instance, we fire off rockets into space in order to categorically verify that other planets have water on them, while our own waters on this planet continue to be polluted and oftentimes barely safe to drink. Likewise, we try to practically envision and financially afford a single space station consisting of a relative handful of travelers. Yet, we let our planet deteriorate to the point that unless a space shuttle can be made that could evacuate a billion people at a time, it is of little practical use.

We have chosen to make ourselves complex when, in actuality, we are all simple beings of Nature, each one of us merely one grain of sand on a beach. A most useful analogy that I want to apply here is from an occasion that I remember while I was growing up. A group of sportswriters gathered around baseball slugger, Tony Perez, trying to inquire what made him such a good hitter…"What makes you such a good hitter? Is it the type of bat you use?…No…Is it the type of swing you have?…No…Is it your stance in the batter's box?…No…Then, it must be your wrist motion, right?…No…Then, what is it that you do so special?" …His simple response: "I see the ball, I hit the ball."...The point to be made here is that we are looking for complex answers to problems, where simple ones will do.

If we want to determine just how far we have strayed from our true selves, we only have to look as far as Nature in order to find the answer. The more we stray from our natural selves, the more we get mired in the proverbial creek without a paddle (which ends up turning into a chopstick the harder and harder that we row).

We cannot delay change much longer, because the clock is ticking, and we all are already on borrowed time. We have the capability and (currently) we still have the capacity of opportunity to correct our situation. It is a matter of whether we have the will to change how we look at the future. Will it be a continuation of our customary, microscopic ways—or one with a broader, macroscopic perspective that potentially can truly solve problems? We are the ones responsible for making the world as it is today, and we are the only ones who will be able to make it whole again in so many ways.

APPENDIX

YEAR	ACCUMULATED NATIONAL DEBT	YEAR	ACCUMULATED NATIONAL DEBT	YEAR	ACCUMULATED NATIONAL DEBT
1860	64,844,000	1902	1,178,031,000	1944	201,008,387,000
1861	90,582,000	1903	1,159,406,000	1945	258,682,187,000
1862	524,178,000	1904	1,136,259,000	1946	269,422,099,000
1863	1,119,774,000	1905	1,132,357,000	1947	258,286,383,000
1864	1,815,831,000	1906	1,142,523,000	1948	252,292,247,000
1865	2,677,929,000	1907	1,147,178,000	1949	252,770,360,000
1866	2,755,764,000	1908	1,177,690,000	1950	257,357,352,000
1867	2,650,168,000	1909	1,148,315,000	1951	255,221,977,000
1868	2,583,446,000	1910	1,146,940,000	1952	259,105,179,000
1869	2,545,111,000	1911	1,153,985,000	1953	266,071,082,000
1870	2,436,453,000	1912	1,193,839,000	1954	271,259,599,000
1871	2,322,052,000	1913	1,193,048,000	1955	274,374,223,000
1872	2,209,991,000	1914	1,188,235,000	1956	272,750,814,000
1873	2,151,210,000	1915	1,191,264,000	1957	270,627,172,000
1874	2,159,933,000	1916	1,225,146,000	1958	276,845,218,000
1875	2,156,277,000	1917	2,975,619,000	1959	284,705,907,000
1876	2,130,846,000	1918	12,455,225,000	1960	286,330,761,000
1877	2,107,760,000	1919	25,484,506,000	1961	288,970,989,000
1878	2,159,418,000	1920	24,299,321,000	1962	295,200,823,000
1879	2,298,913,000	1921	23,977,451,000	1963	305,859,633,000
1880	2,090,909,000	1922	22,963,382,000	1964	311,712,899,000
1881	2,019,286,000	1923	22,349,707,000	1965	317,273,899,000
1882	1,856,916,000	1924	21,250,813,000	1966	319,907,088,000
1883	1,721,959,000	1925	20,516,194,000	1967	326,220,985,000
1884	1,625,307,000	1926	19,643,216,000	1968	347,578,406,000
1885	1,578,551,000	1927	18,511,907,000	1969	352,720,254,000
1886	1,555,660,000	1928	17,604,293,000	1970	370,918,707,000
1887	1,465,485,000	1929	16,931,088,000	1971	408,176,000,000
1888	1,384,632,000	1930	16,185,310,000	1972	435,936,000,000
1889	1,249,471,000	1931	16,801,281,000	1973	466,291,000,000
1890	1,122,397,000	1932	19,487,002,000	1974	483,893,000,000
1891	1,005,807,000	1933	22,538,673,000	1975	541,925,000,000
1892	968,219,000	1934	27,053,141,000	1976	628,970,000,000
1893	961,432,000	1935	28,700,893,000	1977	706,398,000,000
1894	1,016,898,000	1936	33,778,542,000	1978	776,602,000,000
1895	1,096,913,000	1937	36,424,614,000	1979	829,470,000,000
1896	1,222,729,000	1938	37,164,740,000	1980	909,050,000,000
1897	1,226,794,000	1939	40,439,532,000	1981	994,845,000,000
1898	1,232,743,000	1940	42,967,581,000	1982	1,137,345,000,000
1899	1,436,701,000	1941	48,961,444,000	1983	1,371,710,000,000
1900	1,263,417,000	1942	72,422,455,000	1984	1,564,657,000,000
1901	1,221,572,000	1943	135,895,090,000	1985	1,817,521,000,000

1986	2,120,629,000,000	1992	4,002,136,000,000	1998	5,643,400,000,000
1987	2,346,125,000,000	1993	4,351,416,000,000	1999	5,656,270,000,000
1988	2,601,307,000,000	1994	4,643,711,000,000	2000	5,674,178,000,000
1989	2,868,039,000,000	1995	4,961,529,000,000	2001	5,807,463,000,000
1990	3,206,564,000,000	1996	5,181,900,000,000	2002	6,288,235,000,000
1991	3,598,498,000,000	1997	5,369,700,000,000		

Source: 1860 thru 1995 (see Gordon, p.202-04)

Sources: 1996 thru 2002 from Department of the Treasury and Office of Management and Budget.

NOTATIONS

INTRODUCTION (Pages 1 – 5)

1. Wood, p.176
2. Derber, p.123

Chapter 1 – GOVERNMENT (Pages 6 – 30)

1. Tonry & Reiss, Jr. (eds.), p. 208 (Pontell & Calavita chapter)
2. Tonry & Reiss, Jr. (eds.), p. 209 (Pontell & Calavita chapter)
3. Calavita, Pontell, and Tillman, p. 1
4. Gordon, pp. 202-04. Consult his chart if you want to go back as far as 1776.
5. If one were to add the total yearly inflation of the last 25 years, and compare that figure to the added total yearly inflation figure of the previous 200 years—the former total would be small in comparison to the latter total. Therefore, inflation within the last 25 or so years could not be any type of determining factor.
6. U.S. Treasury Department—Interest Public Debt, U.S.
7. Wood, pp. 125-26
8. Clinard, pp. 69, 70, 81
9. Kohut, pp. 9, 12, 99-100, 190-91
10. Baumohl, p. 33
11. Slater, p. 150 (Wealth Addiction)
12. Gross, p. 139 (A Call For Revolution)
13. Lawson & Merkl, p. 286 – Chapter by: Sorauf, Frank J., "Parties and Political Action Committees in American Politics".
14. Lawson & Merkl, p. 538 – Chapter by: Rose, Richard & Mackie, Thomas T., "Do Parties Persist or Fail? The Big Trade-Off Facing Organizations."

Chapter 2 – INDUSTRY (pp. 31 -53)

1. Schmookler, Illusion of Choice, p. 64
2. Wood, p. 220
3. Wood, p. 220

4. Wood, p. 219
5. Kemper & Lutterbeck, p. 23
6. Slater (A Dream Deferred), p. 62
7. Slater (A Dream Deferred), p. 65
8. Schmookler (Fool's Gold), p. 82
9. Wachtel (The Poverty of Affluence), p. 92
10. Wachtel, p. 287 (Quote by Ewen)
11. Kavanaugh, p. 47
12. Schmookler (Illusion of Choice), p. 234
13. Schmookler (Illusion of Choice), p. 165
14. Elgin, pp. 147-48
15. Mahler, p. 29
16. Schmookler (Fool's Gold), p. 127
17. Challenger, p. 66
18. Challenger, p. 67
19. Rifkin (The End of Work), p. 191 – From USA Today, p. 1-B, March 3, 1993, "Cutbacks Fuel Contingent Workforce"
20. Castro, p. 43
21. Rifkin (The End of Work), p. 191 – From Jack Gordon's, "Into the Dark: Rough Ride Ahead for American Workers," *Training*, July, 1993, pp. 24-25.
22. Wright & Smye, p. 61
23. Wright & Smye, p. 35
24. Slater (A Dream Deferred), p. 67
25. Rifkin (The End of Work), p. 102
26. Rifkin (The End of Work), p. 78—quoted from Norbert Weiner. *The Human Use of Human Beings: Cybernetic and Human Beings* (Boston: Houghton Mifflin, 1950).
27. Rifkin (The End of Work), p.88
28. Ibid, p. 174
29. Ibid, p. 36
30. Ibid, p. 288-289

Chapter 3 – EGO, GREED & SOCIETY (Pages 54 – 75)

1. Lasch, p. 53
2. Ibid, p. 54
3. Ibid, p. 53

4. Ibid, p. 5
5. Shames, p. 80
6. Shames, p. 150
7. Wood, p. 252
8. Schmookler (Fool's Gold), p. 61
9. Ibid, p. 61
10. Ibid, p. 17
11. Lasch, p. 29
12. Shames, p. 166
13. Ibid, p. 166-167
14. Ibid, p. 146
15. Slater (Wealth Addiction), p. 28
16. Ibid, pp. 52-53
17. Schmookler (Fool's Gold), p. 22
18. Lasch, p. 74
19. Schmookler (Fool's Gold), pp. 144-145
20. Kavanaugh, pp. 44, 96, 97
21. Shames, p. 133
22. Wood, p. 115
23. Ibid, p. 116
24. Postman, pp. 73, 75, 77
25. Ibid, p. 117
26. Wood, pp. 117-118

Chapter 4 – INDIVIDUAL ABUSES (Pages 76 – 122)

1. Shames, pp. 234, 235, 240
2. Lasch (The Culture of Narcissism), p. 65
3. Ibid, p. 66
4. Derber, p. 121—summarizing a quote from Dr. Benjamin Spock.
5. Gibbs, p. 64
6. Derber, p. 15
7. Ibid, p. 18
8. Wachtel, p. 169—a Studs Terkel quote from Jeremy Seabrook's book, *What Went Wrong?*
9. Wood, p. 136
10. Ibid, p. 137
11. Ibid, pp. 137-138

12. Ibid, p. 137
13. Ibid, pp. 136, 138
14. Milt, p. 39
15. Kritsberg, pp. 21-22
16. Frank & Lynch, pp. 92-93—citing data from FDA Drug Review.
17. Ibid, p. 92—citing evidence from Health & Humane Research.
18. Williams, p. 60
19. Fontana, pp. 125-126
20. Ibid, p. 120
21. Ibid, p. 115
22. Westman, p. 121
23. Conclusions cited in Neely, pp. 103, 105 from Jay Belsky chapter, "Developmental Risks Associated with Infant Day Care: Attachment, Insecurity, Noncompliance, and Aggression?" from the book, *Psychosocial Issues in Day Care*, edited by Shahla S. Chehrazi (Washington, DC: American Psychiatric Press, Inc., 1990).
24. Neely, p. 104
25. Lesly, p. 111
26. Trebach, p. 383
27. McCuan, p. 45
28. Church, p. 54
29. Lasch (Culture of Narcissism), p. 239
30. Schwartz, p. 267
31. Bushong, p. 62
32. Betcher, pp. 15-16
33. Bushong, p. 35
34. Davidson, p. 27
35. Groth & Birnbaum, p. 5
36. Ibid, p. 60
37. Originally categorized by Karl Menninger (a noted psychiatrist in the mid 20th Century), see Lester, pp. 47-48.
38. Wrobleski, p. 55

Chapter 5 – HEALTH CARE (Pages 123 – 152)

1. Konner, p. 17
2. Goodwin, p. 81

3. Whitford, p. 32—quoted from Fred Nahas, M.D.
4. Levitin, p. 91
5. Stewart, p. 56
6. Ibid, p. 76
7. Mechanic, p. 44
8. Finkelstein, p.24
9. Szasz, p.20
10. Stewart, pp. 16, 54—Source for "Number of Physicians" came from World Almanac Fact Book, 2002.
11. Finkelstein, p.25
12. McNamee et al., p.28
13. Finkelstein, p.24
14. Tahmincioglu, p.99
15. Consumer Reports, p.41 (October, 1997)
16. Halvorson, p. 73

Chapter 6 – GUNS AND CRIME (Pages 153 – 171)

1. Kopel, pp.261, 301; Wright, p.64; Weir, p.195—Firearms, death source: National Safety Council.
2. Kopel, pp.76-77
3. Ibid, p. 76
4. Weir, p.208
5. Cozic, p.256—from David Kopel, "Japanese Gun Control Laws Are Oppressive."
6. Ibid, pp.253, 256
7. Neely, pp.113, 115
8. Ibid, p.126
9. Ibid, p.115
10. Kopel, p.419 in reference to research done by Rolf Loeber and Magda Stouthamer-Loeber et al. (See *Child Development*, no. 6 (1982) and *Crime and Justice: An Annual Review of Research*, vol.7 (Chicago: University of Chicago Press, 1986).
11. Neely, pp. 114-115
12. Kopel, p.421 in reference to research done by Douglas Smith and G. Roger Jarjoura (see Journal of Research in Crime and Delinquency, no.1 (1988)).

13. Kopel, p.420 in reference to research done by Joan A. McCord (see *Straight and Devious Pathways*, p.1116).
14. Fontana & Moolman, p.122
15. Peyser & Gegax, p.65
16. Callahan, p.6
17. Ibid, p.7
18. Kopel, p.364
19. Neely, pp.122-123
20. Lord, p.9
21. Kopel, p.357 in reference to studies done by Paul E. Tracy, Marvin E. Wolfgang and Robert M. Figlio in their book, *Delinquency Careers in Two Birth Cohorts* (New York: Plenum, 1990).
    Also see Orange County Probation Department Study, "The Eight Percent Problem," in *Chronic Juvenile Offender Recidivism*, 1994.
22. Kopel, p.356

Chapter 7 – NATURE AND THE ENVIRONMENT (Pages 172 - 191)

1. Schneider & Morton, p.150
2. Ibid, p.158
3. Ibid, p.198
4. Ibid, p.222
5. Wood, p. 159
6. Petitjean. World Press Review, p.8 (February, 2001)
7. Homer-Dixon, p.20 and Rifkin (Biosphere Politics), pp.86-87
8. Homer-Dixon, p.22
9. Rifkin (Biosphere Politics), p.89
10. Luoma, pp. 63, 64, 66
11. Wood, p. 166
12. Fox, p.33
13. Rifkin, (Biosphere Politics), p.79
14. Schmookler (Fool's Gold), p.173—The notion, that a creature that defeats its environment ends up destroying itself, was originally noted by Gregory Bateson in his book, *Steps to An Ecology of Mind*. (New York: Ballantine Books, 1972).

Chapter 8 – THE OVERPOPULATION EFFECT (Pages 192 – 225)

1. Hertsgaard, p.102
2. Science News, Dec.20/27, 1997, p. 396
3. Rifkin (Biosphere Politics), p. 174
4. Homer-Dixon, p.66
5. Schmookler (Illusions of Choice), p.99
6. Berry, p.128
7. Schmookler (Fool's Gold), p.179
8. Braffman-Miller, p. 57
9. Murphy, pp. 133-134
10. Wachtel, p.92
11. Ibid, p.92
12. Wood, p. 55
13. Kassiola, p.44 cited from Herman Arthur, "The Japan Gap: A Country Moves Ahead – But At What Price? *American Educator* (Summer, 1983), p.44 (emphasis in original).
14. Rifkin (Biosphere Politics), p.75
15. Berry, p.72
16. Schmookler (Illusions of Choice), p.110
17. Schmookler (Fool's Gold), p.179
18. Rifkin (Biosphere Politics), p.174
19. Wood, p.160
20. Hertsgaard, p.100
21. Kassiola, p.42—cited from William Leiss, *The Limits to Satisfaction: An Essay on the Problem of Needs and Commodities.* (Toronto: University of Toronto Press, 1976—p.4).
22. Schmookler (Illusions of Choice), p.109
23. Wachtel, p.167—quoting Jeremy Seabrook's book, *What Went Wrong? Why Hasn't Having More Made People Happier?* (New York: Pantheon, 1978).
24. Rifkin (Biosphere Politics), p.175
25. Schmookler (Fool's Gold), pp.33, 87
26. Wood, pp. 45, 126, 127
27. Homer-Dixon, p.68
28. Rifkin (The End of Work), p.207
29. Elgin, p.147

30. Wood, p.162
31. Schmookler (Illusions of Choice), pp. 107, 117, 124
32. Wood, p.127

BIBLIOGRAPHY

Baumohl, Jim (ed.). *Homelessness in America.* (Phoenix: The Oryx Press, 1996).

Beardsley, Tim. "When Nutrients Turn Noxious," *Scientific American*, June, 1997.

Begley, Sharon et al. "Wake Up Call," *Newsweek*, December 22, 1997.

Bender, David and Leone, Bruno and Roleff, Tamara L. (eds.). *The Homeless: Opposing Viewpoints.* (San Diego: Greenhaven Press, Inc., 1996).
 —Mihaly, Lisa. "Homeless Increasingly Affects Families"
 —Zawisza, Kris. "Homeless Is Serious in Rural Areas"
 —Liebow, Elliot. "A Lack of Affordable Housing Causes Homeless."
 —Yeich, Susan. "The Government Contributed to the Homeless Problem."

Berry, Wendell. *Home Economics: Fourteen Essays.* (San Francisco: North Point Press, 1987).

Betcher, William and Macauley, Robie. *The Seven Basic Quarrels of Marriage: Recognize, Defuse, Negotiate and Resolve Your Conflicts.* (New York: Villard Books, 1990).

Birenbaum, Arnold. "Managed Care: Will It Be For Everyone?" *USA Today*, July, 1996.

Birnbaum, Jeffrey H. "Hard Queries About Soft Money." *Fortune*, April 29, 2002.

Braffman-Miller, Judith. "Beware the Rise of Antibiotic-Resistant Microbes," *USA Today*, March, 1997.

Brink, Susan and Shute, Nancy. "Are HMOs The Right Prescription?" *U.S. News & World Report*, October 13, 1997.

Brown, Jay H. *Truth In Governing.* (Evanston, IL: Freedom Publishing Co., 1996).

Brown, Lester. "Food Scarcity: An Environmental Wakeup Call," *The Futurist*, January-February, 1998.

Brown, M.R. "Medical Mayhem." *Black Enterprise*, August, 2001.

Bryant, Adam. "Drowning In a Sea of Debt." *Newsweek*, February 5, 2001.

Buell, John. *Democracy By Other Means: The Politics of Work, Leisure, and Environment.* (Urbana, IL: University of Illinois Press, 1995).

Buell, John. "Harry and Louise: The Sequel," *The Humanist*, September/October, 1996.

Bushong, Carolyn N. *The Seven Dumbest Relationship Mistakes Smart People Make.* (New York: Villard Books, 1997).

Calavita, Kitty and Pontell, Henry N. and Tillman, Robert H. *Big Money Crime: Fraud and Politics in the Savings and Loan Crisis.* (Berkeley: University of California Press, 1997).

Callahan, Sidney. "What We See, We Do," *Commonweal*, January 12, 1996.

Castro, Janice. "Disposable Workers," *Time*, March 29, 1993.

Challenger, James E. "Downsizing Is Bad For Business," *USA Today*, January, 1997.

Church, George J. "Elderscam: Reach Out and Bilk Someone," *Time*, August 25, 1997.

Clinard, Marshall B. *Corporate Corruption: The Abuse of Power.* (New York: Praeger Publishers, 1990).

Cozic, Charles P. and Wekesser, Carol (eds.). *Gun Control.* (San Diego: Greenhaven Press, Inc., 1992).

Davidson, Terry. *Conjugal Crime: Understanding and Changing the Wifebeating Pattern.* (New York: Hawthorn Books, Inc., 1978).

Davis, L.J. "Chronicle of a Debacle Foretold: How Deregulation Begat the S&L Scandal," *Harper's*, September, 1990.

Derber, Charles. *Money, Murder & the American Dream.* (Winchester, MA: Faber and Faber, Inc., 1992).

Dorfman, Andrea. "The World's Next Trouble Spots." (Summit to Save the Earth issue). *Time*, June 1, 1992.

Easterbrook, Gregg. "Healing The Great Divide," *U.S. News & World Report*, October 13, 1997.

Elgin, Duane. *Voluntary Simplicity: Toward A Way of Life That Is Outwardly Simple, Inwardly Rich.* (New York: Quill, 1993).

Elmer-Dewitt, Philip et al. "Rich vs. Poor," (Summit to Save the Earth issue), *Time*, June 1, 1992.

Faltermayer, Charlotte. "Delivered to Their Deaths," *Time*, May 5, 1997.

Figgie, Jr., Harry E. and Swanson, Gerald J. *Bankruptcy 1995: The Coming Collapse of America & How to Stop It.* (Boston: Little, Brown & Co., 1992).

Fineman, Howard. "Everything Will Change, Or Not." *Newsweek*, February 25, 2002.

Finkelstein, Katherine Eban. "The Sick Business," *The New Republic*, December 29, 1997.

Fishkin, Gerald L. *American Dream, American Burnout.* (Los Angeles: Loren Publications, 1994).

Fontana, Vincent J. and Moolman, Valerie. *Save the Family, Save the Child: What We Can Do To Help Children At Risk.* (New York: Dutton, 1991).

Forest, Stephanie Anderson et al. "Revenge of the HMO Patients," *Business Week*, March 17, 1997.

Fox, Michael W. *Returning to Eden: Animals Rights and Human Responsibility.* (Malabar, FL: Krieger Publishing Co., 1986).

Frank, Nancy K. and Lynch, Michael J. *Corporate Crime, Corporate Violence: A Primer.* (Albany, NY: Harrow & Heston, 1992).

Gibbs, Nancy. "How America Has Run Out of Time," *Time*, April 24, 1989.

Gleckman, Howard. "Deficits As Far As the Eye Can See." *Business Week*, May 13, 2002.

Gleick, Elizabeth. "Blackboards As Billboards," *Time*, June 10, 1996.

Goodwin, Jan. "Surgery To Go," *Good Housekeeping*, July, 1997.

Gordon, John Steele. *Hamilton's Blessing: The Extraordinary Life and Times of Our National Debt.* (New York: Walker & Co., 1997).

Greenwald, John. "The Brightest and the Brokest." *Time*, October 5, 1998.

Gross, Martin L. *The Government Racket.* (New York: Bantam Books, 1992).

Gross, Martin L. *A Call For Revolution.* (New York: Ballantine Books, 1993).

Groth, A. Nicholas with Birnbaum, H. Jean. *Men Who Rape: The Psychology of the Offender.* (New York: Plenum Press, 1979).

Hagan, Carolyn. "Health Insurance Hazards: How to Spot Hidden Pitfalls In Your Plan," *American Health*, November, 1996.

Halvorson, George C. *Strong Medicine*. (New York: Random House, 1993).
Hammonds, Keith H. "Hit Where It Hurts," *Business Week*, October 27, 1997.
Harris, Marlys J. "Elder Fraud," *Money*, November, 1995.
Hertsgaard, Mark. "Our Real China Problem," *The Atlantic Monthly*, November, 1997.
Hodgkinson, Liz. *Addictions: What They Are, Why They Happen, How to Help*. (Wellingborough, England: Thorsons Publishing Group, 1986).
Homer-Dixon, Thomas. *Environmental Scarcity and Global Security* (from Headline Series). (New York: Foreign Policy Association, Inc., 1993).
Jenkins, Jr., Kent & et al. "Health Care Politics: The Sequel," *U.S. News & World Report*, December 1, 1997.
Johansen, Bruce E. "Arctic Heat Wave." *The Progressive*, October, 2001.
Kadlec, Daniel. "Power Failure." *Time*, December 10, 2001.
Kaminer, Wendy. "Second Thoughts on the Second Amendment," *The Atlantic Monthly*, March, 1996.
Kassiola, Joel Jay. *The Death of Industrial Civilization: The Limits of Economic Growth and the Repoliticization of Advanced Industrial Society*. (Albany, NY: State University of New York Press, 1990).
Kavanaugh, John Francis. *Following Christ in a Consumer Society*. (Maryknoll, NY: Orbis Books, 1981).
Kemper, Vicki and Deborah Lutterbeck. "The Country Club," *Common Cause*, Spring/Summer, 1996.
King, John L. *Chaos In America*. (Tehachapi, CA: America West Publishers, 1990).
Klass, Perri. "Managing Managed Care," *New York Times Magazine*, October 5, 1997.
Koerner, Brendan I. "From Way Cool to Out of Control." *U.S. News & World Report*, May 3, 1999.
Kohut, John. *Stupid Government Tricks: Outrageous (but, True!) Stories of Bureaucratic Bungling and Washington Waste*. (New York: Plume Books, 1995).
Konner, Melvin. *Dear America, A Concerned Doctor Wants You to Know the Truth About Health Reform*. (Reading, MA: Addison-Wesley Publishing Co., 1993).

Kopel, David B. (ed.) *Guns: Who Should Have Them?* (Amherst, NY: Prometheus Books, 1995).

Kosof, Anna. *Incest: Families In Crisis.* (New York: Franklin Watts, 1985).

Kritsberg, Wayne. *Adult Children of Alcoholics Syndrome: From Discovery to Recovery.* (New York: Bantam Books, 1985).

Lasch, Christopher. *The Culture of Narcissism: American Life In An Age of Diminishing Expectations.* (New York: Norton & Co., 1979).

Lawson, Kay and Merkl, Peter H. (eds.). *When Parties Fail.* (Princeton, NJ: Princeton University Press).
—Sorauf, Frank J., "Parties and Political Action Committees in American Politics."
—Rose, Richard and Mackie, Thomas T., "Do Parties Persist or Fail? The Big off Facing Organizations."

Lesly, Philip. *How We Discommunicate.* (New York: AMACOM, 1979).

Lester, David. *Making Sense of Suicide: An In-Depth Look At Why People Kill Themselves.* (Philadelphia: The Charles Press, Publishers, 1997).

Levitin, Nancy. *America's Health Care Crisis: Who's Responsible?* (New York: Impact Book, 1994).

Lim, Paul J. and Benjamin, Matthew. "Digging Your Way Out of Debt." *U.S. News & World Report*, March 19, 2001.

Linden, Eugene. "Population: The Uninvited Guest," (Summit to Save the Earth issue), *Time*, June 1, 1992.

Linden, Eugene. "Global Fever," *Time*, July 8, 1996.

Littwin, Susan. "A Call For Help! The Untold Story of Elder Abuse Today," *New Choices For Retirement Living*, September, 1995.

Lord, Mary. "They Think We're a Land of Sick Shooters," *U.S. News & World Report*, June 7, 1993.

Luoma, Jon R. "Havoc in the Hormones," *Audubon*, July-August, 1995.

Lustbader, Wendy. "Self-Neglect: A Practitioner's View," *Aging*, 1996.

Mahler, Richard. "While You Wait: T.V. Marketers Hunt Captive Viewers," *Electronic Media*, December 30, 1991.

Mahoney, Richard J. "Revising the Superfund: This Time Let's Get It Right," *USA Today*, January, 1996.

Markley, Oliver W. and McCuan, Walter R. (eds.) *21st Century Earth*. (San Diego: Greenhaven Press, Inc., 1996).

—Stevens, William K. "An Environmental Apocalypse Is Real."

Mayer, Jane. "The Accountants' War." *The New Yorker*, April 22 & 29, 2002.

McCuan, Eloise Rathbone. "Self-Neglect in the Elderly: Knowing When and How to Intervene," *Aging*, 1996.

McGinn, Daniel. "Maxed Out." *Newsweek*, August 27, 2001.

McGinn, Daniel. "The Ripple Effect." *Newsweek*, February 18, 2002.

McNamee, Mike et al. "Health Care Inflation: It's Baaack!" *Business Week*, March 17, 1997.

Mechanic, David. "Managed Mental Health Care," *Society*, November/December, 1997.

Milbrath, Lester W. *Envisioning A Sustainable Society: Learning Our Way Out*. (Albany, NY: State University of New York Press, 1989).

Miles, Jr., Rufus. *Awakening From the American Dream*. (New York: Universe Books, 1976).

Milgram, Gail Gleason. *The Facts About Drinking: Coping With Alcohol Use, Abuse, and Alcoholism*. (Mt. Vernon, NY: Consumers Union, 1990).

Milt, Harry. *Alcoholism, Its Causes and Cure: a new handbook*. (New York: Charles Scribner's Sons, 1976).

Monastersky, Richard. "Health in the Hot Zone," *Science News*, April 6, 1996.

Morreim, E. Haavi. "Let Contracts, Not 'Necessity,' Guide Health System." *Consumers' Research*, December, 2001.

Murphy, Raymond. *Sociology and Nature: Social Action In Context*. (Boulder, Co: Westview Press, 1997).

Neely, Richard. *Tragedies of Our Own Making*. (Urbana, IL: University of Illinois Press, 1994).

Nussbaum, Bruce. "Can You Trust Anybody Anymore?" *Business Week*, January 28, 2002.

Peele, Stanton. *Diseasing of America: Addiction Treatment Out of Control*. (Lexington, MA: Lexington Books, 1989).

Petitjean, Gerard. "The 21st Century: Hot, Hot, Hot." *World Press Review* (reprinted from Le Nouvel Observateur), February, 2001.

Peyser, Marc and Gegax, T. Trent. "A Deadly Late-Night Delivery," *Newsweek*, May 5, 1997.

Postman, Neil. *Technopoly: The Surrender of Culture to Technology*. (New York: Alfred A. Knopf, Inc., 1992).

Rentschler, William H. "Lock 'Em Up and Throw Away the Key: A Policy That Won't Work," *USA Today*, November, 1997.

Rifkin, Jeremy. *Biosphere Politics: A New Consciousness for a New Century*. (New York: Crown Publishers, Inc., 1991).

Rifkin, Jeremy. *The End of Work: The Decline of the Global Labor Force and the Dawn of the Post-Market Era*. (New York: Tarcher/Putnam, 1995).

Ryan, Frank. *Virus X: Tracking the New Killer Plagues Out of the Present and Into the Future*. (Boston: Little, Brown and Company, 1997).

Sagoff, Mark. "Do We Consume Too Much?" *The Atlantic Monthly*, June, 1997.

Samuelson, Robert J. "Is Argentina A Time Bomb?" *Newsweek*, April 23, 2001.

Schaef, Anne Wilson. *When Society Becomes An Addict*. (New York: Harper & Row, 1987).

Schaef, Anne Wilson and Fassel, Diane. *The Addictive Organization*. (San Francisco: Harper & Row, 1988).

Schmookler, Andrew Bard. *Fool's Gold: The Fate of Values in a World of Goods*. (San Francisco: Harper (Division of HarperCollins Publishers), 1993).

Schmookler, Andrew Bard. *The Illusion of Choice: How the Market Economy Shapes Our Destiny*. (Albany, NY: State University of New York Press, 1993).

Schneider, Stephen H. and Morton, Lynne. *The Primordial Bond: Exploring Connections Between Man and Nature Through the Humanities and Sciences*. (New York: Plenum Press, 1981).

Schulhof, Julia. "Cosmetics With A Conscience," *American Health*, November, 1993.

Schwartz, Barry. *The Battle For Human Nature: Science, Morality and Modern Life*. (New York: W.W. Norton & Co., 1986).

Shames, Laurence. *The Hunger For More: Searching For Values in an Age of Greed.* (New York: Times Books, 1989).
Sherrid, Pamela. "Mismanaged Care? Wall Street Takes A Scalpel to HMO Companies," *U.S. News & World Report*, November 24, 1997.
Slater, Philip. *Wealth Addiction.* (New York: E.P. Dutton, 1980).
Slater, Philip. *A Dream Deferred: America's Discontent and the Search For A New Democratic Ideal.* (Boston: Beacon Press, 1991).
Sloan, Allan. "Who Killed Enron?" *Newsweek*, January 21, 2002.
Smil, Vaclav. "Global Population and the Nitrogen Cycle," *Scientific American*, July, 1997.
Stewart, Jr., Charles T. *Healthy, Wealthy or Wise? Issues in American Health Care Policy.* (Armonk, NY: M.E. Sharpe, Inc., 1995).
Stover, Dawn. "The Big Melt." *Popular Science*, May, 2001.
Sugarmann, Josh. "Reverse Fire," *Mother Jones*, January/February, 1994.
Szasz, Thomas. *Our Right To Drugs: The Case For A Free Market.* (New York: Praeger Publishers, 1992).
Tahmincioglu, Eve. "The Catch-22 of Long-Term-Care Insurance," *Kiplinger's Personal Finance*, May, 1997.
Terry, Roger. *Economic Insanity.* (San Francisco: Berrett-Koehler Publishers, Inc., 1995).
Tilman, David et al. "Forecasting Agriculturally Driven Global Environmental Change." *Science*, April 13, 2001.
Tonry, Michael and Reiss, Jr., Albert J. (eds.). *Beyond the Law: Crime in Complex Organizations.* (Chicago: The University of Chicago Press, 1993).
 —Pontell, Henry N. and Calavita, Kitty, "The Savings and Loan Industry."
 —Braithwaite, John, "The Nursing Home Industry."
Trebach, Arnold S. *The Great Drug War: And Radical Proposals That Could Make America Safe Again.* (New York: Macmillan Publishing Co., 1987).
Wachtel, Paul L. *The Poverty of Affluence: A Psychological Portrait of the American Way of Life.* (New York: The Free Press, 1983).
Weir, William. *A Well Regulated Militia: The Battle Over Gun Control.* (North Haven, CT: Archon Book, 1997).

Weiss, Gary. "A Sorry Legacy the Street Can't Shake." *Business Week*, May 13, 2002.

Westman, Jack C. *Licensing Parents: Can We Prevent Child Abuse and Neglect?* (New York: Insight Books, 1994).

Whitford, David. "Now the Doctors Want A Union," *Fortune*, December 8, 1997.

Williams, Joy. "The Inhumanity of the Animal People," *Harper's*, August, 1997.

Witters, Weldon and Venturelli, Peter and Hanson, Glen. *Drugs and Society*. (Boston: Jones and Bartlett Publishers, 1992).

Wolf, Rosalie S. "Understanding Elder Abuse and Neglect," *Aging*, 1996.

Wood, Donald N. *Post-Intellectualism and the Decline of Democracy: The Failure of Reason and Responsibility in the Twentieth Century*. (Westport, CT: Praeger Publishers, 1996).

Wright, James D. "Ten Essential Observations on Guns in America," *Society*, March/April, 1995.

Wright, Lesley and Smye, Marti. *Corporate Abuse: How "Lean and Mean" Robs People and Profits*. (New York: Simon & Schuster Macmillan Co., 1996).

Wrobleski, Adina. *Suicide: Why? 85 Questions and Answers About Suicide*. (Minneapolis: Afterwards Publishing, 1995).

Magazine references that didn't have any specific authors listed.

"A Deadly Clash of Cultures," *Newsweek*, May 31, 1993.

"Death of A Visitor," *People*, November 16, 1992.

"How Will You Pay for Your Old Age?" *Consumer Reports*, October, 1997.

"Pollution Surge From New Chinese Cars." *Science News*, December 20/27, 1997.

INDEX

abuse, 1, 2, 4, 8, 21, 31, 77, 78, 79, 82, 87, 88, 89, 90, 92, 95, 96, 97, 105, 106, 107, 109, 110, 115, 116, 118, 120, 121, 134, 159, 173, 190, 200, 211, 223
Adams, John, 26
Adidas, 43
Andersen, Arthur, 9, 10
Argentina, 220

Belsky, Jay, 100
Berry, Wendell, 197
Betcher, William, 115
Bush, President, 12

China, 5, 35, 180, 194, 195, 208
Civil War, 13
Clinton, President, 104, 105
Colborn, Theo, 185
Columbine school shootings, 162
"commodity way of life", 67
computers, 8, 48, 50, 71, 86, 87, 102, 217
Congress, 6, 11, 12, 15, 16, 27, 33, 52, 105, 129, 144, 148, 153, 188
contingent workers, 47
"corporate memory", 46, 47
cost/benefit, 35, 36, 204

debt, 9, 12, 13, 14, 15, 16, 17, 22, 23, 29, 45, 54, 55, 58, 64, 220
   credit card, 14, 15, 55, 124
Defense Department, 16, 17, 18
Democrats, 19
Depression, 1, 13, 216
Derber, Charles, 83
deregulation, 7, 8, 83
diminishing returns, 1, 42, 80, 202
drug manufacturers, sales & profits of, 138, 139, 140
dysfunctional, 28, 82, 159, 160, 170

Earth, 1, 173, 175, 176, 181, 183, 191, 202, 212
Edwards, Edwin, 166

"ends", 7, 31, 72
Enron, 9, 10, 11
Exxon, 35

Federal Drug Administration (FDA), 94, 139
firearms, number in circulation, 153, 154, 168
Firestone Tire, 80
"floating voters", 29
"fluff" (of life), 3, 63, 64
Founding Fathers, 56, 105
Fry, Michael, 185, 186

gatekeepers, 128, 129
General Accounting Office, 16
"goose market", 38
greed, 2, 10, 37, 56, 57, 59, 80, 83, 179, 208, 211
greenhouse effect, 176, 179, 181, 191
Gross National Product (GNP), 14, 32, 178, 200, 209
Groth and Birnbaum, 117
Guillette, Louis, 185

Hattori, Yoshihiro, 166
Health & Human Services Dept., 20
health expenditure, 46, 123, 124
hedge funds, 8, 9
"hindsight" approach, 4, 6, 187
HMOs, 123, 125, 128, 129, 130, 131, 132, 135, 137, 141, 142, 143, 144, 215
"holistic approach", 20, 22, 187, 223

identity, 2, 4, 39, 66, 70, 71, 72, 73, 82, 97, 106, 210
India, 5, 181, 184, 207
Indonesia, 180, 193
Industrial Age, 1
Information Age, 1, 4, 9, 69, 70, 71, 85
Institutional Momentum (IM), 17, 211
Internet, 14, 72, 73

Japan, 119, 124, 157, 158, 167, 202

Kavanaugh, John, 67
Koren, Edward, 62

Koskovich, Thomas, 160

Lasch, Christopher, 112
Lauren, Ralph, 63
lobbyists, 17, 27, 32, 35, 127, 149, 185

Man, 5, 98, 173, 174, 176, 177, 178, 190, 197, 204
materialism, 3, 60, 66, 179, 210
"means", 7, 31, 72
Medicaid, 145
Medicare, 12, 147
Methyl Tertiary Butyl Ether (MTBE), 186, 214
Mongolia, 197

National Park, 32, 204, 205
Nature, 5, 173, 174, 175, 178, 190, 191, 197, 203, 204, 205, 210, 211, 212, 213, 219, 221, 224, 225
"needs", 3, 41, 59, 65, 131, 139, 218
Neely, Richard, 158
"new and improved", 38, 140
Nike, 43
nursing home, 109, 145, 146, 147, 148

oil companies, 36
Orwell, George, 126
overcompetitiveness, 3, 76, 78, 79, 80, 121, 222
overconsumption, 13, 37

Paradoxes
  #1 - ignoring waste and fraud, 17
  #2 - federal agencies' dilemma, 23
  #3 - political party bases of support, 28
  #4 - overconsumption, 37, 69
  #5 - needs vs. wants, 41
  #6 - lack of corporate and worker loyalty, 49
  #7 - automation vs. loss of jobs, 52
  #8 - security vs. insecurity of material goods, 59
  #9 - life vs. lifestyle, 61
  #10 - success vs. failure using money as criterion, 77

#11 - parents' time, 81
#12 - health-insurer middlemen, 127
#13 - medical payment plans, 130
#14 - mental vs. physical health, 135
#15 - quality health care at affordable price, 145
#16 - parenting and juvenile delinquency, 159
#17 - worldwide environmental standards, 190
#18 - overproductivity and demise of human species, 202
#19 - high-tech world vs. overpopulating one, 216
#20 - production of goods vs. world's limited resources, 219
"paralysis by analysis", 174
"patchwork approach", 20, 187, 221
Patients Bill of Rights, 129
Perez, Tony, 224
Perot, Ross, 29
"Pez", 39
plutocracy, 6
"portrayed" violence, 162
Postman, Neil, 72
PPMs/PPOs, 143

Reagan, President, 7, 8, 18
Republicans, 19
robotons, 4, 202

"safety net", 15, 19, 148
savings and loan, 4, 7, 8, 16, 18, 83
Schmookler, Andrew, 191, 222
Securities and Exchange Commission, 11
self-esteem, 21, 25, 39, 72, 88, 110
"self-made man", 54, 55
Senate, 6, 9, 18
Shames, Laurence, 62
Slater, Philip, 34
"soft" money, 33
special interest groups, 5, 17, 28, 32, 33
Springer, Jerry, 105
standard of living, 14, 51, 56, 60, 155, 180, 206, 208
"stuff", 37, 55, 61
Superfund, 188

Taylor, John, 26
Third World, 34, 53
transgenism, 215
two-party system, 4, 19, 26, 28, 30

United States (U.S.), 38, 53, 124, 133, 157, 223
"upgraded" technology, 38, 49, 60, 70,

Vietnam War, 13
Vreeland, Jayson, 160

"wants", 3, 41, 56, 59, 64, 65, 70, 99, 112, 131, 139, 177, 206, 218
wealth, 3, 13, 26, 31, 54, 56, 57, 58, 59, 60, 63, 99, 191, 207, 208, 222, 223
Weiner, Norbert, 51
West Virginia, 158
"whistleblower", 33
Whittle Communications, 44
"whole", 3, 96, 131, 191, 201, 204, 210
"wilding", 83
Williams, Joy, 95
"window of opportunity", 7, 192, 212
Wood, Donald, 17, 87, 201, 211
workforce, 16, 36, 45, 47, 48, 52, 121
World War II, 1, 136, 153, 186, 200, 223

Printed in the United States
1339900004B/58-504